APPLYING SOCIAL PSYCHOLOGY

Applying Social Psychology

**John Kremer, Noel Sheehy,
Jacqueline Reilly, Karen Trew
and Orla Muldoon**

First published 2003 by
PALGRAVE MACMILLAN
Houndmills, Basingstoke, Hampshire RG21 6XS and
175 Fifth Avenue, New York, N. Y. 10010
Companies and representatives throughout the world

PALGRAVE MACMILLAN is the global academic imprint of the Palgrave Macmillan division of St. Martin's Press, LLC and of Palgrave Macmillan Ltd. Macmillan® is a registered trademark in the United States, United Kingdom and other countries. Palgrave is a registered trademark in the European Union and other countries.

ISBN 0–333–77617–8

This book is printed on paper suitable for recycling and made from fully managed and sustained forest sources.

A catalogue record for this book is available from the British Library.

A catalogue record for this book is available from the Library of Congress.

10   9   8   7   6   5   4   3   2   1
12 11 10 09 08 07 06 05 04 03

Printed and bound in Great Britain by
Creative Print & Design (Wales), Ebbw Vale

Contents

List of Figures and Table

Figures

Table

Preface

Skim quickly over the pages of any standard introductory textbook and what should strike you immediately is social psychology's remarkable potential for offering insight into so many aspects of our daily lives. Unfortunately while the potential of the subject matter may be enormous, in reality many social psychologists have not always afforded a high priority to the practical application of their work to everyday concerns. To help counter this trend, in this book we have decided to adopt an alternative starting point by deliberately focusing attention on the application of social psychological knowledge to the world in which we live. Each chapter is devoted to an important aspect of our social world thereby providing an opportunity to consider the contribution which the subdiscipline is able to make to understanding different facets of social life. In this way we hope to show how the theory and the practice of social psychology can work in harmony to inform discussion of applied and relevant social topics.

We hope that in combination the chapters will be able to provide you with insight into concerns which daily occupy our thoughts and our actions. As the Contents page reveals, all life is here, including our education, work, leisure and health, as well as our involvement with the environment, the media, crime, conflict and the economic world. Taken together it is our hope that the chapters can witness the breadth of material which social psychology has at its disposal to inform understanding. Taken singly we hope that each chapter can shed light on the topic in question while at the same time revealing how social psychology has gone about its business. In this way the text may either be used as a primary text for a course or module dealing with applied social psychology or to provide background material for a particular applied topic.

To help those using the text to accompany a course on applied social psychology we have deliberately structured each chapter around a number of common subheadings. Following the **Introduction** to the general area, we felt it was important to provide some description of the **History and Development** of the subject area, including significant influences within and without the discipline of psychology. The following section then brings the reader up to date by focusing attention on **Contemporary Priorities** or those issues which occupy greatest attention from social psychologists working today. The third section is entitled **Concepts, Models and Theories** and, as the name suggests, outlines the most important theoretical contributions which continue to inform developments in the chosen field. The emphasis then shifts towards the application of this material in **Practical Issues,** where the dominant theme is the application of our knowledge to real life concerns and including intervention strategies and examples of action research. Finally, **The Way Forward** is designed to offer a speculative glimpse into the future, to consider where it is likely that trends will evolve or develop.

Assuming that many readers will be students of psychology, we have tried to include examples which are relevant to student life. At the start of each chapter you will find a case study (**Once upon a Time**) which is based on the type of situation which a student could encounter and where the material covered in the chapter may be of relevance in helping understand the thoughts, feelings and actions associated with that scenario. Many of the class activities are also designed to make the material as relevant as possible to the experiences of the reader, thus hopefully making the subject matter as accessible and entertaining as possible.

For teachers of psychology, we have included a number of key readings which could be assigned to students prior to group discussions, tutorials or seminars, along with short questions and class activities which could form part of a range of interactive sessions. For those who decide to adopt the text for teaching purposes we would be most interested in your feedback to learn how we can continue to improve the product, in the process using practice to inform theory, so underlining a central theme of the text.

JOHN KREMER
NOEL SHEEHY
JACQUELINE REILLY
KAREN TREW
ORLA MULDOON

Introduction

1

Knowledge of the world is only to be acquired in the world, and not in a closet.
(Lord Chesterfield, 1774)

ONCE UPON A TIME...

Joe was a student who had left school with reasonable grades but with little idea of what he wanted to study at university other than something that he found personally engaging. He had seen a few psychologists on television and thought that their work seemed interesting as he felt it dealt with real world concerns. For this reason he decided that he wanted to become a psychologist. In his first year at Arcadia University he studied a number of subjects alongside psychology including sociology, economics, politics and social anthropology. He found all these subjects interesting but was surprised that each discipline tended to work in isolation; indeed he felt they often used different jargon to describe similar social topics and did not engage with the literature outside their own fields. To pass his examinations, the easiest way was to follow the lead of his lecturers and keep each subject in its own box. In his psychology course he found the emphasis on applied work was not strong. By the end of first year he had some idea of how the central nervous system worked and how our social identity was constructed, but the world of psychology which he had imagined in his schooldays seemed quite distant. Joe continued with his degree and only saw occasional glimpses of how the material could be applied to the real world. He left university, married, had three children and became a manager with a multinational company but is still not entirely sure in what way his degree has relevance to his work or his life.

Introduction

This book is concerned with the appliance of science or, to be more precise, how the science of social psychology can be applied so as to help further our understanding of significant social concerns. When dealing with real world issues, an appreciation of the relationship between theory and practice assumes immediate importance. Indeed, across many disciplines one issue continues to be rehearsed during discussions of applied social research, namely the role which has been played (or more often not played) by theory. While problem-driven research may direct attention to the heart of a social problem, at the same time this focus may mean that theoretical considerations are asked to take a back seat. As a consequence, short-term answers and solutions can emerge but arguably at the expense of the long-term growth and prosperity of the discipline as a whole. In the words of Proshanky (1981), 'Psychologists in general, including those of us concerned with complex human and social problems, are not very good at developing and employing theoretical analysis and using the products of such analysis' (p. 102).

This may have been true in the past but is it inevitable that this always has to be the way of applied research? The answer must be no, for when all is said and written the real world must provide the crucial litmus test for any social theory. The now famous remark of Kurt Lewin that there is nothing so practical as a good theory (Lewin, 1951) has become something of a cliché in the world of applied psychology. We would not argue with Lewin's under-lying sentiment, but this is only half the story, as he himself acknowledged (p. 169) – there is also nothing so good for theory as the experience of sound practice and application. Both propositions are equally significant – has a particular theory been able to tell us anything about real world phenomena and, beyond this, in what ways has the real world helped to foster, modify or facilitate the development of theory?

A happy marriage between good theory and good practice has to be the most stable relationship in both the short and the long term. To achieve this balance the relationship between theory and practice should aim to be sym-biotic, with both anticipating that benefits will accrue from shared experiences. Using a social exchange analysis (based on an economic consideration of relationships in terms of interacting rewards and costs), although the out-comes for each partner may be different both should perceive that the rewards which they receive will have outweighed the costs that they have incurred. This interaction must be kept firmly in mind. Sometimes this is straightforward as theoretical foundations are well-established in applied areas. More frequently, links and relationships are buried at some distance below the surface but significant connections can be unearthed to reveal the importance of applied research to the development of mainstream social psychology.

Defining social psychology

Before considering the mechanics of applying social psychology, it would seem sensible to set the main parameters and terms of reference. To begin at the beginning, how can the subject matter of social psychology be defined and where do its boundaries lie? These are not easy questions to answer. In truth it is possible only to state that through an examination of their work it would appear that social psychologists selectively deal with social behaviour and experience and most often human behaviour and experience. Taken in its entirety this represents a very wide brief and a truly massive undertaking. It is little wonder that social psychologists have not been able to spread themselves uniformly across the spectrum of potential areas of interest to include all those behaviours, actions, emotions and cognitions which make humankind so specially social.

To many social psychologists the process of selectivity has become interesting in its own right. Why is it that certain topics have been placed under the glare of the research spotlight while we are left groping in the dark trying to understand other aspects of everyday life? What processes are at work bringing different areas and topics into and out of vogue? These are fascinating questions, touching on a great many political, social, economic and historical concerns. These are also questions which social psychologists are increasingly turning towards as the history of the subject becomes recognized as a legitimate topic of interest (Sahakian, 1982; Jaspars, 1986; Ibanez, 1990; Jones, 1998).

Returning to the issue of definition, even to describe social psychology as the scientific study of social behaviour and experience creates difficulties (Shotter, 1975). Many would argue that history reveals how aspiring to follow a scientific road has led to a series of irresolvable dilemmas concerning the goals of the subject and what methods must be employed to reach these goals. These concerns would be echoed by many feminists in social psychology who have often reacted strongly to traditional, and predominantly masculine, psychological methods (Squire, 1989; Wilkinson, 1986), variously labelled as reductionist, positivist and/or determinist, and who have made such a positive contribution to the development of the subdiscipline in recent years by their challenge to the status quo.

Over the last thirty years, the general principle of adhering to a scientific or pseudo-scientific model has increasingly been called into question. If social psychology is to be labelled a science it must be thought of as a special sort of science, poised somewhere within both the social sciences and the human sciences. In view of the wide and ever-increasing diversity of interests and activities of social psychologists, any definition of social psychology which moves beyond the bland and the non-specific is likely to cause offence to somebody. As a consequence it is thereby likely to inhibit rather than facilitate research activity, and so for now the issue of definition is perhaps best left as an unopened can of worms.

History and development

Defining the subject is difficult; in comparison, tracing its formal history is relatively easy, or at least from the time people began to describe themselves as social psychologists (Allport, 1985). Before that time the sources of influence were many and varied, and all made an impact in different ways (Jackson, 1988). After all, anyone and everyone who has offered insight into what it is that makes us human or social can legitimately be described as an applied social psychologist. Each in their own way has presented a social psychological theory, model or hypothesis. In the words of Fritz Heider (1958), all humans are naive psychologists, each presenting a unique psychological interpretation of their world.

This point is not in dispute, but embedded in this proposition lies one of the most thorny problems which confronts the subject. Everyone is a practicing social psychologist, each with their own ideas and theories about what makes us human and what makes us social. We cannot and should not ignore this fact, but the consequences cannot be ignored. For example, it can be proposed that, leaving aside the jargon, applied social psychology reaffirms nothing more than we already knew – it is a formalized version of common sense. In mitigation, it can be suggested that there are as many naive psychologists as there are competing versions of common sense. A scan through the *Oxford Dictionary of Quotations* supports this point. To give a few examples, if 'Many hands make light work' why do 'Too many cooks spoil the broth'; when 'To travel hopefully is better than to arrive' should it be that 'A bird in the hand is worth two in the bush'; 'You can't judge a book by its cover' yet 'Beauty is only skin deep'. Which truisms are true? This is not an idle question, but one which good social psychological research should try to address.

Throughout its short history, social psychology has successfully challenged or disproved many popular versions of common sense. Often this has been the case despite the common-sense or intuitive hypotheses which social psychologists themselves brought to their research. Citing some of the most famous social psychology experiments, Stanley Milgram (1974) did not expect that a majority of his subjects would administer 440 volts of electricity to a complete stranger simply because they were expected to do so by a man in a brown laboratory coat. Solomon Asch (1956) did not anticipate that his subjects would go against the evidence of their own eyes and conform with an obviously incorrect majority in a visual perception task when no obvious reward was offered. James Stoner did not hypothesize that his experimental groups would consistently adopt more extreme decisions than individuals making choices in isolation. Philip Zimbardo did not expect that he would have to discontinue his field experiment involving students playing out the roles of prisoners and guards because of the zeal or 'enthusiasm' of his student 'correctional officers'.

Moving beyond the laboratory, when the world has been stunned by events which disconfirm our common-sense views of who we are, social psychology has been on hand to offer insight. With this in mind, specific incidents have often been very significant in the history of social psychology. The horrific public murder of Kitty Genovese in New York and its impact on altruism and bystander-intervention research immediately springs to mind. Likewise, the Jonestown mass suicide and other cult activities have continued to stimulate interest in social influence. On a much more global scale, the treatment of Jews in Nazi Germany has left its indelible mark in so many ways on social psychology, including the influence which European Jewish psychologists brought to American social psychology in the 1940s and 1950s.

These influences must be set against the backcloth of long-term historical developments in psychology. Trends have often reflected upon widescale societal forces and changes, for just as the person in the street is a social psychologist, so the social psychologist is also the person in the street, also buffeted by the *zeitgeist* or spirit of the times. These social, economic and political trends will intrinsically affect researchers' motivations and orientation towards topics. In a more pragmatic vein, they also make their mark on the availability of research funds and possibilities for publication.

The subject of social psychology which we are left with today has continued to change and grow through these experiences, often dividing and then multiplying as it has come to terms with conflicting pressures and influences. Some of these divisions have long and distinguished histories, the most noteworthy being that between what is loosely described as sociological and psychological social psychology (Armistead, 1974). This division has its roots in the origins of the subject. Wilhelm Wundt (1897) (following on from Lazarus and Steinthal) began to discuss what was then known as *Volkerpsychologie*, which roughly translates as the relationship between the individual and his or her community/state, and by 1908 two books had appeared which marked the introduction of the term social psychology into the English language (although Gabriel Tarde's book, *Etudes de Psychologie Sociale* had already appeared in French in 1898 [Pepitone, 1981]).

The two texts were William McDougall's *Introduction to Social Psychology* (1908), and Edward Ross's *Social Psychology* (1908). In all honesty, the actual content of these books has justifiably faded into history (Jaspars, 1986), but both are still cited as the earliest identifiable ancestors of the two traditions. Ross was concerned with the social and structural context of behaviour, or collective social psychology, and he was rooted very much within a sociological tradition. McDougall's concern was with the individual in his or her social world and the instinctual bases of social behaviour. It was this tradition, with roots extending back to Wundt's *Volkerpsychologie*, which has come to dominate the discipline during this century, namely the study of the individual and how the social world impacts upon the individual.

In terms of significant influences since that time, it is not practical to dwell on all possible historical factors. Stating the obvious, behaviourism had its inevitable influence in terms of experimental methods and laboratory orientation. Alongside this, the Gestalt tradition has been vital, influenced so significantly by European social psychologists who emigrated to America, including Solomon Asch, Fritz Heider, Kurt Lewin and Muzafer Sherif. These pioneers operated within the existing American experimental tradition, but at the same time they successfully paved the way for social cognitive approaches which have now come to dominate the literature so powerfully on both sides of the Atlantic.

As regards the sociological tradition, as typified by Edward Ross, it would probably be fair to say that the majority of psychologists and many social psychologists, have experienced only fleeting exchanges with much of this material, embedded as it is within another academic discipline, sociology. One classic example would be the work of George Herbert Mead and his theory of symbolic interactionism (Mead, 1950). Formerly Mead's work was often neglected within psychology as a whole but more recently the true significance of his work has come to be recognized. In some respects Mead must be seen as being before his time and particularly as regards recent developments in social cognition, arguably the main plank of contemporary social psychology. Erving Goffman's writing (for example *Asylums; Stigma; Presentation of Self in Everyday Life*) would undoubtedly be more familiar to students of social psychology, past and present, but it is also true that his dramaturgical model and frame analysis would still sit uneasily in most general social psychology texts.

For most of this century the psychological and the sociological traditions have tended to run parallel but apart. From a teaching point of view this separate development was convenient, as the ways in which each tradition described the world, their areas of concern, their methodologies and their terminologies were so different. To attempt a synthesis would not have been easy. However, during the 1960s and 1970s writers began to evaluate alternative approaches and simultaneously began to engage in critical introspection, looking more carefully at the approaches which had been followed in the past and asking if there was a better way in the future.

At the same time, European social psychologists also began to find their feet and sought to develop an identity apart from the USA. Over the years, European social psychologists have continued to migrate across the Atlantic. Undoubtedly they have wielded influence in their adopted country but simultaneously they have become entrenched within the American academic system. During the 1960s and through into the 1970s, European-based social psychologists such as Henri Tajfel and Serge Moscovici began to show unease with US traditions, and especially the almost exclusive focus on the individual within social psychology (Israel and Tajfel, 1972). Some have described this period around the early 1970s as marking a crisis in social psychology (Smith, 1972; Strickland *et al.*, 1974). It was maintained that social psychology should recognize and perhaps do penance for its over-dependence on human psychology, its focus on behaviour not experience, and its overreliance on mechanistic, positivist and experimental approaches. Instead, humanism, phenomenology and Marxism were heralded as beacons to light the way forward (Armistead, 1974).

An identity crisis may have occurred at this time, but with the benefit of hindsight it may have been more a drama than a real crisis of confidence for the discipline as a whole. This was a drama which the main actors and supporting cast thought was highly significant but one which was often being played to an empty house. It was also a drama without a satisfactory conclusion for it is interesting, even disappointing, to recognize very similar arguments being advanced almost twenty years later, as debate was once more rekindled. On this occasion, the position of social psychology in the postmodern world was being critically assessed (Parker, 1989; Gough and McFadden, 2001). Social psychology's failure to take on board the lessons of the 1970s led some writers to talk not of restructuring the discipline, but of deconstructing social psychology (Ibanez, 1990; Parker and Shotter, 1990). However, whether such attacks strike the death knell for social psychology as we know it, or whether they can be seen more positively as part of an ongoing process of self-evaluation remains to be seen.

During the 1970s, 1980s and 1990s, it is probably true to say that applied social psychology progressed with merely token regard to such debates, and in America in particular mainstream social psychology continued with little more than a sideways glance. Rather than revolution there were signs of rebellion but, together with other more significant developments and reconstructions across psychology at that time and since, there was sufficient disturbance to eventually change how people thought about social psychology and its subject matter. This shift in orientation has presented wonderful opportunities for opening the boundaries of the subject wider and for shedding the blinkers which often served to limit topics of interest.

Concepts, models and theories

Through these debates, and despite continuing protestations about the dominance of American individualism, the individual in his or her social world still remains the central character in mainstream social psychology, as it was fifty years ago. Who this person or social animal is thought to be has changed substantially however. The individual is now recognized as a person with a social biography and a social and group identity. He or she is an interpreter or formulator of ideology, a social representor or constructor, and an engager in rhetoric and discourse. Instead of being seen as the passive recipient of social influences, the individual is now perceived as an active interpreter of information, making deliberate choices between alternatives, acting in a meaningful way as he or she deciphers and reconstructs social reality.

One research area which vividly highlights this change in focus is that dealing with attitudes. From Allport's work in the 1930s onwards (Allport, 1935), tremendous effort has been expended in trying to accurately measure attitudes. This was in the belief that once the problem of measurement was overcome, then it would be possible to use attitudes to predict behaviour. Unfortunately this endeavour continued apace without ever really coming to grips with two fundamental problems – what an attitude really is, and how attitudes relate to behaviour.

To begin with, the concept of 'an attitude' is problematic. Just because social psychologists spend so much time describing attitudes it is dangerous to assume that attitudes are ever present. We may often not hold an attitude or attitudes on many issues, and even if we do we may then behave in a number of ways which are not necessarily related to that attitude (Fazio, 1990). At other times the cart may come before the horse. If asked we may claim that we hold a particular attitude because in the past we have behaved in a particular way. Here the behaviour precedes the cognition and helps us to make sense of our actions (Bem, 1967). On other occasions it may be that we behave despite our attitudes; on other occasions we may construct an attitude because it helps us deal with inconsistencies in our lives, whether these are cognitive, emotional or behavioural.

Beyond the attitude/behaviour relationship, we then encounter the problem of measurement. Should we focus on the cognition, the emotion, or rather perversely should we begin at the end and measure the resulting behaviour? Do we look at what people do, what they say they do, or do we accept what they say as what they do?

In this climate it is very understandable that one theory which has repeatedly tried to untangle these mind games has returned to prominence, namely cognitive dissonance theory (Festinger, 1957). Festinger's theory is underpinned by the belief that we strive for consistency between what we do, how we feel and our perception of the world, and we will engage in all sorts of mental gymnastics to attain consistency. The work of Ajzen and Fishbein (1980), again built on a cognitive consistency model, is also very important in contemporary discussion, describing the interaction between our attitudes, our beliefs (subjective norms), our intentions to act, and finally, but not inevitably, our actions.

As complex multivariate statistical techniques have become more accessible, there open up many opportunities for looking at the multitude of personal and social factors which ultimately determine behaviour, and for unravelling the complex interactions between these mediating variables. As these predictive models have become more and more refined, inevitably they have become increasingly complex. Although often bewildering, this complexity has to be welcomed as thereby the models more accurately reflect the underlying complexity of human cognition, along with our idiosyncrasies as information processors.

Where the end of this trail leads is difficult to predict, but one thing is certain: to the person in the street attitude research has become less and less comprehensible. One real life example may serve to illustrate the increasing sophistication of this research, where the difficulties in trying to use attitudes to predict behaviour is vividly shown by work on voting behaviour. In the past, possibly in more stable times, voting was looked at in terms of a small number of key variables, many couched in terms of political socialization. These were seen as capable of explaining most of the variance in voting behaviour, the classic example being the Michigan model of vote choice (Campbell *et al.*, 1960). In comparison, later models of voting behaviour such as that developed by the London School of Economics in the 1980s included a multitude of personal and social factors all interacting in bewildering ways to determine where the cross is finally placed on the voting card (Himmelweit *et al.*, 1985).

Practical issues

When taken together, where does this leave modern-day applied social psychology? Probably at no other time have the intricacies and vagaries of social behaviour been more recognizable. Current research takes cognizance of this complexity, but eventually may demonstrate not how much we know but how little. In order to fill the gaps in our knowledge, social psychologists may have to broaden their horizons yet further. Other social sciences and humanities should not be regarded as off-limits, but as happy hunting grounds for both methodological and theoretical contributions. This cross-fertilization and interdisciplinary enthusiasm can be extremely invigorating and rewarding. At the same time caution must operate to ensure that a little knowledge does not become a dangerous thing. It is important to keep in mind the traditional boundaries of the subject, and to recognize the limits of knowledge and competence of those brought up within its borders. Moving beyond traditional fences may be necessary, even essential, but often progress can only be made in the hands of an expert guide. The need for research teams drawn from many disciplines therefore becomes a priority.

Such projects may help to develop comprehensive answers to a range of social questions, but they cannot aim to be too ambitious. Applied social psychology has rarely been concerned with providing large answers to large questions, and within social psychology as a whole there is now less concern with establishing general laws and sovereign principles (Proshansky, 1981), nor with exclusive reliance on single theories. Complementary theories and models have proliferated in this climate of pluralism, simultaneously demonstrating a greater appreciation of how each individual interprets and understands their world. Again, using a familiar example from experimental social psychology, while 30 per cent of subjects may have conformed on at least one trial in the classic Asch experiment, what about the 70 per cent who did not and the reasons why they did not? When subjects did conform, why did they and what did it really mean to them? So models and theories have generally become more person-centred, sometimes at the expense of nomothetic approaches concerned with general and universal laws. This is not to deny that on many occasions it is important to know something of general population trends and probabilities, but a spirit of methodological and theoretical pluralism is now far more acceptable to answer different questions in different ways (Bryant *et al.*, 1992).

One casualty of this shift has been the traditional laboratory experiment. Experimental research still dominates many journals, and experiments without doubt remain extremely powerful research tools, but in general the popularity of laboratory-based research has shown something of a decline. One example highlighting this trend is the literature devoted to experimental gaming. These studies filled various social psychology journals in the 1960s, 70s and early 80s but then became extremely thin on the ground (before enjoying a more limited resurgence in interest over the last few years). Against this overall trend, many advances in social cognition have been predicated upon experimental laboratory studies. Witness the emphasis which was placed on laboratory work by Tajfel when developing his ideas on social identity (for example the minimal group paradigm), or Asch when laying the foundations for modern theories of social cognition by his work on impression formation and central traits. What is undoubtedly true is that the costs as well as the benefits of laboratory experiments are now taken into account, and there is accordingly a greater reluctance to generalize findings beyond the walls of the laboratory to various aspects of everyday life.

As experimental methods have been looked at more closely, so unitary or simple and sovereign research strategies have often been replaced by multi-faceted designs in applied research. It would be more and more common to see, for example, quantitative and qualitative approaches co-existing in a multi-perspective research enterprise. The strengths and weaknesses of a variety of approaches may become complementary when used in combination. In this way, it would be possible to see unstructured interviews sitting happily alongside standard psychometric tests as part of a research project, and this mix-and-match approach would be recognized as having positive advantages.

The commercial world has also taken on board this modern eclecticism. Taking the case of market-research organizations, most commercial companies now offer their clients not only large-scale survey techniques and sampling frames but also suggest running small focus-group sessions where selected individuals, possibly chosen to represent opinion in key customer groups, discuss the product under the guidance of a discussant or facilitator. In a curious way this commercial example also typifies one important shift in orientation already mentioned. It is no longer unacceptable to ask people what they think – what people say is recognized as just as significant in its own way as what they do. Understandably, discourse analysis has grown in importance during this period (Potter and Wetherall, 1987), alongside other qualitative methodologies which focus on individual interpretation, included grounded theory.

As applied research has become less hidebound, the more it has become apparent that restricting analysis to one level, be it the individual, the interpersonal, the group, the societal, the political, the economic or the historical, is never going to reveal the full picture (Doise, 1986). Accordingly, it may be that social psychology can reap benefits from maintaining a foothold in both general psychology and the social sciences, as it is thereby well-placed to move easily within and across different traditions in an attempt to understand any social phenomena.

To illustrate this point, the chapter on peace and conflict (Chapter 5) will endeavour to show how prejudice, discrimination and community relations cannot be explained solely with reference to personality or individual differences, nor interpersonal style, group membership, social institutions, history, politics nor economics, but only by a fusion of contributions operating at different levels of analysis. At the level of the individual it would be appropriate to consider the behaviour, attitudes, motivations, aspirations and expectations of individuals. At the interpersonal level, who people talk with, marry, socialize with, where they work, where they spend their leisure time, their family life, all become important. Groups within the community may be looked at and how these groups interact. Relationships between these groups and individual community members and then between groups/individuals and other institutions are all worthy of attention. The influence of community leaders can be considered and how the community relates to the wider society – whether it represents a particular minority, and the value systems in operation and whether they are in conflict or harmony. Only by working through these various levels of analysis is it possible to develop a full understanding – take away any one part and the jigsaw is incomplete.

With this in mind, one very important component which also cannot be ignored is the frame or context in which the jigsaw itself resides (Furnham, 1986), including culture (Matsumoto, 2000). Laboratory research was often criticized for isolating behaviour from social context, and there is now widespread recognition that social behaviour is intricately bound up with its environment, and behaviour cannot be divorced from its surroundings and still be meaningfully understood (see Chapter 2). Hence, theories and models must be dynamic so as to explain changing behaviour in shifting contexts. The further development of contingency models and theories is therefore of paramount importance, perhaps predicated upon longitudinal rather than snapshot research (see Chapter 3). Using the example of sport, as described in Chapter 10, recent findings suggest that the most effective coaches constantly evaluate and reevaluate personal characteristics of their athletes, their training and their competition schedules, before deciding how best to motivate and manage over time.

The way forward

Taking all these points together, what are the implications for applied social psychology? Without question this branch of the discipline has continued to grow in stature and, despite the reservations in certain quarters (Helmreich, 1975), will hopefully continue to flourish given the current onus on accountable, cost-effective and applicable research. Too often in the past problem-driven or topical research was seen as some sort of second-class citizen – the soft or dirty end of social psychology. Nowadays the majority of funded research is problem-driven, drawing on theories and methods as appropriate but with the social problem or issue as the binding agent.

For better or worse, pragmatism must rule the day when conducting applied research. Irrespective of theoretical niceties, sponsors or customers will often want specific answers to specific questions. How is it possible to balance this demand with recent advances in social psychology which emphasize the complexities and idiosyncrasies of social behaviour? The answer has to be not to bury your head in the sand and pretend the problem does not exist but instead to try to strike a delicate balance. This will ensure that the research does not neglect current theory, but at the same time it is able to concurrently address the customer's needs. On some occasions conflicts of interest will not necessarily arise; at other times the conflict must be recognized and managed in terms of immediate priorities.

Returning to the theme which was introduced at the beginning of this chapter, with care and attention it should be possible to serve more than one master. Because research is problem or topic-driven, the methods and procedures do not have to be exclusively packaged to offer short-term answers while ignoring more complex and searching longer-term solutions and theoretical concerns. The acceptance of multi-perspective approaches positively encourages elaborate, integrative and imaginative research designs. At the same time, in this climate social psychology is able to offer itself as a very marketable product, standing at the interface of so many social and human sciences.

Time alone will tell if the subject can continue to deliver the goods, and will ever be able to come to terms with explaining and interpreting the complexities of social behaviour. In the meanwhile, it is the responsibility of those who carry out applied research to ensure that their research accurately reflects upon and is informed by developments across the subject as a whole, and in turn their research must go on to make its own impact on the social psychological literature. It is in this spirit that the following chapters are offered.

SHORT QUESTIONS

1 Review the development of social psychology over the last hundred years, highlighting the effects of key historical and cultural landmarks along the way.
2 'There is nothing so practical as a good theory.' Critically evaluate a social psychological theory of your choice with reference to Lewin's famous quotation.

SHORT QUESTIONS (cont'd)

3 To what extent is the history of social psychology reflected in its current priorities?
4 Does the subject matter of social psychology reflect more on the culture within which the research is undertaken or on universals of human social behaviour and experience?
5 Compare and contrast the interests of European and US social psychologists. Suggest why these differences may have come about and evaluate the extent to which they continue to exist.

CLASS ACTIVITIES

1 Thinking back over the last week, make a list of the three most important events which happened to you. Now skim through a standard social psychology textbook and identify material which would be helpful in understanding what happened and why. In what ways does the material help you understand the experience and what is missing?
2 Bring a number of recent newspapers to class. Scan the papers and choose a number of topics which are 'hitting the headlines' at the moment before discussing the following questions:

   ■ Which social psychological theories help in understanding the phenomenon in question?
   ■ Which methods do you think could be employed to help further our understanding?
   ■ What sort of intervention, based on social psychological principles, could be used to deal with issues/problems associated with this topic?

FURTHER READING

Bryant, F.B., Edwards, J., Scott Tindale, R., Posavac, E.J., Heath, L., Henderson, E. and Suarez-Balcazar, Y. (1992) *Methodological Issues in Applied Social Psychology*. New York: Plenum Press.

Jackson, J.M. (1988) *Social Psychology: Past and Present: An Integrative Orientation.* Hillsdale, NJ: Lawrence Erlbaum.

Oskamp, S. and Schultz, P.W. (1998) *Applying Social Psychology* (2nd edn). Upper Saddle River, NJ: Prentice Hall.

Sadawa, S.W. and McCreary, D.R. (1997) *Applied Social Psychology.* Upper Saddle River, NJ: Prentice Hall.

Sahakian, W. (1982) *History and Systems of Social Psychology.* New York: Hemisphere Publishing.

The Environment 2

We cannot solve the significant problems we face by working at the same level we were at when they were created.

(Albert Einstein)

ONCE UPON A TIME...

Fiona, a mature student, heard of a proposal to site a waste disposal facility close to her home. She decided to become actively involved in a local campaign to oppose the proposal and to have the facility sited elsewhere. A number of alternative sites were identified but each was in an area close to the homes of either friends, relatives or fellow students. These individuals in turn mounted vociferous objections to the proposal. While everyone agreed that recycling and other waste-reduction practices offered the best long-term solution, the community was faced with the reality of a growing mountain of waste. A compromise was finally reached: the facility would be sited on some old industrial land, close to a deprived area of town where its presence would be least noticed and where the residents did not have the capacity to mount an effective opposition to the plan.

Introduction

Environmental psychology is concerned with understanding people–environment relationships. These relationships are considered from two perspectives. Behaviour always occurs in a context so one perspective is concerned with understanding environments as settings in which people think, feel and act. This perspective starts from the premise that it is impossible to understand or predict how people will feel or behave without regard for the milieu in which emotions are experienced or intentions enacted. For example, fear responses can only be understood in the context of a person's perception of the potential threat posed to them by someone or something in his or her environment. From this perspective environmental psychology is similar to social or developmental psychology. The environment is thought to provide meaning and to influence behaviour in much the same way as social settings or developmental stages provide frameworks for understanding behaviour.

From a different perspective environmental psychology is concerned with the consequences of human behaviour for the environment. This includes a concern for large-scale environmental problems, such as the contribution of human behaviour to global warming, and potential solutions such as encouraging people to embrace improved waste-management practices (for example re-use and recycling) and adopt lifestyles that will minimize adverse environmental impacts. This perspective is concerned with understanding how people can alter the contexts in which they live in subtle yet profoundly important ways, and with approaches to promoting attitudes, values and behaviours that will minimize environmental impacts that may threaten the well-being of humans and other species. This perspective emphasizes how human behaviour and the environment mutually influence one another.

Although environmental psychology shares many features with other branches of the discipline, particularly social psychology, it has several distinguishing characteristics (Gifford, 1996). The first concerns its approach to studying its subject matter. Since environments influence individual and group behaviour it is considered particularly important to study behaviour in naturalistic settings. At a practical level this means the environments chosen for study are usually away from conventional laboratory settings and include streets, shopping centres, public parks, beaches and so on. However, it would be wrong to infer that environmental psychologists are disinterested in studying phenomena under laboratory conditions. They often do, for example by examining the effects of carefully controlled changes in noise or lighting on human behaviour. Laboratory settings are interesting for another reason: they are contrived social settings and as such the social environment of the laboratory is worthy of consideration in its own right.

A second characteristic of environmental psychology is the way it treats environment–behaviour relationships as a unit rather than conceptually distinct components. For example, a visitor to planet earth might not be able to deduce the purpose of buildings containing rows of shelves stocked with a multitude of containers, vegetables and animal parts. However, their function may become more apparent when people are observed to visit them and collect some of their contents for consumption elsewhere. This may seem like a strange way to describe 'shopping in supermarkets' but it illustrates what environmental psychologists mean when they say they study behaviour–environment relationships as a unit. The concept of 'a supermarket' is based on a shared understanding of appropriate ways to behave in that particular environment; supermarket shopping is more than a collection of individual shopping episodes. Consumers in that environment interact with and influence one another, so in this sense the environmental setting both facilitates and constrains the behaviours that occur within it. Thus, if the behaviour of the shoppers is studied abstractly, in isolation from particular environmental conditions, the conclusions derived will inevitably be limited.

A third characteristic of environmental psychology is that environment–behaviour relationships are treated as interrelationships. The environment influences and constrains behaviour, but the behaviour also leads to changes in the environment. For instance, the availability of particular fuels (for example coal or timber) in the environment will influence the types of energy-producing behaviour that will occur. That in turn will shape the type of pollution that is likely to result and the kinds of health problems that may arise for the fuel users. The strength of the interrelationships that can exist between people and the natural environment is also illustrated in the way people will commonly report being able to perceive the impressions that particular cultures leave on the landscape. As one phenomenologist (Ortega, 1972) put it: 'To walk then, through an orchard, sown field, or stubble field, through an olive grove laid out in diagonal rows or methodically planned grove of pine oaks, is to follow man travelling within himself.' You may have noticed that it is often possible to distinguish between photographs of French, American, Norwegian and English landscapes because they have been modified over centuries to reflect the interrelationships that communities have developed with their natural surroundings.

A fourth characteristic of environmental psychology is that it is less likely to draw sharp distinctions between basic and applied research than other sub-disciplines of psychology. The fuzziness of the distinction arises because environmental psychologists usually undertake particular research investigations for both practical and theoretical purposes. Environmental psychology is problem-focused; it is intended to inform solutions to practical problems, such as changing environmentally destructive behaviours.

A fifth characteristic of environmental psychology is that it is strongly inter-disciplinary. Landscape architects, urban planners, builders and environmental scientists share a professional interest in the study, management and development of natural and built environments. More generally, encouraging people to change environmentally destructive behaviours is a matter of concern for governments and voluntary organizations, such as Friends of the Earth, throughout the world. This means that environmental psychology also has a distinctly international flavour.

These five characteristics combine to give the application of social psychology to environmental issues a particular quality. Thus, many psychologists working on environmental issues call themselves 'environmental psychologists', rather than applied social psychologists, in order to signal the equal importance they attach to environmental and social forces. For the remainder of this chapter we will use the term 'environmental psychology' as a synonym for the application of social psychology to environmental problems and concerns.

History and development

The history of the study of environment behaviour interrelationships grew out of an interdisciplinary movement associated with the work or five pioneers: Roger Barker, Edward Hall, Kevin Lynch, Robert Sommer and Christopher Alexander. The earliest pioneer was Roger G. Barker. He was a student of the social psychologist Kurt Lewin, who regarded the environment as a key determinant of behaviour. Even though Lewin is primarily associated with the analysis of social environments much of his theoretical work was informed by an early interest in 'the phenomenology of landscape' (Lewin, 1917) that arose from his observations of battlefields during the First World War.

The major part of Barker's career was devoted to investigating the everyday lives of children and adults with a particular emphasis on identifying, describing and measuring the environments in which they live. In 1947 he established, in the small town of Oskaloosa, Kansas, the Midwest Psychological Field Station. Its mission was to investigate the everyday lives of the children of the town; what happens to them (their environments) and how they react (their behaviour). Two kinds of data resulted from the two methods he used: specimen record data and behaviour-setting data. Specimen records are minute by minute, day-long narratives of the personal environments and social behaviour of individual children as seen and recorded on the spot by teams of skilled observers. Behaviour settings are the stable, environmental enclaves (for example the doctors' offices, the basketball games) a community provides its citizens. Barker regarded behaviour settings as 'geo-physical-behavioural' entities with characteristic patterns of activity and forces that coerce people to behave appropriately. Barker pioneered the analysis of behaviour–environment units but did not consider psychology capable of explaining behaviour-setting data because of its focuses on behaviour to the neglect of the environment. He developed a corpus of 'eco-behavioural' concepts and theories he considered more appropriate to the task. These are considered later in this chapter.

Conceptualizations of the term 'environment' have changed since the work of pioneers such as Barker. The early focus was on studying relationships between behaviour and the built environment. Interest was extended to natural environments, including ecological disasters, during the 1980s and 1990s when a large number of disciplines were converging on concerns about the global environmental implications of human population growth, the cumulative effects of depletion of natural resources and the consequences of progressive industrialization across the world. Thus, environmental psychology defines the term environment very broadly and includes both the built and natural environments. However, the remainder of this chapter focuses mainly on concerns with the natural environment.

Contemporary priorities

The 'tragedy of the commons' refers to a social dilemma that has had an important influence on contemporary priorities within environmental psychology (Hardin, 1968). The commons was the green area of the New England village where every member of the village could graze their livestock. The commons was owned by everyone in the village, so everyone could rightfully use it. However, when one person would begin grazing more than the average share of livestock it would be to the detriment of everyone because, if others did the same, the commons would be exhausted and all would suffer. What is so compelling about this dilemma is that it is perfectly possible that an individual might increase their livestock and assume that others will not do the same because others would recognize that, if they did so, the commons would be quickly depleted. However, others may not see it like this and respond by increasing their herds too. Hardin argued that this dilemma can be taken as a metaphor for planet earth with each country competing for its limited resources, until it is exhausted and we all perish. The dilemma raises a fundamentally important question: What attitudes and values do people have toward their environment?

Environmental attitudes

Many environmental controversies focus on disagreements about acceptable levels of chemical toxins or other hazards in the environment. What is tolerable to one person or group may be quite unacceptable to another. These differences reflect contrasting attitudes that have emerged from variations in experience, learning and background. A particularly influential approach to conceptualizing variations in environmental attitudes distinguishes between the human exceptionist paradigm (HEP) and a new environmental paradigm (NEP). The two paradigms discriminate between those who are willing to invest effort in saving the natural environment from those who are unwilling to take part in conservation activities because they regard humans as in some sense falling outside nature's influence. Those whose attitudes are closer to the HEP are more likely to regard concentrations of chemical toxins as an industrial rather than an environmental problem and something to be repaired by inventing and applying appropriate technological solutions. Those who are closer to the NEP are likely to be more concerned about the long-term consequences of delaying any clean-up of chemical toxins and more critical of industrial activities that wait for environmental problems to appear rather than minimizing the likelihood that they will arise in the first place. Dunlap and Van Liere (1978) developed a 12-item questionnaire that is often used as a standard starting point for assessing basic attitudes towards environmental issues. Their short questionnaire is reproduced at the end of this chapter.

One of the limitations of the HEP–NEP questionnaire is that it predefines two types of environmental attitude and requires respondents to endorse or reject statements reflecting just these two positions. Environmental attitudes are usually more complex and varied than this, and Gray (1985) has proposed a more sophisticated model. The elements of his model include the following:

1 General environmental concerns, including acceptance of a pressing need for humanity to act together to address a range of global environmental problems.
2 Primitive beliefs, including the belief that humanity is in some sense apart from nature and that there is little or no interdependency between different life forms. Another primitive belief regards progress and growth as fundamental to enriching the quality of life: bigger is always better and, whatever happens, science and medicine will create new technologies and cures to overcome any problem.
3 Costs/benefits, this includes both long-term and short-term aspects of the magnitude of any personal or societal threat posed by damage to the environment.
4 Locus of responsibility and control. This refers to the difference we feel our own actions can make and the extent to which we believe we can influence the attitudes and beliefs of others.

Gray's model treats attitudes towards conservation, pollution and population growth as derived from these more basic elements. Conservation, defined as attempts to achieve harmony with nature, is derived from general environmental concerns, an appreciation of costs and benefits and a strong sense of responsibility and control. Attitudes towards pollution, defined as the intrusion of novel synthetic substances into nature, are derived from primitive beliefs about the degree of interdependency between humankind, beliefs about the long-term consequences posed by a possible accumulation of pollutants and one's sense of responsibility and control in influencing levels of pollution at a local level. Attitudes towards population growth are thought to be derived from general environmental concern and primitive beliefs.

A somewhat different perspective on environmental attitudes has been developed by McKechnie (1978) whose environmental response inventory (ERI) is intended to classify personal dispositions towards the environment. He contends that there are seven major dispositions:

- *Pastoralism* is characterized by a concern for population growth, the preservation of natural resources and negative attitudes towards industrialization.
- *Urbanism* values density living, the variety of cultural and interpersonal experiences made possible by the growth of large cities.
- *Environmental* adaptation regards the environment as something to be exploited for the creation of wealth; it is associated with opposition to government controls on environmental matters and with promoting the use of technology to solve environmental problems.
- *Environmental trust* refers to a disposition whereby people feel positive, confident and safe in their environment, rather than fearful of hazards that might be lurking therein.
- *Antiquarian* refers to values and attitudes that treasure heritage and history and may be reflected in a penchant for collecting historical artefacts.
- *Need for privacy* is indicated by a need for physical isolation, a preference for wilderness and the enjoyment of solitude.
- *Mechanical orientation* refers to the enjoyment of manual work including construction and an interest in technology.

While there is ample evidence that meaningful distinctions can be made between different kinds of attitudes and dispositions to the environment, even large differences may disappear whenever a community is faced with the prospect of a hazardous waste facility being located in its midst. The reaction is usually: 'Not in my back yard!' This stock response has been dubbed the 'NIMBY principle'. It is often provoked by fears that, for example, hazardous waste will accumulate on the site and pose a long-term threat to the health of the community and to the quality of the environment. The NIMBY principle embodies some of the elements presented in the tragedy of the commons. Many important social choice problems involve selecting a single community (the 'host') to bear the cost of an environmental project that will yield net benefits for society as a whole. While everyone may agree that 'something must be done with the waste' every local community may attempt to show that some other community would be better placed to do what needs to be done. Moreover, a community that might be willing to host a site may be deterred by fears that, having agreed to a site on one occasion, they will be unfairly treated in the future and expected to take on more of their fair share of responsibility for waste disposal. However well-meaning the NIMBY principle may be, it can prevent the construction of environmentally sound waste disposal sites and encourage less suitable construction on older, contaminated sites located in depleted neighbourhoods.

Concepts, models and theories

Environmental psychologists believe that when trying to understand human–environment interactions, whether global, national or local, it is important to have a model that predicts how people will behave within and towards their environment under particular constraints and conditions. The development of such a model is still some way off but there is general agreement about the kinds of things the model should account for. These include: *Attention* – understanding how people notice the environment; *Perception and cognitive maps* – How people construct mental representations of the natural environment; *Preferred environments* – understanding the characteristics of places where people feel comfortable and confident; *Environmental stress and coping* – how people respond to hazardous environments; *Participation* – what motivates people to become involved in designing and managing their environment; and *Conservation* – the values people place on creating an ecologically sustainable environment.

Environmental psychology sets out to understand the nature of human–environment interrelationships by conducting systematic observations and attempting to identify statistical associations that can be used to make predictions. When a sufficient number of predictions have been supported the process of theory building commences in order to achieve a greater focus for research and to provide explanations as to why some behaviour–environment relationships develop as they do. Although environmental psychology is a relatively new sub-discipline several theoretical perspectives have been developed to account for a number of conspicuous regularities in human–behaviour interactions over time: arousal theory, load theory, adaptation level theory, behaviour constraint theory, stress theory and ecological theory. The emphasis in each of these is on how people respond to environmental stressors hazards or major structural changes.

Arousal theory

Arousal theory is concerned with understanding how people respond to varying levels of environmental stimulation. This approach suggests that increased environmental stimulation leads to increased arousal which requires people to make sense of this newly-noticed change. Thus, they may ask whether the increased arousal is pleasant or unpleasant. Social comparison processes can be particularly important in making sense of the increased arousal: do I seem to be better or worse-off than others who have also noticed the change? According to the Yerkes–Dodson law, increased arousal will facilitate or impair behaviour, depending on whether the individual's arousal is below or above an optimal level. The law states that behaviour is optimized at an intermediate level of arousal and becomes gradually worse when arousal becomes progressively greater or lesser than the optimum. Arousal theory is particularly effective in explaining why people respond to large changes in crowding, noise, smell or heat. For instance, a firm may introduce a more energy-efficient manufacturing process that leads to an increase in malodorous but harmless emissions. Arousal theory predicts that local communities will accept the new process provided they agree that the increase is barely noticeable and completely innocuous. The change in the environment will be noticed but good relationships between the local community and the manufacturer will remain unaltered. However, a conspicuous increase in malodorous emissions, or a belief that the new manufacturing process may not be as harmless as its predecessor, will provoke a large arousal response – the community will object to the new environment and poor community–industry relationships will ensue.

While arousal theory makes intuitive sense a major limitation relates to the measurement of 'arousal'. In the case of a manufacturing process that produces harmless but unpleasant smells it would be almost impossible to predict whether a specific increase in emissions will be perceived as an unacceptable change to environmental conditions. Familiarity with a smell, proximity to the source and individual variations in olfactory sensitivity all add to the complexity of assessing what will contribute to a change in arousal. In reality one usually has to wait for people to change their behaviour in order to determine the point at which an optimal level of arousal has been exceeded. Once exceeded a new, unknown optimum level of arousal may be established making further predictions very difficult. This means that, at a practical level, arousal theory is limited by the fact that it relies on the benefit of hindsight.

Load theory

The concept of information overload is based on the limited capacity of people to process information. This limitation means that people will use strategies, such as ignoring irrelevant information, in order to attend to more important characteristics of the environment. Conversely, very monotonous environments can lead to information underload and to stress caused by unremitting boredom. Under these circumstances people will usually expend some effort in making their surroundings more stimulating. The concept of overload can be particularly useful in understanding what motivates people to make use of leisure spaces. For example, some people enjoy taking their lunch breaks in local parks and gardens in order to 'get away from it all'. Many people use recreational spaces at the week-end to 'recharge their batteries'. Information overload can also be used to account for the fact that as the amount of vegetation in a neighbourhood increases so do property values but only up to a point, after which the settings as seen as unkempt and as a potential source of damage to surrounding houses (Stern, 1992). One of the limitations of the information overload perspective is that 'monotony' is a psychological response that varies from person to person. Some people might regard a journey across moorland or a desert as terribly monotonous, while others would regard it as hugely stimulating. Moreover, like arousal theory, it is usually impossible to predict an optimum level of information load in advance of that level being exceeded.

Adaptation level theory

Adaptation level theory (Wohwill, 1974) attempts to address a limitation common to arousal and information overload theories by emphasizing the importance of individual differences in adaptation level: stimulation above or below an individual's adaptation level will be experienced as unpleasant and provoke a matching response either to increase or decrease the level of environmental stimulation. Adaptation level is particularly useful in accounting for three types of environment–behaviour relationships: sensory stimulation, social stimulation and movement. Too much (e.g. noise) or too little (e.g. silence) sensory stimulation can be unpleasant. Similarly, too much or too little social contact can be undesirable, as can too much or too little movement in the environment. Wohwill argues that these three types of environment–behaviour relationship vary along three dimensions: *patterning, intensity* and *diversity*. Patterning refers to the extent to which anything we perceive has both structure (predictability) and uncertainty. For example, you have probably been in buildings or cities that you have experienced as extremely 'confusing'. A sense of being 'lost' can be unpleasant and stressful because of the absence of structure and predictability in your surroundings. Intensity refers to the quantity of sensory of stimulation of which a person is aware. Living or working in extremely noisy environments can be just as taxing as those experienced as 'eerily quiet'; very dark locales can be as stressful as others that are dazzling bright. Diversity refers to the degree of variety in an environment. Too much variety, as in the proliferation of shops in a local neighbourhood, can be experienced as an ugly eyesore, whereas too little is associated with a sense of environmental dreariness.

Wohwill introduced an important caveat to arousal theory to reflect the fact that there are large individual differences in preferred levels of stimulation: people do not share the same adaptation level and an individual's adaptation level will vary over time. For example, if you have moved from a rural to an urban environment you may have found the initial experience quite stressful: the levels of noise and movements of people and vehicles can be intrusive and somewhat overwhelming. Similarly, if you have lived in a city for a long period of time and then spent some time in a secluded rural area you may have experienced the absence of noise and people as somewhat disorienting. A person's adaptation level is strongly influenced by their previous experiences – the kinds of settings in which they have routinely lived and worked. Paradoxically, adding this caveat seems entirely sensible but it limits the usefulness of the theory. Because adaptation level theory accommodates so much individual variation it can explain every response but not predict how a particular person will experience a specific change to their environment. Moreover, like arousal and overload theories, it is very difficult to predict the adaptation level which a person or group of people require. The only sure way to identify an adaptation level is to exceed it.

Behaviour constraint theory

Behaviour constraint theory focuses on things that people experience as imposing limitations on their intentions, actions or preferences. It emphasizes the importance of perceived control: to what extent do people *perceive* constraints and to what extent do they believe they can influence restrictions on their lives. Perceived loss of control over the environment, such as may be experienced in a prison, can lead to reactance – a sense of discomfort than can prompt efforts to regain a sense of control or, in some cases, learned helplessness. If repeated attempts to regain a sense of control are unsuccessful people may feel there is little they can do to improve their situation and thereby 'learn' to be helpless. For instance, a local community that has failed to change emissions from local factories may feel that there is little they can do to improve their circumstances which may, in time, lead to further depletion of environment. This model is particularly useful in predicting the cumulative effects of a perceived loss of control. However, it does not recognize that an increased sense of control can actually lead to problems too: if people feel that they can avert many environmental disasters that could potentially befall them, they may expend endless hours of worry and effort attempting to control forces of nature that are rarely likely to impact on them. People may feel a sense of responsibility to influence things that are in reality beyond their control.

Stress theory

Stress theory suggests that once stimuli within the environment have been evaluated as threatening, coping strategies are brought into play. These strategies are often beneficial because they allow people to deal with the perceived threat. However, prolonged exposure to stress can produce enduring aftereffects including psychological ill-health and lowered resistance to stress. The stress model is very effective in predicting the consequences of long-term environmental stress; however, the identification of a stressor is problematic because it requires someone to show a stress response in order to identify whether something is stressful. Ironically, failure to express a stress response may have negative long-term consequences. For instance, a local community that has become accustomed to emissions from a nearby factory may allow toxins to build up to such a level that serious ill-health problems only become apparent many years later. Stress theory does not indicate which aspects of an environment have the potential to be more stressful than others.

Ecology theory

Barker (1968), one of the pioneers of environmental psychology, emphasized behaviour setting as a single environment–behaviour unit of study. For example, when examining the ecological psychology of the classroom, he was particularly interested in understanding the number of people required to maintain that setting. How many children are required? How many teachers and assistants are needed? What happens if there are too many children or too few assistants? In examining these questions, Barker developed Staffing Theory (or manning theory as it was first coined). The core idea is that every environment–behaviour unit requires a *maintenance minimum*. The largest number of people a setting can accommodate is its *capacity*. People who qualify for membership or admission to a setting are referred to as *applicants*. If the number of applicants to a behaviour setting falls below a maintenance minimum, then people who are already in the setting must take on additional roles in order to maintain it. Barker distinguished between people who took on primary responsibility for managing the maintenance of a setting, *performers*, and those who took on secondary roles, *non-performers*. In a classroom setting the teacher would be regarded as the performer and her pupils the non-performers. The maintenance minimum for performers could be the minimum number of teachers required in a class, for non-performers it could be the smallest number of pupils needed to keep the class going. Barker's approach is particularly effective in understanding relationships between groups and the environment. For example, it provides a general framework for understanding challenges that arise when attempting to maintain particular settings, such as preserving the quality of beaches and other environmental amenities. It also provides a method that can be used to produce very detailed descriptive analyses of any environment–behaviour interrelationship. However, it is so broad in its scope that it has the potential to account for everything that might attract the interest of an environmental psychologist while being of limited practical value in predicting or helping to manage changes in environment–behaviour interrelationships.

Practical issues

Ethics and environmental psychology

Many techniques and measurement approaches preferred by environmental psychologists require research to be conducted in naturalistic settings in which the research participants are usually completely unaware that an investigation is taking place. While unobtrusive observation frequently improves the validity of research in a number of ways, it also raises significant ethical questions regarding informed consent and the invasion of privacy. Before conducting covert observational studies it is essential to undertake an assessment of the extent to which human dignity may be jeopardized and that threat must be weighed against the value of the study. What major issues will be clarified by the study? If the study is so designed that its value may only become apparent after the data have been analysed, then one must ask whether psychologists should be involved in research where the end (the nature of the results) will be used to justify the methods.

A related question concerns whether people who may be included in observational studies should be alerted to the fact, for example through use of public notices, that they are entering an area that will be monitored for research purposes? Is it better to leave people unaware so that they will not be upset by the realization of having been included in an investigation? It may be possible to inform participants when they are leaving the research environment (for example as they are about to depart from a shop), but that may over-sensitise them to the possibility of future covert observations taking place in other everyday settings. Some people may be genuinely distressed at the prospect of being unwitting participants in psychological research.

What is the rationale for assuming it to be permissible under some conditions to observe people without their knowledge? People in public settings, such as on footpaths, realize they are under constant informal observation by others and for this reason most researchers argue that systematic observation should be no more threatening. Moreover, in many environments such as shops and railway stations, people have become accustomed to the presence of security cameras. However, if research participants in a public setting become aware of being observed for research purposes, rather than to maintain security, there are good reasons to alert them to the dual purpose of the cameras and to provide them with an alternative route or area that is not being monitored by a research team. While potentially this leads to selection bias in people involved in the study, it does protect their right to privacy. The assumption that under some conditions researchers have the 'right' to observe people always requires environmental psychologists to judge when the behaviour falls in the public domain and when it should be considered private.

Assessing perceptions of environmental quality

Perceptions of the quality of an environment are usually better predictors of attitudes and behaviour than objective indicators, such as pollution levels. For example, compared to the levels of pollution associated with cities, the countryside is often perceived to be relatively unspoiled and clean. Consequently, public concerns about the quality of urban environments are typically stronger than worries about the quality of rural settings. In reality the economic pressures on farmers to produce larger quantities of cheap food have forced many of them to rely ever more heavily on chemical sprays to achieve greater crop yields. Thus, on some objective indicators, such as the concentration levels of nitrogen in the soil, agricultural land should be regarded as heavily polluted. Although the implications of agri-chemical pollution for the survival of wildlife, as well as the water quality of lakes, rivers and streams, should be a cause for concern, public *perceptions* of rural environments as 'natural' and 'clean' mean that environmental problems in rural areas tend to go unnoticed.

Perceptions of environmental quality are reflected in their perceived economic value. For example, estimates of the value of basically identical houses with different landscaping have been found to result in an average increase of 7 per cent (Orland, Vining and Ebreo, 1992). People are willing to pay for more aesthetically pleasing environments; environmental quality has real economic worth. Orland *et al.* also found that properties located close to wooded areas are often sought after, and 'treed' neighbourhoods are highly valued. In a study inspired by labelling theory, Anderson (1981) investigated how different labels could affect people's perception of a landscape. She found that areas labelled as 'wilderness' and 'national parks' received higher ratings on landscape quality than did others labelled as 'timber stands' and 'leased grazing areas'. This suggests that labels create expectations of a quality of a scene and when the landscape confirms these expectations the effect of the label is more pronounced than when the scene does not fit the expectation. Labels such as 'wilderness', 'national park' and 'national forest' imply naturalness, a quality that has been consistently reported as being preferred to 'treated' or 'artificial' landscapes (Hodgson and Thayer, 1980).

How are perceptions of environmental quality measured? Daniel and Vining (1983) describe five perspectives on the assessment of environmental quality:

1   The ecological perspective emphasizes the physical and biological features of the environment, such as the diversity of flora and fauna in a particular area;
2   The aesthetic perspective relies on the judgments of experts (e.g. landscape planners) to assess the aesthetic value of an area of land;
3   The psychophysical perspective measures how people perceive the environment to discover whether there are mathematical relationships between geometrical and geographical characteristics of the landscape and positive perceptions of quality;
4   The psychological perspective examines the feelings and perceptions of those who encounter the landscape;
5   The phenomenological perspective is concerned with examining the world that exists prior to our conceptualizing it, and emphasizes the need to continually examine and reexamine our biases and presuppositions.

Each perspective has advantages and disadvantages. For example, the ecological perspective runs into difficulties in attempting to establish an 'appropriate' variety of flora and fauna and in trying to account for the range of values, from little to very great, that people place on bio-diversity. The aesthetic perspective can be criticized for relying too heavily on expert testimony, while the phenomenological approach fails to attend to important details of the psychological processes involved in assessing quality.

Several methods have been developed to assess the scenic quality of an environmental vista because visual appearance usually plays a particularly important role in judgments of environmental quality. These most frequently used methods are descriptive inventories, questionnaire surveys and evaluations of perceptual preference (Daniel and Boster, 1976). The various methods are sensitive to different aspects of environmental quality.

Descriptive inventories are based on lists of landscape features, such as rivers and trees, thought to be particularly relevant to judgments of scenic beauty. The presence or absence of each feature is noted, their number counted, and in some instances, a numerical value assigned to each feature. This feature-based inventory is then used to quantify scenic quality. If an appropriate list of relevant features can be established a wide variety of landscape types (such as urban, coastal, mountainous) can be described in comparable terms. An obvious difficulty is that the features used must be sufficiently flexible to allow application to a number of quite different landscapes. They must also be sufficiently precise to discriminate within groups of similar landscapes. For example, they must be able to discriminate between the scenic quality of a number of mountainous landscapes. In practice descriptive inventories can be used to reliably quantify large differences in scenic quality, as between very pleasant and very unpleasant urban landscapes, but they are much less effective in discriminating between scenes at an intermediate level of pleasantness where most realistic landscape management alternatives lie. The effectiveness of descriptive inventories depends to a great extent on the expertise and judgment of the user, and on the relevance of the descriptive features included in the inventory. Perhaps their greatest weakness has been a failure to relate the features included in most inventories to independently validated measures of scenic beauty (Daniel and Boster, 1976).

Surveys and questionnaires are commonly used to gauge public perceptions of environmental quality. These techniques presume that preferences expressed by respondents are directly related to their perceptions of landscape beauty: the greater the preference for one landscape over another, the greater the implied beauty. In reality the relationship between ones preference for a landscape and its perceived beauty is usually more complex than this. For example, landscapes are often populated by people: a piece of wasteland may be a recreation site favoured by local children. Survey respondents may indicate that they regard the public park as scenically superior to the wasteland, but they may also judge it to be a less valuable environmental resource for their community. The wasteland may be preferred because it is considered safer for the reason that it is closer to children's homes and allows parents to supervise their children more easily. The specific wording of a questionnaire can also be critically important because responses may be determined as much by the way a landscape is represented in a question as by its actual characteristics. For example, a local river may be bounded by derelict warehouses on one side and a public park on the other. A question such as: 'What are your feelings about the river running beside the derelict warehouses?' may elicit less favourable responses than: 'What are your feelings about the river running beside the public park?' There is no simple way to determine the most appropriate phrasing of a question. Neither is there is a simple way of determining the 'true meaning' of respondent's replies, especially from open ended questions.

Perceptual preference assessments attempt to address some of the limitations in survey questionnaires by representing landscapes more directly to respondents either in the form of photographs, video recordings or, less frequently, by visits to specific sites. Determining vantage points and which photos should represent an entire landscape are some of the decisions that have to be made. If samples of photographs are shown against photographic criteria such as composition, colour, lighting and framing, substantial bias may be introduced. Random sampling from a large number of photographs may reduce this potential source of bias but random sampling may not be possible when particular areas include prominent features or well-known panoramic views.

Perceptual preference assessments typically require respondents to make a forced choice between two scenes or to rank their preferences for several scenes. These procedures generally yield an ordinal ranking of preferences and reveal little if anything of relative preference intensities. For example, respondents may consider their top two preferred scenes to be vastly more preferable to their third-ranked preference, but simple ordinal ranking will not reveal this. Further, only a small number of scenes can be effectively managed with this procedure. By using an individual rating procedure a much larger number of landscapes can be efficiently evaluated, and an indication of the relative differences between landscapes (rather than simple rankings) can be obtained. However, the interpretation of rating responses often requires mathematical transformations or complex statistical analysis to adjust for each observer's idiosyncratic use of the response scale. Notwithstanding these limitations, because perceptual preference assessments represent the landscape more directly than verbal descriptions, they offer distinct advantages over questionnaire surveys.

Measuring scenic beauty

Imagine you read of a proposal to construct a new road to a remote forest recreation area. The road must provide access and attractive vistas but should not be an unpleasant intrusion for either inhabitants or tourists. How can the road be constructed so as to keep the scenic quality unchanged? The answer to this question illustrates how applied social psychologists draw on diverse psychological concepts as well as ideas and approaches from other disciplines.

Many of the most widely applied principles for landscape assessment and management evolved from the design tradition of landscape architecture. This approach emphasises the importance of contrasts in lines, forms, colours or textures that are likely to draw attention. It is broadly consonant with what psychologists know about how people visually process information. For example, the human visual system is especially sensitive to the presence of contrasts and can readily detect certain simple lines or shapes. Given that these principles help to determine what will receive attention, what determines whether the scene is evaluated as pleasant or unpleasant? Scenes in which contrast is high often receive positive evaluations, for example the contrast of snow-capped mountain peaks with the green valleys at their feet, and this probably contributes to their visual appeal. However, given that people generally prefer natural landscapes to those produced by human engineering, one would probably wish to minimize contrasts that draw attention to industrial sites or the presence of electricity transmission cables and supporting pylons.

Berlyne's (1960) work on aesthetic judgement provided a foundation for much of the research carried out on environmental aesthetics over the last 25 years. Berlyne was particularly interested in human exploratory activity when viewing environments, and especially the role of 'collative properties' (those that create perceptual conflict) of environmental stimuli. Collative properties include: complexity, the degree to which a variety of components make up an environment; novelty, the extent to which there is a mismatch between an environmental factor and its content; and 'surprisingness', the extent to which we are presented with the unexpected. These collative properties relate to the uncertainty contained within an environment and accordingly an environment elicits responses to reduce the uncertainty caused. Berlyne's general hypothesis, supported by a large corpus of empirical evidence, is that people engage in voluntary, active exploration of an environment in direct proportion to the amount of uncertainty and conflict it engenders. A person's tendency to engage in exploration is highest for environments relatively rich in collative properties.

Although Berlyne's work was highly influential, it was criticized for not attending to individual differences in perceptions of environmental aesthetics and for presuming that the scenically beautiful and aesthetically pleasing will always be valued more highly. Kaplan and Kaplan (1979) attempted to address some of these limitations and argued that in order to understand environmental preferences one must first understand how people react to things and spaces. They identified two persisting purposes, 'making sense' and 'involvement'. We should prefer environments that we can understand – 'make sense'– and stimulate or 'involve' us. Four major variables, similar to those described by Berlyne in his work on aesthetics, are identified by the Kaplans:

- *Coherence*: the extent to which an environment has structure and organization, or how it 'hangs together'; more coherent environments are preferred.
- *Complexity*: how much is going on in the environment; the greater the complexity the stronger the preference.
- *Legibility*: the degree to which a landscape or scene can be recognized and classified; the greater the legibility the stronger the preference.
- *Mystery*: the degree to which an environment contains hidden information or the promise of new sights and experiences; the greater the mystery the stronger the preference.

The Kaplans' approach has been particularly useful in estimating public reactions to the management and development of landscapes that contain high levels of variety. However, some landscapes, such as forest parks, are quite monotonous and public perceptions of their quality and value cannot be accurately predicted using their approach. To address this problem Ulrich (1977) proposed that it is possible to scale landscapes according to the extent that certain other variables are present. These variables are components of the theoretical concepts of legibility and mystery. He proposed that a landscape will be highly legible, and thus preferred, if:

- Its visual complexity is moderate to high;
- Complexity is patterned and helps to establish a focal point (focality);
- The ground surface texture is even; and
- Visual depth is moderate to high and is unrestricted.

In one study Ulrich assembled 53 photographs of landscapes chosen by a panel of experts to reflect varying degrees of legibility. Respondents were asked to rate each photograph on a six-point preference scale. He found statistically significant correlations between the preference ratings given by the respondents and the values for the model variables obtained from the panel of judges ratings for focality, ground texture, depth and mystery, but not complexity.

Statistical methods can do a very respectable job of predicting subjective assessments of environmental scenes and have been frequently applied by environment resource managers though rarely by designers. However, a shortcoming of the physical-perceptual approach is that the predictors – the measures that are used to statistically estimate people's evaluations of a landscape – do not always make intuitive or theoretical sense. This criticism is not fatal but it means that the predictive equations developed in one environmental setting may not generalize to other, ostensibly similar landscapes. Although this approach is attractive because it emphasizes objective characteristics of the environment, psychologists are also intrigued by the possibility that measures of more purely psychological processes, such as memory of a particular landscape, may be effective at identifying constructs that can be applied to human experience across a wide range of environments.

The way forward

Today's children will be tomorrow's decision-makers, and our environmental bequest includes a plethora of problems with serious implications for social, economic and cultural development. We are obliged to include in that legacy a repertoire of problem-solving skills commensurate with the scale of the environmental problems they will confront. While there is a good deal of evidence that children hold encouraging attitudes towards a range of environmental issues, positive attitudes will not necessarily lead in any direct way to changes in the way people think about the environmental consequences of their actions, nor to more creative approaches to solving environmental problems. Thus, environmental psychologists have turned their attention to examining children's understanding of complex environmental processes and to the development of techniques that may help foster children's environmental problem-solving.

Environments are systems, and environmental education entails imparting concepts from systems theory, including systems analysis and management. However, the theoretical and empirical literature on the developmental progress of the child's concept of system is sparse, possibly because talking about systems is demanding both cognitively and linguistically and we may have wrongly presumed that children do not approach an appropriate level of sophistication until adolescence. Since the natural environment is a system, helping children to develop a sophisticated understanding of many environmental issues, global or local, should be based on attempts to support their systems thinking. What is it that children are doing when they are engaged in systems thinking?

Sterman (1994) described systems thinking as the ability to see the world as a complex system, in which we understand that 'you can't do just one thing' and that 'everything is connected to everything else.' Espego (1994) proposed that systemic thinking involves an understanding of how: (1) the parts of an environment relate to each other and constitute large wholes, (2) interactive processes constitute wholes at multiple levels, (3) an environmental process works, and (4) local, specific behaviour can affect the whole system, and vice versa. Wiley *et al.* (1998) have suggested that young children are able to engage in systems thinking much earlier than much of the traditional developmental literature would seem to suggest. They argue that the thinking system of the child – *how* the child thinks about environmental systems rather than *what* they know – should be the basis for understanding how children learn to think of the environment as a system. For example, they emphasize the importance of understanding the ways in which children explain *how* air pollution comes about and *how* they would solve this problem, rather than the technical or scientific accuracy of their answers. Wylie *et al.* (1998) found that pictorial materials can make it easier for children to show how they think about environmental systems because they reduce the burden on the child to express what they are thinking through language. However, pictures are static representations against which interactions, consequences and so on must be imagined, thus making it difficult for the child to articulate what they know about systems behaviour. A better approach involves using systems to understand children's systems thinking and support its development.

Computer-based environmental simulations can offer children opportunities to manage dynamic systems and to demonstrate their systems thinking through their interactions with the simulation in ways that further reduce language demands. Sheehy *et al.* (2000) developed a computer-based simulation to examine how eight and 11-year-old children would solve environmental dilemmas. One dilemma involved a forest depletion problem and another a water shortage. Although the complexity of the final simulations for the two groups of children were broadly similar, older children were better able to forestall the depletion of both the forest and water resources, suggesting they had managed the resources somewhat better. Younger children appeared to work from the principle that 'biggest is best' and attempted to solve environmental problems by creating larger resources, either by planting larger forests or creating larger water reservoirs. Older children appeared to work from the premise that 'small is beautiful' and attempted to minimize the use of scarce resources. Thus, younger children focused their efforts on parts of the problem at the source (that is, planting more forests) or end of the life-cycle (creating larger waste sites), whereas older children concentrated more on improving the use of paper products between production and disposal. In other words, when attempting to research solutions to environmental dilemmas, older children focused on changing aspects of social behaviour that would have beneficial environmental impacts. They used their knowledge about human behaviour and *social* systems to intervene in the enrichment of *environmental* systems and in so doing demonstrated what environmental psychology is about: understanding the consequences of human behaviour for the environment and changing human behaviour in ways that will enrich environmental and social systems. Future work must continue to develop approaches based on children's ability to learn to solve *environmental* problems through *social* interventions. To borrow from Einstein's quotation: we cannot expect the next generation to solve the significant environmental problems we have bequeathed to them by working at the same level of sophistication which operated when we created them.

SHORT QUESTIONS

1 A fellow student studying landscape planning and management tells you she has heard about environmental psychology and asks you what psychologists can contribute to the management of the natural environment. What would you tell her, and why?

2 Is it possible to produce an objective measure of scenic beauty?

3 Which of the major theories of environmental psychology considered in this chapter do you regard as the best? Justify your choice.

4 Look around the room you are in right now. To what extent can it be described as an environmental system?

5 If you were planning to conduct an observational study of children's use of a public playground what ethical precautions would you take, and why?

CLASS ACTIVITIES

I   Complete the HEP–NEP attitude questionnaire. Ask some of your friends to do the same and compare your respective positions.

The HEP–NEP Attitude Questionnaire

	Strongly agree 4	Mildly agree 3	Mildly disagree 2	Strongly disagree 1
1. We are approaching the limit of the number of people the earth can support.				
2. The balance of nature is very delicate and easily upset.				
3. Humans have the right to modify the natural environment to suit their needs.*				
4. Mankind was created to rule over the rest of nature.*				
5. When humans interfere with nature it often produces disastrous consequences.				
6. Plants and animals exist primarily to be used by humans.*				
7. To maintain a healthy economy, we will have to develop a 'steady state' economy where industrial growth is controlled.				
8. Humans must live in harmony with nature in order to survive.				
9. The earth is like a spaceship with only limited room and resources.				
10. Humans need not adapt to the natural environment because they can remake it to suit their own needs.*				
11. There are limits to growth beyond which our industrialized society cannot expand.				
12. Mankind is severely abusing the environment.				

*These questions are reverse scored.

A total score of 12 indicates a complete rejection of the new environmental paradigm and reflects a strong belief that the natural environment is there for human beings to do with what they wish. A score of 48 indicates a strong commitment to the new paradigm.

2   Assemble some photographs of four or five outdoor locations that you think of as aesthetically pleasing. When you think of those locations to what extent do you think they can be described in terms of their:

(1)   *Coherence*: the extent to each location has structure and organization, or how it 'hangs together';

(2)   *Complexity*: how much is going on in each environment;

(3)   *Legibility*: the degree to which each location can be recognized and classified according to its distinctive features;

(4)   *Mystery*: the degree to which each environment contains hidden information or the promise of new sights and experiences.

3   What psychological factors are at work in the NIMBY principle? Can their influence be reduced?

FURTHER READING

Bell, P.A., Greene, T.C., Fisher, J.D. and Baum, A. (2000) *Environmental Psychology*. London: Harcourt.

Cassidy, T. (2002) *Psychology in Practice: Environment*. London: Hodder & Stoughton.

Stern, P.C. (1992) 'Psychological Determinants of Global Environmental Change', *Annual Review of Psychology*, vol. 43, pp. 269–302.

Wapner, S., Demick, J., Takiji, Y., Minami, H. and Yamamoto, C.T. (1999) *Theoretical Perspectives in Environment–Behavior Research*. New York: Plenum.

Work

To travel hopefully is a better thing than to arrive, and the true success is to labour.
(Robert Louis Stevenson, 1881)

ONCE UPON A TIME...

Joe came to the end of his second year at university with an overdraft which his bank manager described as 'truly awesome'. In his defence Joe had worked hard at his studies after receiving a poor set of examination results after Christmas and so had given up his part-time job in a local supermarket having decided that his degree must come first and that somehow he could survive until the summer. After his June examinations Joe returned to work at the supermarket but was disappointed to find that his old supervisor had left, to be replaced by an individual who made no effort to relate to new staff and especially students. Joe's previous supervisor had worked hard to integrate new staff into his 'team' and although he made jokes about students, he appeared to like working with people who were different. In stark contrast the new supervisor clearly had his favourites, who invariably were established staff and he was quick to make fun of any newcomers. Very often he would deliberately assign the more onerous tasks to students and would be intolerant of any mistakes which they made, in particular taking great pleasure in calling into question their intelligence. While Joe would have been conscientious, in this new environment increasingly he 'did enough and no more' and hence his relationship with the supervisor went from bad to worse. Eventually, and despite still being in debt, Joe handed in his notice.

Introduction

Most adults spend around half of their waking lives at work and usually in the presence of others who are also working. As a consequence you could easily assume that work-related issues would feature prominently in the affairs of social psychology. To test this hypothesis try skimming through the subject index of any introductory social psychology text or consider the number of social psychology experiments relating to employment with which you are familiar. The reality is that the field of paid employment has largely remained out of bounds to the day-to-day interests of most social psychologists. For whatever reason, those who define themselves as social psychologists have often drawn a boundary around employment matters, leaving this field to their colleagues in occupational or industrial psychology. Perhaps this avoids any accusation of poaching or may simply reflect personal priorities or values. Whatever has been the case this chapter intends to reverse this trend by reflecting on the insights which social psychology has made and can make to understanding the world of employment.

The chapter will aim to explore and evaluate the processes whereby social psychological knowledge can impact on the labour market, along the way focusing on areas including leadership, work motivation and group processes, and touching on other concerns such as recruitment and selection and the management of diversity. Rather than focusing exclusively on material derived from psychology, it is hoped to set this work in a wider context by drawing on literature from a number of relevant disciplines, thereby highlighting a core theme of the book, the value of a multidisciplinary approach when applying social psychology to the real world.

History and development

Before the industrial revolution in the Western world (the late eighteenth and nineteenth centuries), the concept of employment was quite different from that which we take for granted today. Before that time the line of demarcation between paid work and other life domains was not clear-cut, with domestic life and employment often naturally intertwining in small-scale businesses and cottage industries. However, with the continuing growth of the industrial process the split between the home and the place of work became ever wider, and at this time increasing attention was afforded to where paid employment featured as a distinct activity in the social order.

Although this was a major theme for many Victorian authors, this was by no means new territory. Many centuries earlier, both Plato and Aristotle had argued that there was a natural order which characterized society and which determined gainful employment within that society. Plato described three primary social strata which he labelled *guardians* (the aristocracy), *warriors* and *artisans* (the workers). Likewise Aristotle identified three, in his case the *very rich* (who did not have to work), the *very poor* (who often were unable to work) and the *middle classes* (who worked). Furthermore Aristotle argued that self-realization was only attainable within the stratum which was appropriate to that person's innate psychological make-up – in his world view we each have a rightful place and we should know that place. While neither Plato nor Aristotle would have been described as social psychologists, as is so often the case with hindsight we can see that they were presenting social psychological theories dealing with the individual in social context and in particular as defined by the person's employment status. It is also worth bearing in mind that those who occupy the highest social strata are those who are removed from the burden of work, they are seen as above such activity, thereby identifying work as something which we may aspire not to do!

The idea that our psychological well-being hinges on occupancy of one's rightful position in the social pecking order as reflected in employment status, is also reflected in nineteenth-century theorizing on matters which today would also be described as social psychological. One example is Social Darwinism, a theory which sat easily with or even excused the brutal excesses of the early industrial process. Derived from the work of both Herbert Spencer (1820–1903) and Charles Darwin (1809–82), Social Darwinism postulated that the social order is a consequence of natural evolutionary forces and especially the survival of the fittest. Nature dictates that the strong will flourish and the weak will go to the wall, and accordingly social advantage and disadvantage merely reflect the workings of nature. Indeed, it would be flying in the face of nature to interfere with this process, for example by promoting social welfare. In many respects Social Darwinism and related social and political theories at that stage in our history helped provide a 'scientific' rationale for permitting market forces to rage unfettered during and beyond the industrial revolution, and in the process allowed a blind eye to be turned to welfare issues in and out of work. The appalling conditions endured by workers during the nineteenth and early twentieth century, as witnessed by popular Victorian writers such as Charles Dickens, bear stark testimony to the pervasiveness of such views.

Beyond popular fiction, in the nineteenth century perhaps the most insight-ful and critical analyses of the relationship between the individual and the labour market came not from psychology but from those outside the discipline. For example the German sociologist Max Weber (1864–1920) related the growth of modern industrial capitalism to a particular personality type which he linked with protestantism or, more specifically, Calvinism. The protestant work ethic, as he dubbed it, was founded on a set of religious beliefs which not only tolerated but actively encouraged the accumulation of wealth, which valued industry for its own sake and which disavowed worldly pleasures. According to Weber this mind-set provided a recipe for the growth of capitalism and its associated industrial forms (Abraham, 1973).

Writing at the same time, the influential French sociologist Emile Durkheim (1858–1917) described two types of solidarity which he felt characterized societies pre and post the industrial age. These were based on types of division of labour which in turn were reflected in different types of individual consciousness. The first, 'mechanistic solidarity', characterized non-industrialized societies where, 'Solidarity which comes from likenesses is at its maximum when the collective conscious completely envelopes our own conscience' (*The Division of Labour in Society*, The Free Press, 1947). In contrast, industrialized societies, characterized by high degrees of differentiation in relation to the division of labour, foster 'organic solidarity' where the whole is greater than the sum of its parts and where the individual can often feel psychologically distant and apart from the place of work.

As sociologists, both these writers focused their attentions on social structures but at the same time their analyses were underpinned by social psychological assumptions about personality, relationships and the nature of 'human nature'. Likewise, while Marx, Engels and Hegel would each have regarded the human condition as primarily a reflection on economic forces operating at any moment in history, they also considered that condition in relation to different means of production. In the words of Marx, 'Man is...not only a social animal but an animal which can develop into an individual only in society' (*A Contribution to the Critique of Political Economy*, 1904, p. 266). Marx believed that modern industrial or bourgeois society had surplanted feudalism, characterized by many different classes, and had distilled class divisions down to two, the bourgeoisie (the owners) and the proletariat (the workers). And what of the human condition at work in capitalist societies? According to Marx,

> The work of the proletarians has lost all individual character, and consequently, all charm for the workman. He becomes an appendage of the machine. Not only are they the slaves of the bourgeois class...they are daily and hourly enslaved by the machine, by the over-looker and, above all, by the individual bourgeois manufacturer himself. (*Manifesto of the Communist Party*, 1888, p. 21)

These writers created the backcloth against which psychologists began to ply their trade. In the early part of the twentieth century a small number of psychologists started to consider business and industry, but generally with scant regard to the grand political, economic or sociological concerns as outlined above. Perhaps these psychologists are best described as technicians rather than social commentators or theorists, not concerned with 'macro' issues of social order but the 'micro' environment of the workplace. As early psychology focused on the laboratory, so early industrial psychologists focused on the factory. As one example, Hugo Munsterberg (1863–1916), a former student of William James and his successor as director of the psychology laboratory at Harvard University, published what is regarded by many as the first textbook on the psychology of work, entitled *Psychology and Industrial Efficiency* (New York: Houghton, 1913). It is interesting that his three core themes (personnel selection; ergonomics; marketing and consumer research) would still resonate in today's industrial psychology texts, but equally the book contains few mentions of wider social issues beyond the factory gates.

From within industry itself, one character came to play a very significant role in the development of the psychology of work around this time. Perhaps not coincidentally, Frederick Winslow Taylor (1856–1917) was an engineer by training. His first post was as a labourer with the Midvale Steel Works but he quickly rose to the post of chief engineer before moving to the Bethlehem Steel Works. Here was a man who used his practical experience to inform theory. His famous text, *Principles of Scientific Management*, was published in 1911, but even as early as 1895 he had presented papers on the effects of different wage systems on performance (and his first text called *Shop Management* had appeared in 1903).

Taylor's theory of scientific management was based on four principles. First, the development of a true science of work (knowing what is a 'fair day's work' but using this yardstick to establish a 'large daily task' and offering reward for this greater productivity); second, the use of scientific selection procedures and progressive development of each recruit when in work (that is, the need to identify and train those capable of above-average work); third, combining the science of work with scientifically selected and trained workers (through a 'mental revolution' in management); and fourth, the constant and intimate cooperation of management and workers (the two work in harmony for what he described as their common good – increased productivity).

Taylor's ideas were greeted enthusiastically by several captains of industry, not surprisingly given the huge short-term increases in productivity which he had proved were possible using these methods. To Taylor, workers were characterized as little more than trained circus animals, driven solely by greed and self-interest. It took over twenty years for this simplistic view to be challenged but yet again here was a psychological theory which sat easily with the means of production at that time, and hence the motivation for challenge was not strong. Indeed, when the challenge did arrive it came from a quite unexpected quarter.

The Hawthorne Studies, as they came to be known, were conducted principally by researchers based in the Harvard Graduate School of Business Administration and most notably Elton Mayo (1880–1949). The original research at the Hawthorne Works of the Western Electric Company of Chicago began in 1924 and was designed to investigate not social phenomena but the effects of environmental factors, including illumination, on productivity. To everyone's surprise, including the research team, regardless of changing conditions in both the experimental and control conditions it was found that productivity continued to improve over time. A further series of field experiments was then conducted between 1927 and 1932, chiefly involving the manipulation of the conditions under which a small group of women workers assembled electrical relays and electric motors. Once more physical changes in the environment had little influence on productivity. Instead, far more important appeared to be the response of the employees to their special treatment – in a nutshell, they responded by behaving specially (now known as the 'Hawthorne Effect'). Two further studies, one a survey of 21 000 employees, the other a consideration of group processes in the 'bank wiring observation room' confirmed that social considerations were of great significance in determining job satisfaction, morale and productivity. Here was a research project which naturally evolved over time but which in the process brought together a host of techniques – some experimental, others observational; some quantitative, others qualitative – which in combination threw a clear light on the emerging issues. Here were multiple perspectives in action.

This work was and is vitally important in the history of applied psychology for several reasons, but two in particular are worthy of mention. First, it established the significant role which social factors played in the workplace and in the process kick-started the human relations movement (HRM) which later revolutionized the practice of management. Second, it marked an end to a reliance on simplistic and very often demeaning interpretations of workers' behaviour and motivation which had characterized the literature previously. It also resonated with other developments at that time which had finally focused attention on workers' welfare rather than their crude exploitation. A good example was the pioneering work carried out in relation to welfare and employees' well-being in the 1920s by both Cadbury's at their

Bournville factory outside Birmingham and Rowntree's cocoa works outside York in England (Bunn, 2001).

From that time onwards it was no longer possible to ignore the complexities of social behaviour and experience at work. No one individual came to exemplify how best to develop this understanding more than Kurt Lewin (1890–1947), frequently described as the most important figure in the history of applied social psychology. Lewin was trained in Berlin but moved to Cornell University in the USA in 1933, from where he developed an academic career which had such a profound influence on the development of social psychology. Through his research and writing Lewin took issue with many psychological traditions of the time, including Taylor's principles of scientific management. For example, Lewin argued that work must be psychologically satisfying if productivity was to remain high in the longer term. Hence psychology's task was not to manipulate but to understand why work is or is not personally satisfying for the individual worker. Lewin's field theory (Lewin, 1951) remains influential to this day. According to Lewin, a field is all the forces which have an effect on an individual and in particular the life space which a person occupies. Lewin's applied work before and during the Second World War then focused on how different components of the life space interact to produce behaviour, for example in relation to particular leadership styles, new foodstuffs or changing production styles at work. Lewin first coined the term 'action research' to describe this work, as the research process was always necessarily linked with social change and was by definition never far removed from the problem at hand. For example, one of his most famous projects involved understanding and then changing attitudes and behaviour in the USA towards the consumption of offal during the war.

Contemporary priorities

Lewin was the epitome of a practical theorist and this pragmatic tradition has continued to inform this particular field through to the present day, with the focus of attention continuing to fall on the practical concerns of those who manage people at work. In industrial psychology these concerns tend to focus on a relatively small core of social psychological themes, including most notably leadership, work motivation, selection and recruitment and group processes.

Leadership

An interest in leadership had never waned from the time that industrialists in the early twentieth century (later supported by military leaders during the First

World War) turned to psychology for help in identifying potential leadership material (Bass, 1990). The earliest leadership approach in psychology (the trait approach) reflected an existing Victorian literature which described 'great men' with special talents and visions as central to the development of world history. This approach also reflected a positivist perspective as psychology's dominant 'metatheory' throughout most of its history. Positivism holds that through careful control and experimentation it will be possible to develop generalizable laws of behaviour which can define relationships between variables, and in particular can define cause and effect relationships between two or more variables. The fact that so much of our social behaviour still defies prediction highlights the shortcomings of a strong positivist standpoint, but its appeal continues to draw those who believe that the goal of prediction and control is realizable

In accordance with this perspective, the task undertaken by those adopting the 'great man' or trait approach to leadership was to provide the formula which could define a successful leader in terms of both psychological and physical attributes. Literally hundreds of studies have been undertaken over the last 100 years in an attempt to unearth this formula, but it will probably come as no surprise to learn that the task has been less than successful (Bass, 1990). Leaders come in all shapes and sizes, and there is no blueprint for success as the pages of history and of business bear witness.

An alternative position held that it is context that determines who will emerge to influence or lead. The *zeitgeist* (spirit of the times) or situational approach suggests that a search for traits is doomed to failure because context is the key. According to this perspective, if political leaders had not risen to power at key moments in history then some other leader with similar outlooks and values would have emerged in order to fit the bill at that particular time. Yet again, history has shown this approach to be too simplistic. Instead, since the 1950s there has been a succession of projects which have considered the behaviour of leaders in various situations, to determine which combinations of people and places are most successful, otherwise known as contingency approaches.

The scene for this work was established by two significant applied projects. First, Lewin and his co-workers considered the effects of different styles of supervision (authoritarian, democratic or *laissez-faire*) on 'social climate' in four clubs of 10-year-old boys. They found that the three styles indeed had a differential impact on both climate and productivity, with the democratic style generally yielding the most positive responses from the boys. Second, in the 1950s researchers from both Ohio State and Michigan Universities used a range of techniques, including factor analysis, to identify behaviours of supervisors in business and industry. These behaviours appeared to cluster around two dimensions labelled at the time as *consideration* (the extent to which the supervisor/leader focuses on people) and *initiating structure* (the extent to which the supervisor/leader focuses on the task). Although these constructs have been given a host of different names by successive theories and models of leadership, the two core dimensions (task and socio-emotional) continue to feature in virtually all perspectives to this day.

From the 1950s onwards, a multitude of contingency theories have been developed (Shackelton, 1995), each endeavouring to throw light on the multifaceted ways in which we influence and are influenced by others, and primarily in the context of work. A number of the more influential models are briefly summarized later in the chapter, but most of these approaches whether modern or traditional have one common feature – they assume that leadership is in itself an integral and necessary part of organizational life. More radically, it can be argued that these approaches are all predicated on masculine models of group life, presupposing that organizations function most effectively when there are individuals with defined authority working in ordered, hierarchical structures. With this in mind, it is interesting to monitor recent approaches in organizations on the cutting-edge of technology. These environments aim to suppress leadership and associated group structures as it is felt that these structures could stand in the way of innovation and change by suppressing individuality.

Work motivation

The history of research on work motivation reveals a lack of consensus about the fundamental nature of the phenomenon, as well as a shortage of research which tests theory in practice (Steers and Porter, 1991). Early work, such as that of Maslow and Alderfer, focused not on the process of motivation but on 'content' or the factors which do or do not motivate people at work. One example is Maslow's famous Hierarchy of Needs which has been translated across to the world of employment. The theory proposes that working towards self-actualization in employment (that is, challenging job, opportunities for creativity, achievement in work, advancement in organization) is only possible once other needs have been satisfied (in order, physiological needs [pay, working conditions], safety needs [working conditions, benefits, job security], social needs [work group, supervision, associations], esteem needs [recognition, job title, job status, feedback]).

In his ERG theory, Alderfer condensed these five needs down to three (ERG = Existence, Relatedness and Growth) but also presented a hierarchy of needs, and likewise failed to attract much support from empirical research. Following in this tradition, Herzberg's two-factor theory adopted a rather more sophisticated approach, maintaining that there are two types of needs which determine job satisfaction. These were labelled *hygiene factors* and *motivators*, each operating quite independently. Hygiene factors such as job security, working conditions, benefits and pay can lead to dissatisfaction if they are not well-managed, but they can never lead to positive feelings towards work. In contrast, the motivators, such as striving for growth, achievement, recognition and individual expression, can produce positive feelings of job satisfaction. Once more, while the approach has intuitive appeal, the empirical evidence has been far from convincing, and the reason is all too familiar, each fails to accommodate individual differences.

Faced with the idiosyncracies rather than commonalities of individual motivation, contemporary approaches have generally abandoned the search for the 'content' of motivation and instead have focused on the 'process' which links effort to performance to reward to job satisfaction. A number of alternative models have been developed since the 1960s which describe the relationship between cognitive and structural factors, but it is difficult to detect a genuine convergence of opinion as to what work motivation is and how it can best be described. What this research does indicate, however, is the growing recognition of the significance of social cognition in understanding behaviour in the workplace.

Selection and recruitment

Turning briefly to selection procedures, the majority of effort has been devoted to the task of finding the best techniques for identifying the best candidate for appointment or promotion. It would be impossible to summarize this extensive literature here (see Smith and Robertson, 1993; Herriot, 1989), other than to say that two conclusions from this work are first that the closer the techniques are able to match actual job performance then the more reliable they will be as selection procedures, and second that traditional techniques, and most notably interviews, are notoriously unreliable as selection devices (Cooper and Robertson, 1995). Increasingly the interview has come under close scrutiny, not only evaluating the role of the interview as a selection device, but also considering the dynamics of the two-way interaction itself, including how aspects of verbal and non-verbal behaviour may be perceived and come to influence outcome (Breakwell, 1990).

Concepts, models and theories

Historically the individual at work was viewed as object rather than agent, to be manipulated by the employer in order to maximize productivity and minimize costs. This perspective is exemplified in Taylor's principles of scientific management. Taylor's model of the person was very simplistic – we are motivated to earn as much as we can but if we are left to our own devices we will be inefficient and lazy and so we require constant supervision in order to achieve an acceptable level of productivity. Later work, enshrined in the human relations movement and more latterly in concepts such as job enrichment and job enlargement, served to demonstrate that the person at work is far more complex, with a range of intrinsic psychological factors determining job satisfaction and in turn productivity.

In tune with this sentiment, Lewin had maintained that the 'life space' of each individual was idiosyncratic and one task of psychology was to understand the different worlds that we each occupy. Lewin adopted a gestalt orientation, to him each person's life space comprised 'the totality of facts which determine the behaviour (B) of an individual at a certain moment. The life space (L) represents the totality of possible events. The life space includes the person (P) and the environment (E)' (Lewin, 1936, p. 216). According to Lewin, $B=f(P,E)$, that is behaviour is a function of the person and the environment in which s/he is found. This simple formula paved the way for a radical reevaluation of the concept of the person at work. Implicitly, modern industrial psychology now recognizes that each person is an active and thoughtful decision-maker and judge, driven by idiosyncratic needs or motives and evaluating rewards and costs in unique ways.

At the same time, and reflecting gender biases in employment, it would be fair to say that the concept of the person at work has also been, and continues to be, predominantly masculine. Contemporary feminist authors would point to the significance of historical forces in laying down the blueprint for the gendered labour market which characterized much of the twentieth century. As work became increasingly divorced from the home, so men were cast in the role of primary breadwinner while women's primary responsibility was seen to lie within the home and with the family (Rowbotham, 1977). Hence the primacy afforded to the nuclear family arose alongside the process of industrialization, and immediately cast women as players in the secondary sector of the labour market, a role which continues to influence perceptions to this day. The discrimination which women encounter in the workplace is manifest in many ways, including persistent pay differentials between men and women (known as the 'gender gap'), the absence of family-friendly policies, glass ceilings which prevent women climbing the corporate ladder and gender-hostile work environments which foster gender harassment (Kremer and Montgomery, 1993). Other research shows how harassment remains a significant problem for large numbers of working women, although the sex-discrimination legislation in the UK and elsewhere now affords the potential for protection when supported by appropriate policies and procedures (Kremer, Steele, Cassidy and Jones, 1999).

Overall, disparity between men and women in employment still reflects in significant psychological constructs. One of the most intriguing is the concept of personal entitlement, or what the person regards as 'fair' in relation to pay, status and working conditions. There is evidence to suggest that women may continue to be satisfied with less from work than men, and so accept the status quo rather than challenge it as would be expected (Major, McFarlin and Gagnon, 1984).

This masculine model could also reflect in the preoccupation which industry has with leadership and hierarchies. As previously mentioned, the literature continues to abound with models and theories of leadership, and a number of the most influential are described briefly below.

Fiedler's contingency model of leadership effectiveness

Focus – situational control and personality

Using a device known as the Least Preferred Co-Worker (LPC) Scale, individuals are characterized as either being 'high LPC' or 'low LPC', depending on their rating of the person they least preferred working with in the past, that is their least preferred co-worker. The situational control of the leader is then defined typically in terms of three elements (position power; leader–member relations; task structure), and the model then predicts the situations when high or low-LPC leaders will be more or less effective. On the basis of a considerable number of studies, Fiedler claims that low-LPC leaders are more effective when there is either high or low situational control, but that high LPC leaders are more effective when there is moderate situational control. According to this model, LPC score defines a predisposition to respond or even a personality trait and the task of the leader is not to change him/herself but to change the situation to match his or her preferred style, leading to Fiedler's intervention strategy known as Leader Match.

Vroom and Yetton's normative decision-making model

Focus – leadership style and decision-making

Adopting a different tack, this model argues that a primary function of leadership is decision-making, and each time a leader makes a decision two concerns must be balanced – the quality of the decision (task dimension) and acceptance of that decision by subordinates (socio-emotional dimension). The combination of these two concerns then determines the particular leadership style to be employed (whether autocratic, democratic, consultative or group). Typically, the model is operationalized using a decision-making tree where answers to a series of questions relating to decision quality and acceptance lead sequentially to a node or endpoint signifying the appropriate leadership style(s).

House's path–goal theory

Focus – leadership style and motivation

As with the normative model, this theory once more argues that leaders must adopt one of a number of leadership styles (labelled instrumental, supportive, participative and achievement-oriented) in order to best motivate followers. The theory is derived from a process theory of motivation known as expectancy theory (see later), and locates the leader centrally in this process, helping subordinates recognize and then achieve their goals by clarifying objectives and removing obstacles to progress. The contingencies which determine the most effective style include characteristics of the situation (that is, task structure, formal authority system and primary work group) and the followers (that is, ability, need for affiliation, authoritarianism and locus of control).

Hersey and Blanchard's situational leadership theory

Focus – leadership style and followers' maturity

As yet another alternative, Hersey and Blanchard maintain that a good leader should employ one of four leadership styles (structuring, coaching, encouraging and delegating) depending on the maturity of the people to be led. The latter is defined in terms of both job maturity (previous experience, current knowledge, meeting deadlines, ability to take responsibility, problem-solving ability, awareness of political implications) and psychological maturity (persistence, independence, achievement orientation, attitude to work and willingness to take responsibility).

The above four approaches have a great many similarities when the surface structure is scraped away. When taken together, all reveal how leadership involves a great many functions, and that good leaders have to be responsive to ever-changing contexts in order to be successful. With the exception of Fiedler's model, it is also acknowledged that the onus is on the leader to respond or change style to suit circumstances rather than vice versa. Each also includes reference to the fundamental distinction (first identified in the Ohio State and Michigan studies as initiating structure and consideration), between task and socio-emotional concerns. While the terminology which each uses is unique, this enduring distinction remains central to understanding leadership behaviour. Finally, it would be fair to admit that the empirical support for each approach is less than substantial (Yukl, 1994; Shackleton, 1995), but at the same time the popularity and intuitive appeal of each cannot be denied. In Lewinian terms they are practical theories, but are they good theories? The fact that so many approaches continue to vie for support and have spawned so many types of practical intervention could be seen as a positive sign of complementarity. Equally it could point to a lack of clarity in relation to fundamental underlying constructs, including what we mean by the term leadership.

At present, the leadership literature shows a greater diversity than at any time in the past as this issue of definition has failed to be resolved. For example, there is now a considerable focus on the social cognitive processes associated with the exercise of power and influence (Brotherton, 1999). This includes implicit leadership theory (Lord and Maher, 1991) which considers the schemata which are associated with different styles of leadership and their effect on the perception of leadership effectiveness. As another example the leadership attributional model (Green and Mitchell, 1979) deals with the influence of causal attributions (whether internal or external) on leaders' subsequent behaviours towards subordinates. The literature is also character-ized by two alternative perspectives on leadership, the transactional and the transformational. The former is characterized as the more traditional, where the leader is seen in the context of the transactions which go to define group and organizational life. A social-exchange perspective typifies the transactional approach, arguing that leaders must constantly respond to the needs and values of the group in order to achieve results, and will only be given scope to influence their followers so long as the rewards which accrue from their leading are greater than the costs which are incurred by the followers when following. Transformational leadership is sometimes referred to as charismatic leadership. It has been described as a reinvention of the trait approach insofar as it considers how certain leadership styles can transform individual performance in the context of a special relationship between the leader and other group mem-bers. According to Bass (Bass and Avolio, 1992), the '4 Is' of transformational leadership are:

- *Individualized consideration* (leadership by developing people);
- *Intellectual stimulation* (leadership by stimulating people to think);

■ *Inspirational motivation* (leadership by inspiring people);
■ *Idealized influence* (leadership by charisma).

It would be encouraging to see an emerging consensus in this field, but this seems a distant prospect. Instead, the rather nebulous concept of leadership continues to nurture multiple perspectives, each focusing attention on a different aspect of social influence, each using a unique terminology and each applying different methods.

Cognitive and affective factors

A number of theories which reflect on social cognition have become extremely influential within occupational psychology. Among these, attribution theories have helped understand leadership processes (see above) as well as issues associated with equity. For example, Turner and Pratkanis (1994) found that from a psychological viewpoint affirmative-action programmes (where preference may be shown to members of underrepresented groups during selection), unless carefully managed, may be counterproductive insofar as those selected (and their co-workers) may come to value themselves less highly, in line with predictions from theories of causal attribution.

Adams' equity theory (1965) continues to play a prominent role in understanding employees' perceptions of their work and their motivation. The theory argues that how much we are paid (either underpayment, equity or overpayment), how we are paid (piece rate, hourly or salary) and how much we receive in comparison with others will all have a significant effect on how we view our work and hence how hard we work. Underpinned by principles of social exchange, the theory assumes that we aim to achieve a state of balance between our inputs and our outcomes relative to others, that is 'equity'. For example, if an assembly-line worker is paid too little s/he may come to value the work less highly and so exert less effort. On the other hand, if the person is paid too much s/he may then invest too much energy in the production of each item and hence slow down.

This theory also appears in what is the most important theory of work motivation to date, expectancy theory. This is an approach which genuinely embraces cognitive and affective factors in order to understand the complex worker. Although there have been many variations, the core of the approach is now well-established and originates from the work of Vroom in the 1960s. The theory assumes that we are rational decision-makers who will choose to invest energy in certain activities if we believe that we can influence our performance (the expectancy component), that our performance will be rewarded (instrumentality) and that we value these rewards (valence). Porter and Lawler's (1968) model describes the relationship between each variable, with the spine of the model being the relationship between effort, performance, reward and finally job satisfaction. The link between effort and performance is mediated not only by our ability and traits but also by the role which we play within the organization. In turn, the evaluation of the rewards we receive for our performance accommodates both intrinsic and extrinsic factors along with whether the rewards are equitable, in comparison with those which others receive for similar performance. Job satisfaction hinges on this evaluation and the amount of effort we will then continue to exert will be influenced by our experience of the process. An extensive literature dealing with expectancy theory indicates the positive support which the theory enjoys from both academics and practitioners alike. Paraphrasing Kurt Lewin, this does appear to be a good example of a practical theory.

Social and organizational factors

As the previous sections should indicate, all behaviour in work has typically been considered within its social context, and hence a consideration of social and organizational factors naturally pervades this literature. In particular, two levels of analysis tend to feature prominently, the organizational and the group.

From the nineteenth century, there has been an interest in organizational design and the effects of design on productivity. According to Max Weber, the 'ideal type' (meaning that which characterizes the pure form but which does not imply that it is the best) business organization is one founded on bureaucratic principles, with a rigid hierarchical structure, clear rules of behaviour, a strict division of labour and relationships characterized by formality and lack of favour or emotion. As time has shown, very often such structures are inappropriate as they do not maximize the potential of staff, are resistant to change and innovation and can be notoriously inefficient. Today the emphasis in organizational design is towards a contingency approach, matching the type of structure (e.g. tall vs flat; centralized vs decentralized; function-based vs product-based vs location-based; mechanistic vs organic; project vs matrix vs free-form) with the environment in which the work is carried out. The vast literature in this field not only demonstrates the huge impact which design can have on organizational effectiveness, but also the psychological costs and benefits attached to different structures. With this in mind it is interesting that many high-technology organizations deliberately suppress structures (free-form organizations) so as to maximize responsiveness and flexibility, albeit aware that such environments can create feelings of insecurity and 'homelessness' among staff.

At a more micro level of analysis, small groups have been of interest from at least the time of the 'Hawthorne Studies. The human-relations movement has continued to emphasize the importance of the small group or team in work, sometimes leading to radical changes in working practices. One of the most famous involved the production of Volvo cars in Kalmar, Sweden. Following principles of job enrichment, the method of production switched from a standard assembly line to small, independent work teams. While the scheme was costly to implement, in the short to medium term at least it significantly reduced absenteeism and staff turnover (Gyllenhammer, 1977), although the longer-term benefits were not as dramatic.

During the 1970s there was an explosion of interest in group structures, including possibilities for communication between group members and the degree of centrality of particular roles. The conclusions reached from this highly empirical, laboratory-based work were predictable. For example, on certain tasks where work is able to be delegated or subdivided, then groups with limited scope for communication are often more effective than those where there is too much communication or where certain communication channels become saturated (Forsyth, 1999).

A more interesting and sophisticated literature has slowly evolved around the dynamics of groups in work organizations, including the circumstances when 'team spirit' and group cohesion may or may not increase efficiency and effectiveness. The literature in mainstream social psychology on social influence has long suggested that groups have the potential to stifle individuality, and yet the message has taken a long time to filter through to managers. By way of example, brainstorming as a technique for generating new ideas enjoyed uncritical acclaim in the advertising industry from the 1950s. Members were instructed to generate as many ideas as possible, to be freethinking, to encourage others and to use ideas as stepping stones to new suggestions. In the 1970s, laboratory research finally challenged the consensus by demonstrating that individuals working alone were often more productive. This work showed that there was nothing inherent in group membership which fostered individual creativity, although we prefer group work and we believe that we are more creative in group settings (Paulus et al., 1993). On this occasion it was the laboratory that provided the test for practice, rather than vice versa as is more often the case.

As a further challenge to groups as necessarily the most effective way of doing business, from the 1970s work on group polarization and groupthink has demonstrated the downside of fostering 'tight' work groups. The former research has shown that groups will often support more extreme decisions than individuals working alone, while the latter research highlights the dangerous processes which can characterize cohesive groups and the bizarre decisions which they can subsequently endorse if not carefully controlled. Originally based on Janis's analysis of international fiascos precipitated by faulty group decision-making (Janis, 1982), it has also been shown that groupthink adversely affects decision-making in the world of work (Sims, 1992).

While teams and team-building may have been management buzz-words in the 1980s, there is now a more considered approach to the circumstances where teams may or may not facilitate individual performance at work. If any one group or culture comes to dominate an organization, then the organization will remain partisan and will find it difficult to acknowledge the contributions of those who may be different, however that difference may be defined. 'Majority rule' in these organizations, unless challenged effectively, can stifle change and voices of constructive dissent, and the result can be poor decision-making and inefficient organizations.

With this in mind there is now greater emphasis on the positive role which conflict is able to play in effective organizations, and how conflict should not be avoided but managed in order to enhance effectiveness (Keashly, 1997; Thomas, 1992). In turn, this literature is at last dovetailing with other discussions around diversity at work. The management of diversity is now recognized as an integral part of effective organizational life (Ross and Schneider, 1992). As one example, Kandola and Fullerton (1994) have been instrumental in developing a model (based on the analogy of a mosaic) which describes how best to strategically implement a diversity policy and to ensure that the policy genuinely mainstreams with the business of the organization.

Practical issues

Intervention strategies and action research

The work of Kandola and Fullerton is one illustration of how almost all research in this field necessarily involves some form of intervention. Indeed, the term action research itself originated with Kurt Lewin and it would be hard to find examples of research dealing with paid employment which has not been influenced by this orientation. Many theories of organizational behaviour have been put to the test in work settings, but in truth few have survived that ordeal unscathed; the complexities of behaviour at work continue to defy simple and sovereign explanations. The literature on work motivation and leadership, as previously described, are both cases in point.

In relation to group processes, it is noteworthy that business and industry now routinely embrace alternatives to standard group decision-making procedures so as to avoid the pitfalls of social influence. The nominal group technique (where the meeting is structured to allow each person's ideas to be given equal consideration by the group until a consensus is reached) and the Delphi technique (where ideas are shared and evaluated but not in face-to-face meetings) are two examples (Van de Ven and Delbecq, 1974).

The close relationship between theory and practice is commendable, but sometimes the narrow theoretical focus of particular research projects has prevented a fuller understanding of the topic in question. A fascinating counter-example involved a group of social psychologists in Uruguay in the 1970s who were asked to help sell curtains in very unfavourable trading conditions. Using a combination of approaches derived straight from mainstream social psychology (and including cognitive dissonance theory, Brehm's theory of reactance and the foot-in-the-door technique), the team were successful in tripling sales (Zimbardo and Ebbeson, 1970).

On the one hand, the world of work presents tremendous opportunities for considering a wide range of social phenomena in 'natural' field settings. On the other hand, there are a number of factors which combine to determine the types of research which are actually carried out, and here market forces cannot be ignored. The employer will generally cooperate in return for a tangible benefit and often a short-term benefit. Publication of sensitive findings can also be problematic and some employers may demand the right to control access to research findings.

Allied with these concerns, if the research can only be carried out with the cooperation of the employer then fundamental ethical issues arise. As with any research which has policy implications, it is not sufficient to argue 'she who pays the piper picks the tune', and especially where welfare matters may be involved. Typically research in this field has not wrestled with this problem but has tended to support the status quo. From an alternative perspective, while the employer may be interested primarily for selfish reasons, nevertheless much of the research is likely to have positive effects on the quality of working life through increasing job satisfaction and reducing stress.

The way forward

It is very likely that this particular field will continue to be dominated by a small number of topics. Occupational psychologists have not been slow in the past to draw on accumulated knowledge across psychology to help develop practical solutions to problems at work, and it is likely that this trend will continue. The primacy of sophisticated socio-cognitive models of behaviour and motivation shows a genuine willingness to engage with the complexity of human behaviour and experience, and there is little sign that this task is nearing completion. Instead it is likely that ever-more sophisticated models will develop, based increasingly on integrated approaches which are able to move beyond small answers to small questions. In this way psychological knowledge can help inform organizational development in the real world where the management of people continues to present a fascinating challenge.

SHORT QUESTIONS

1 In what ways did the human-relations movement revolutionalize the way in which we think of people at work?
2 Are leaders born or are they made?
3 Outline the advantages and the disadvantages of team-building for both job satisfaction and productivity at work.
4 Compare and contrast at least two theories of work motivation.
5 Discuss the effects of organizational structures on motivation and performance at work.

CLASS ACTIVITIES

1 Reflecting on your experiences of paid work, which managers have you found most and least acceptable and why? Consider their management styles in relation to existing theories and models when trying to understand your perceptions.
2 Drawing on relevant theories and your own experiences of work, discuss practical steps which a manager can take to maximize the motivation of people at work.
3 Draw up a list of factors which have the potential to create either glass walls or glass ceilings for people who happen to be different from those they work with. Now outline practical steps which can be put in place to remedy each of these issues in turn, and describe likely obstacles to progress.

FURTHER READING

Brotherton, C. (1999) *Social Psychology and Management: Issues for a Changing Society*. Buckingham: Open University Press.

Cooper, D. and Robertson, I.T. (1995) *The Psychology of Personnel Selection*. London: Routledge.

Kandola, B. and Fullerton, J. (1994) *Managing the Mosaic: Diversity in Action*. London: Institute of Personnel Development.

Keashly, L. (1997) 'Conflict and Conflict Management', In S.W. Savada and D.R. McCreary (eds), *Applying Social Psychology* (pp. 248–73). Upper Saddle River, NJ: Prentice Hall.

Shackelton, V. (1995) *Business Leadership*. London: Routledge.

Steers, R.M. and Porter, L.W. (1991) *Motivation and Work Behavior*. New York: McGraw-Hill.

Health and Illness

Illness is the night-side of life, a more onerous citizenship. Everyone who is born holds dual citizenship, in the kingdom of the well and the kingdom of the sick. Although we all prefer to use only the good passport, sooner or later each of us is obliged, at least for a spell, to identify ourselves as citizens of that other place

(Susan Sontag, 1978)

ONCE UPON A TIME...

Janet was a student who was finding it difficult to settle in to university life. Living away from home, she missed her family and her wide circle of familiar friends. All of her classmates seemed to be having a much better time; Janet was never invited to the parties they talked about after classes. Janet didn't want to worry her parents so she never mentioned her loneliness when she telephoned home. She tried to be more outgoing and approached several people about going out socially but they were too busy and she soon gave up. She tried to concentrate on her studies but found this difficult and she fell behind in her work. She was not going out much and often didn't bother going down to meals, snacking in her room instead. She gained weight and always seemed to have a cough or a cold. When she did go home for a weekend her mother was shocked at the changes in her appearance and demeanour, and urged her to visit a doctor. Janet cried and felt that her parents just didn't understand but eventually she agreed. Depression was diagnosed and cognitive behavioural therapy arranged. Some months later Janet had made a few friends, lost some weight and regained her health and vitality. She was looking forward to the rest of her university life.

Introduction

In contemporary industrialized societies, psychological aspects of health and illness are readily acknowledged and there is widespread acceptance of the idea that mental and physical health are intimately related. This acceptance is evident in a variety of contexts, from the preponderance of self-help books in the average bookshop to more formal provision of psychological services such as bereavement counselling within the wider healthcare system.

What is less evident is that the acceptance of this relationship has waxed and waned throughout history and indeed has a relatively short recent history. Only a century ago, medical doctors tended to view health as the absence of disease, and to regard illness as a physiological matter. The idea that an individual may act to improve their own health by psychological means would have been derided by these professionals as a misunderstanding of the accepted mechanisms by which the healthy body became ill, as revealed by scientific means.

Current acceptance of the relationship between psychology and health reflects broader issues such as our concepts of health, of illness and of the person. Such social constructions represent the ways in which individuals and indeed medical professionals locate the sources of health and illness. These issues have a profound impact both at the societal and the individual level, influencing policy-making and medical practice as well as individual lifestyles and health-related behaviours. These constructions also guide research into the causes and consequences of illness and the interpretation of empirical findings. They also inform the conceptual models currently prevalent in health psychology, which are crucial for the meaningful synthesis of empirical findings. Social psychological theories and evidence have been widely utilized in the construction of these conceptual models which facilitate the analysis of the complex relationships between mental and physical health and illness.

This chapter will consider only selected contributions made by social psychologists to the understanding of health and illness. While huge progress has been made in some respects, there remain many areas where understanding remains limited. However, given that psychologists have relatively recently begun to examine relationships between psychosocial factors and illness, and even more recently initiated similar research into wellness, the potential for social psychology to further illuminate important issues in the area of health and illness is clear.

History and development

Historically and culturally, social constructions of health and illness have varied considerably. These constructions have ranged from those which attribute an individual's health status to forces beyond control of the individual to those which hold the individual to be responsible for his or her own physical and mental health. In the nineteenth century, great progress in the scientific study of medicine was reflected in the predominance of a biomedical model to guide understanding of disease. This approach was consistent with Darwin's theory of evolution, given that humans were re-conceptualized as biological beings similar to, rather than qualitatively distinct from, other animals. Thus, the health status of an individual came to be regarded as a physiological matter, with social psychological factors relegated to the status of possible consequences of illness. This view was also congruent with the prevalent health problems of the nineteenth century, including infectious diseases such as typhoid, tuberculosis and diphtheria, along with a conception of health as simply the absence of disease. Clearly this model, which prevailed well into the twentieth century, allowed little need or scope for applying social psychological theory to health and illness or indeed for the development of a psychology of health.

In stark contrast to this earlier approach, health is now typically defined in terms of biological, psychological and social aspects of well-being. This biopsychosocial model of health is consistent with contemporary thought which recognizes the importance of social psychological factors in every aspect of the experiences of health and illness. A variety of factors have had an influence on the development of this modern perspective. For example, patterns of mortality and morbidity show that life expectancy increased considerably during the last century, with many of the health problems most prevalent as we enter the twenty-first century either related to lifestyle (such as lung cancer) or diseases of old age (such as dementia). Both categories are readily amenable to psychological research, and indeed psychological approaches have been employed extensively in these areas. Moreover, the addition of psychological and social elements to definitions of health including relatively new concepts such as social capital (see later) have broadened both research and theorizing in relation to health and illness, principally within the field of health psychology. Health psychology, which has developed only since the 1970s, represents one of the most rapidly developing areas of modern psychology, mirroring the importance which psychologists in general now attach to health as an area of investigation.

Contemporary priorities

One priority for psychologists interested in health and illness has been establishing the relative significance of physiological, psychological, social and behavioural factors to an individual's current and future health status. Thus, health psychology continues to examine factors such as gender, ethnicity and socioeconomic status in relation to health. Particular emphasis has been placed on stress as a factor in the development and experience of illness within the emerging field of psychoneuroimmunology. In addition, health promotion has been prioritized, at least in part reflecting on the growing costs of providing sophisticated but expensive medical treatments. Naturally, it will be cost-effective for any health service to prevent rather than treat illness and, with this in mind, health promotion has made extensive use of social psychological research on topics such as persuasion and attitudinal/behavioural change. In addition, with the increased numbers of elderly people in the developed world, psychosocial aspects of the ageing process have become a 'hot topic' for research. However, the application of social psychology to health and illness does not merely address specific problems; it has also led to the development of theories and models which further understanding of health and illness in more social and cultural contexts. Concepts such as social capital illustrate the importance of this approach. In combination, these trends have been reflected in a move to reject psychology's traditional emphasis on dysfunction and instead to investigate the factors which may promote 'the good life' or thriving, as exemplified in the 'Positive Psychology' movement (Seligman and Csikszentmihalyi, 2001).

Concepts, models and theories

The biomedical model

The biomedical model of disease, which dominated research into health and illness in the early years of the twentieth century, had important implications for beliefs about the causes, consequences and treatment of illness. The causes of illness within a biomedical model can be classified as either internal (such as degenerative diseases) or external (such as infection), but in either case are regarded as beyond the control of the individual. Treatment is logically focused on changing the physical condition of the body from an unhealthy to a healthy state, and thus is best offered by experts on the body, namely qualified medical doctors. The status of the ill body is also viewed as qualitatively different from that of the healthy body and there is a clear Cartesian split between the mind and the body. Within this model, the role of social psychological factors is confined to the possible social consequences (such as unemployment) and psychological consequences (such as depression) of physical illness, with the person viewed as subject to, rather than integral to, the disease process.

Through the course of the last century, this model was challenged by several developments, including the emergence of psychosomatic medicine. For example, as knowledge of the nervous system increased so it became clear that some complaints, such as 'glove anaesthesia', could not have physiological causes because symptoms were inconsistent with existing knowledge of the physical structures involved. Instead, Freudian theory formed the basis of psychological explanations for such complaints. Through such research it became increasingly clear that the mind and body were related in ways which were incompatible with the Cartesian split between mind and body and hence with the biomedical model itself. Instead, the accumulated evidence suggested strongly that mind and body are intricately and intimately inter-related, and hence a more inclusive model was needed to account for these developments. However, despite these shifts in focus over time, it should not be forgotten that the biomedical model remains hugely influential in health research and especially medical research.

The biopsychosocial model

The development of the psychosocial model has been important for several reasons, not least because of the implications for health promotion and for approaches to treatment. The biopsychosocial model incorporates the inter-action of biological influences (such as genetic vulnerability to particular diseases) with both psychological and social influences on health. Given the interactive nature of these influences, opportunities for interventions aimed at a psychological or social level then presented themselves. It is important to remember, however, that certain constraints operate within this model. For example, genetically determined diseases would not be amenable to a psychological intervention, although such an intervention may improve coping strategies and so improve the quality of life for the affected individual.

As medical research discovered links between some behaviours (such as smoking and eating animal fats) and the development of particular diseases (such as coronary heart disease) it also became clear that eliminating or reducing these behaviours would reduce the individual's risk of disease. Within the behavioural perspective, which was especially influential in psychology until the 1970s, such changes are not only possible but there are also prescribed ways of achieving them, mainly based on conditioning schedules. More recently, cognitive-behavioural techniques have been influential, combining features derived from cognitive psychology alongside behaviourist principles to develop a variety of effective interventions. These techniques are consistent with a biopsychosocial model which incorporates biological (such as genetic vulnerability and physical condition), psychological (for example individual differences) and social factors (for example socioeconomic status, group norms).

Models of health-related behaviour

Within the health sciences generally, a radical reconceptualization of the individual in relation to health status can be mapped onto a biopsychosocial model of health and illness. Social factors play a significant role within this model, and consequently a plethora of models describing health-related behaviour have emerged over recent years. The most widely used of these models draw directly on social psychological theory and research, citing factors including norms, reference groups and social support as important elements in the development, course and consequences of health and illness. Conner and Norman (1996) have been particularly influential in arguing that social factors as well as cognitive factors exert an important influence on experiences of health and illness. Cognition, they argue, does not take place in a social vacuum, but instead is embedded in a social context rich in factors which may influence perception, attributions, attitudes, decision-making and other cognitive processes important in determining health-related behaviours.

Armitage and Conner (2000) have reviewed a number of social cognition models in terms of how they account for variations in health, whether in terms of motivation or behaviour, and the authors have concluded that each had inherent strengths but also weaknesses. They argue that a consensus approach would be useful in helping to integrate existing theory and research. However, such an approach has not been forthcoming, perhaps in part because each approach has demonstrated at least some utility and hence empirical research is able to provide sufficient confirmation which thereby acts as a defence for each separate theory or model (Weinstein, 1993).

Two theories falling under the heading of social cognition were originally developed within mainstream social psychology in order to describe the complex relationship between our attitudes and our behaviour. The theory of reasoned action (TRA) and in particular the theory of planned behaviour (TPB) both include social factors which may influence an individual's assessment of potential threat (including illness or disease) and the perceived efficacy of actions that may be taken to avert that threat (Ajzen, 1991; Azjen and Fishbein, 1977). In this respect they differ from theories and models specifically designed to predict health behaviours, such as Protection Motivation Theory and the Health Belief Model, neither of which emphasizes the more social dimensions of health-related behaviours. To date, empirical testing has shown that models of behaviour which include social factors are more predictive of health-related behaviours than models specifically devised to do so but which neglect social factors (Stroebe, 2000).

The TRA, for example, includes outcome beliefs and outcome evaluations which together help to form an attitude to the health behaviour in question. Also included in this model are normative beliefs and motivation to comply with these beliefs which together form subjective norms. The normative beliefs are the assessment by the individual of the extent to which significant others believe they should, for example, stop smoking or go on a diet. Weinstein (1993) notes that by explicitly incorporating social influence in this way, the TRA differs from several other popular models attempting to predict the likelihood of health-related behavioural change. At the same time, it has been argued that the TRA best predicts behavioural change for behaviours that are under voluntary control, and unfortunately many health-related behaviours are not volitional, being either habitual (for example smoking) or dependent on resources (skills, money, time).

The TPB was developed in order to address these issues and accordingly incorporates control beliefs or perceived behavioural control, roughly comparable to Bandura's (1977) concept of self-efficacy. Empirical tests indicate that this modification has improved the predictive validity of the model for health behaviours not entirely under volitional control. Nevertheless, while these models have proved useful, they are vulnerable to criticism insofar as they may not predict behaviour itself but rather behavioural intentions, which are not always a reliable guide to action itself. Until the so-called attitude–behaviour gap is fully understood, the predictive utility of these theories is likely to remain limited.

These developments, and others such as transtheoretical models (see for example Prochaska and DiClemente's, 1983, stages-of-change model) clearly show a contemporary view of the person as an active decision-maker in relation to health-related behaviour, thereby reflecting current social psychological models of the person. The practical benefits of such an approach are evident in that by examining the stages of change (that is, precontemplation, contemplation, action, maintenance and possibly relapse) in relation to the processes of change, it is possible to increase the effectiveness of programmes aiming to change behaviour and also to maximize self-help approaches.

Sheeran, Conner and Norman (2001) have recently noted that the transtheoretical model may provide insights into additional variables which, if incorporated into the TPB, would improve its predictive validity yet further. Their study of the TBP in relation to health screening found that the theory did predict both attendance and frequency of attendance. It also distinguished between those who refused screening and those who agreed, but was not able to distinguish between participants who attended screening appointments regularly, those who delayed attending and those who attended only once. They suggest that considering implementation intentions and processes of change may help predict these behaviours. Clearly, as research evidence accumulates so the models of health-related behaviour will have to be extended and refined in order to improve their utility, with corresponding benefits for those practitioners who are interested in actually promoting healthy behaviours.

Attributions, stress and coping

Various factors associated with social cognition have been related to health and illness. For example, in order to experience illness then the individual must interpret symptoms as being indicative of a health problem and this labelling process is of interest to health professionals. Equally, the causal attributions associated with prevalent diseases are of interest. For example, French, Senior, Weinman and Marteau (2001) reported that cardiac patients were more likely to attribute cardiac disease to luck or to stress than non-patients, who thought that factors including being overweight or having high blood pressure were more important. French *et al.* maintain that such findings may reflect a basic actor–observer bias, in this case the actor (patient) attributing the disease to factors external to him/herself (luck, stress) while the observer (non-patient) attributes the disease to internal factors of the patient (overweight, hypertension). They also note that in such studies, patients usually comment on the causes of their own disease while non-patients will tend only to comment on the causes of the disease generally.

Attributional styles have also been related to depression and to the ability to cope with stressful life events. While the health consequences of stress may be attributable to concomitant physiological changes (in the endocrine, immune and autonomic nervous systems), stress has also been shown to be related to changes in health-related behaviour such as increased consumption of alcohol. The work of Lazarus and Folkman (1984) in relation to cognitive appraisal has been particularly influential in this respect, offering a framework for understanding individual differences in stress responsivity. For example, they have described cognitive appraisal in terms of three specific elements, primary appraisal (assessment of a situation in terms of its significance to the individual); secondary appraisal (the potential threat in relation to perceived coping resources and options); and reappraisal (in the light of new information and the effects of coping behaviours). Moreover, Lazarus and Folkman's descriptions of coping as either problem-focused (directed at managing the threatening situation) or emotion-focused (directed at altering emotional responses to the perceived threat) have been useful for those interested in understanding individual differences in response to stress, whereby some individuals may become depressed whereas others do not.

Seligman (1975) first proposed a learned helplessness model of reactive depression which looked on the illness in terms of responses seen in animals which had been exposed to unavoidable aversive stimuli. When later exposed to avoidable aversive stimuli these animals did not try to escape, signifying that repeated experience of uncontrollable events had taught them to expect that future events would also be uncontrollable (that is, learned helplessness). This model was later revised by Abramson *et al.* (1978) to incorporate causal attributions, whereby individuals attributing a negative life event to stable, internal and global causes are more likely to become depressed than those who attribute such events to external, unstable and specific causes.

Overall, the most significant contribution of social psychology in this area appears to come from the research examining coping resources, in particular that relating to social support (Cohen and Wills, 1985). Typically, research examines social support in terms of the structure of the support sources available to the individual (often called the social network) and also the functions of the support (for example emotional support, instrumental support, informational support and appraisal support). It has been argued not only that social support reduces the risk of depression by buffering the effects of stress, but also that the general health benefits of social support can extend to a reduced risk of mortality (House *et al.*, 1988), fewer complications in childbirth (Oakley, 1992) and an increased immune function among unemployed women (Arnetz *et al.*, 1987).

Social capital

Many social and organizational factors interact in complex ways to influence health and illness (Bennett and Murphy, 1997). Wilkinson (1996) goes so far as to state that

> Medical science can address the biological pathways involved in disease, the pathology and the opportunities for treatment, but to the extent that health is a social product and some forms of social organisations are healthier than others, advances in our understanding of health will depend on social research. (p. 1)

Wilkinson points out that factors such as gender, race and position in the social hierarchy are related by a variety of pathways not only to standard of living but also to health itself. By way of example, those in lower-paid occupational positions may be subject to more stress and hence may be more vulnerable to stress-related disease than those who occupy a position further up the occupational and social hierarchy. In addition, those who have lower household incomes tend also to be those who have fewer educational qualifications and both of these factors are associated with increased risk in terms of a variety of lifestyle-related illnesses. Indeed there is a wealth of evidence suggesting a strong negative relationship between social class and both illness and mortality (Adler *et al.*, 1994).

At the same time the seemingly straightforward relationship between socioeconomic status and health is complicated by the fact that health has been shown to be related to relative living standards within but not between societies. Within any given society, those with a relatively high standard of living tend to be healthier than those with a lower living standard. However, when considering differences in health between societies, these are found to be related to differences in the extent of inequality rather than to differences in average living standards between the societies. Therefore in a society where the income gap between rich and poor is relatively small, then health tends to be better on average than in a society where the gap is large, independently of average living standards in each. In other words, as Wilkinson (1996) points out, in general terms it is the most egalitarian rather than the richest societies which have the best health.

Alongside these findings, it should be remembered that social support is a key factor in determining the health of the individual, buffering the effects of stress and conferring a variety of health-related benefits (see above). The concept of social capital has emerged relatively recently and is a useful way to synthesize much of this evidence. Hawe and Shiell (2000) note how the debate on social inequality and health has prompted this conceptual development which incorporates relational (e.g. trust, social networks), material (e.g. resources, environmental quality) and political (e.g. social equality, civic engagement) aspects. In general it is maintained that communities and societies with a high degree of social capital will have better health than those with low social capital. However, Hawe and Shiell note that social capital research has not yet addressed the issue of the relationship between macro (or contextual) and micro (or individual) factors. In relation to research on social capital and children, Morrow (1999) notes that the concept has been defined in a variety of ways and hence is problematic. Despite these criticisms, which perhaps may be resolved by further refinement of the concept and more research into relationships between its components, this approach is a promising one capable of integrating much of the existing evidence.

A case study – gender and health

Gender differences in health are now well-established and provide a useful vehicle for considering how a biopsychosocial approach to health and illness can operate. In industrialized countries, women live between five and seven years longer than men but during their lives experience higher rates of morbidity than men, including higher rates of acute and chronic conditions, more days of restricted activity, more visits to physicians and more discharges from short-stay hospitals. These gender differences are evident even after controlling for the higher number of reproductive problems reported by women. Equally, in terms of mental health, females are more likely than males to be admitted to psychiatric hospitals at all stages of the life-span, an exception being during childhood, and consistently report higher levels of psychological distress than their male counterparts (Gove, 1984). In other words, women may become sick but men die.

Many explanations have been advanced for gender differences in health, variously emphasizing either biological, social or psychological factors. In reality, these explanations are not likely to be mutually exclusive and so accepting the role of one does not necessarily negate the utility of another. This is evident when gender differences in mortality and morbidity associated with coronary heart disease are examined. Cardiovascular disease is the most common cause of death in the industrialized world for women as well as men. However, women, and especially younger women, show a lower incidence of cardiac-related death than men of the same age. Despite this apparent advantage, cardiovascular disease is nonetheless the primary cause of premature disability and death in women as well as in men (Light and Girdler, 1993).

Biological explanations for these observed differences focus on the protection that female reproductive hormones, especially oestrogen, may afford women. For example, there is a 100 per cent increase in coronary mortality rates in women between the ages of 48 and 53, a period of life during which approximately two-thirds of women reach the menopause. In addition, research suggests that oestrogen replacement therapy following menopause may halve the risk of coronary death. Oestrogens are believed to lower the blood levels of total cholesterol and low-density lipoprotein cholesterol, two known risk factors for cardiac disease (Stampfer and Colditz, 1991).

At the same time, other gender-specific risk factors need to be considered in order to develop a comprehensive understanding of the phenomenon. For instance, men's cardiovascular health is disadvantaged by behavioural risk factors which they acquire in greater numbers than women, such as smoking, drinking and being excessively overweight (Verbrugge, 1989). Furthermore, the increased rate of morbidity from coronary heart disease in women has been linked to a gender bias in the management of coronary heart disease. Healy (1991) suggests that a widespread belief among physicians that heart disease is a 'man's condition' has resulted in women receiving inadequate treatment for the condition; until such time as a woman demonstrates she is just like a man, for example by having a major coronary attack, she may not receive appropriate treatment (for a full review of the factors that explain gender differences in heart disease morbidity and mortality rates see Light and Girdler, 1993). In effect a full understanding of gender differences in relation to coronary heart disease necessitates consideration of a wide range of biopsychosocial factors.

Other gender differences in health provide similar examples. Available evidence from non-Western cultures suggests that patterns of morbidity and mortality related to gender vary widely (Hraba, Lorenz, Lee and Pechacova, 1996; Okojie, 1994). The health disadvantage of females relative to males in developing countries has been attributed to inequalities in health which begin in childhood and continue to old age. Because of the differential social evaluation of sons and daughters in some societies, within the family girls are likely to be discriminated against in terms of both the allocation of food and available healthcare resources. The health implications of such discriminatory practices in developing countries are severe, correlations of female/male mortality ratios and indices of son preference being .51 for infants and .41 for young children (Waldron, 1987). These findings illustrate the problems inherent in privileging biological over social and psychological explanations when attempting to explain gender differences in physical health.

Other gender differences can be found in developed countries. For example, the higher rates of female morbidity across all stages of the lifespan cannot be accounted for by women's advantage in terms of longevity (Haavio-Mannila, 1986). Gove (1984) suggests that higher rates of female morbidity are related to the differing social roles played by men and women. In particular the nurturing role often assumed by women may result in increased and diffuse social demands and stresses. However, these demands, unlike occupational stresses, are not circumscribed but pervasive and hence this nurturing role is pinpointed as being especially pathogenic. Gove also suggests that the quality and quantity of roles that individuals hold will have a direct impact on both physical and mental health. In general, studies have shown that people who hold multiple social roles tend to exhibit better physical and mental health (Crosby, 1987). While the beneficial effects of increased number of social roles do not always hold across various demographic groups (Rushing and Schwabe, 1995), the addition of a paid occupational role does appear to have a consistent and positive effect on the mental and physical health of both men and women (Cochrane and Stopes-Roe, 1981; Jin, 1995). The difference in the number of social roles occupied by men and women, and in particular the traditional absence of a paid occupational role outside the home for women, therefore has also been suggested as a reason for higher rates of female morbidity. Empirical support for this argument is considerable; married women in paid employment tend to have better mental and physical health than their counterparts with a single role as homemaker (Cochrane and Stopes-Roe, 1981; Dennerstein, 1995).

Despite research suggesting that both men's and in particular women's health is enhanced by additional social roles, gender differences in health persist even when only women and men in paid employment are compared (Hughes and Galinsky, 1994). This clearly should not be the case if the *quantity* of social roles was the primary explanation of gender differences in health. Findings such as these point to the importance of the *quality* of social roles as well as the quantity. Gove's (1984) early work in this area highlighted the importance of role quality by suggesting that a nurturing role such as wife and mother often permeates all areas of life. More recently the issue of role quality has been addressed by examining topics such as the personal salience of the role (Thoits, 1995) and the meaning the role has for an individual (Simon, 1995). The results of an initial study on the influence of role-meaning appear particularly interesting in this regard. These findings would suggest that the reason married women fail to capitalize fully on the health benefits of paid employment is related to role-meaning. Qualitative analyses of the meanings which married, employed men and women ascribe to their various roles illustrate that men tend to view their roles as spouse, parent and worker as compatible or interdependent. Women, on the other hand, tend to view these roles as independent, giving rise to feelings of guilt, inadequacy and ambivalence in particular about their roles as wife and mother (Simon, 1995). Clearly this is an area where further research is needed if the relationships between gender, health and social roles are to be fully understood.

It is also worth bearing in mind at this point that biological sex does not preclude females from being characterized as psychologically masculine (male gender-role orientation) or males from being characterized as psychologically feminine (female gender-role orientation). These gender-role classifications reflect on social constructions ascribed to men and women from birth, and once more illustrate the complex interaction between the social and the psychological which operates at the level of the individual. Psychologically masculine individuals may tend to engage in unhealthy behaviours such as smoking and drinking (Shifren, Bauserman and Carter, 1993), while Wech (1983) found that feminine individuals reported greater physical health problems than either androgynous or masculine females. Such findings suggest that gender role identity may explain lifestyle and health choices more fully than biological sex *per se*. Further to this, these choices may well represent a critical link in the chain that ties gender to physical and mental health.

In terms of understanding gender differences in health, evidently the influence of social factors such as socioeconomic status, social equality, gender differences in social roles and occupational participation (and more recently the meanings attached to these issues by the individual) interact with biological and cultural factors in determining physical and mental health.

Practical issues

Research issues

Within the health sciences generally, the 'gold standard' for empirical evidence is that obtained from randomized, double blind, placebo-controlled trials. Ideally, such evidence is gathered by randomly assigning individuals to either a control or a treatment group without telling the researchers or the individuals of this assignation, followed by the administration of either the treatment or a placebo, again without the knowledge of the individuals or the researchers (hence 'double blind'). Pre and post-testing may therefore be compared, and statistically significant differences between the groups may be presumed to be attributable solely to the treatment rather than to knowledge on the part of either the researcher or the participants as to whether they were receiving the experimental treatment or a placebo. However, while this experimental format works well within a biomedical model of disease, it is often impossible to achieve the necessary degree of control when working from a biopsychosocial perspective. Many studies adopting a biopsychosocial approach utilize a correlational design, which may reveal associations but cannot establish causation. However, this is often the only ethical and practical way to investigate health problems from this perspective. Researchers cannot randomly assign participants to a higher or a lower socioeconomic status, and can achieve only limited control (often statistical control) over other variables which vary systematically by social class such as education, income and living standards. Hence, research findings from such studies are often regarded as less compelling than those from experimental studies.

From a practical point of view there has been much health-related research which has resulted in complex arrays of often conflicting findings. A good example of this phenomenon is in relation to obesity research, with researchers frequently divided over issues such as whether there are any health benefits associated with losing weight. Traditionally the answer to this question has been that in terms of reduced risk of late-onset diabetes, heart disease, vascular disease and mortality, weight loss pays health dividends for those who are significantly overweight. More recently, however, this received wisdom has been questioned, and the available statistics have been used not only to question the supposed benefits of weight loss (Ernsberger and Koletsky, 1999) but also to raise serious questions as to the impact on health of many methods which are used to achieve weight loss, whether dietary or pharmacological. From the point of view of the individual, this lack of consensus among researchers may result either in confusion as to which behaviours are likely to improve health, or loss of motivation to change behaviour.

Over recent years there has been an increase in the use of qualitative methods in health research. These methods examine not simply health-related behaviours but also the meanings behind these behaviours. Given the close links between health psychology and social psychology this is unsurprising (Murray, 2000), and reflects to some extent the aftermath of the 'crisis' in social psychology in the 1970s (Armistead, 1974). At that time many researchers rejected a positivist framework and explored alternative approaches. In terms of furthering understanding of the social and psychological processes involved in the experience of health and illness, such research has great potential to provide insights which are complementary to the findings of quantitative studies.

Intervention strategies

Given the contemporary emphasis on social and psychological factors as significant determinants of health, it is not surprising that social psychological theories have been applied in a wide variety of interventions aimed at modifying health-related behaviours. The field of health promotion utilizes models of attitude change and theories of persuasion, for example in publicity campaigns and community heath programmes urging individuals to eat more healthily, take up regular exercise, reduce alcohol intake and stop smoking. Such initiatives, aimed at the general population, have tended to have limited impact (Bennett and Murphy, 1997), and it has been argued that intervention approaches at this level may be less effective than those targeting specific individuals with several reasons advanced by way of explanation.

First, as Weinstein (1987) points out, most people are biased in the direction of false optimism about their own chances. Coupled with a general tendency to overestimate behavioural risks, such false optimism leads individuals to assess their own risk of a particular health problem as lower than that of the average person but often higher than is actually the case. Second, another factor which may limit the efficacy of large-scale attempts to change health-related behaviours may be the content of public-health intervention materials. According to the theory of planned behaviour, in order to be persuasive an argument must influence the attitudes, norms and control perceptions relevant to the behaviour which is targeted for change. These may in fact vary widely across a large group such as a community or a population. For example, some individuals may continue to smoke because they feel unable to stop, others may be subject to group norms that promote smoking while others may perceive positive benefits from smoking. In order to achieve behavioural change, health promotion communications would need to address all of these issues. In practice this is clearly a difficult if not impossible task and hence it has become more common to see campaigns directed at specific groups. For example the young are generally agreed to have less interest than older people in health-related information, but are known to be peer-oriented and motivated to be attractive. Hence several campaigns aimed at reducing smoking in young people have focused on the impact of cigarette consumption on appearance as well as on health.

Given the limitations of health-promotion campaigns it is not surprising that an alternative strategy for initiating and maintaining behavioural change has involved the use of therapy at either an individual or small group level. Particularly popular have been approaches based on learning theories, although contemporary approaches tend to be more broad-based and include elements of skills training and cognitive restructuring as well as conditioning techniques. While these approaches can be useful, Bennett and Murphy (1998) point out that population-based interventions can often be more cost-effective. Workplace initiatives have been shown not only to be conveni-ent but also to provide individuals with social support as they endeavour to make changes in their health-related behaviour. Moreover, within the work-place environmental change may be initiated to support such changes and indeed may be a prerequisite for successful intervention.

Various intervention strategies, then, have been developed ranging from the focused, individual therapeutic approach, through to population-based initiatives. As indicated above, the success of large campaigns aimed at modifying health-related behaviour seems to be limited for reasons that are explicable in terms of the social psychological theories which underpin them. However, even at the level of individual intervention, limitations to the effectiveness of interventions are numerous and range from the genetic to the social and psychological. For example, in the case of coronary heart disease an individual who has a genetic predisposition and adopts an exemplary lifestyle encompassing a healthy diet, regular exercise, moderate alcohol intake and not smoking may nevertheless suffer a heart attack at a relatively young age. Hence even where behavioural change is achieved this may not have the anticipated health benefits.

Most interventions aimed at modifying health-related behaviours have low to moderate success rates. Given that individuals who present themselves for therapeutic intervention have already decided that they wish to modify the behaviour in question (and that many may already have tried to do so alone before seeking help), the high rates of relapse may indicate gaps in our understanding of the processes involved. However, given the relationship between social psychological theories and the various models of health-related behaviour it may well be that many of the gaps in understanding are at least in part symptomatic of the well-known 'attitude–behaviour' gap which has remained problematic for social psychology as a whole. Nevertheless, as research proceeds and the exchange of information between health psychology and social psychology promotes better understanding, it is likely that interventions will be further refined and become even more effective than is currently the case.

One often cited example of a highly effective intervention strategy is that of the AIDS education and prevention campaigns which were targeted at gay and bisexual males in the United States in the 1980s. Several indicators of efficacy were noted, including reduced rates of infection and decreased risky behaviours. However, it has been noted that this success may have been largely due to the nature of the targeted group, which was already highly organized and politically active and hence was ideally placed to play a proactive role in the strategy. Thus, social factors relating to the nature of the target group will always play a significant part in the success of any intervention.

The way forward

The advent of the biopsychosocial approach within health psychology has opened up possibilities for new understanding of health and illness which includes perspectives drawn from social psychology. Stroebe (2000) notes that currently there is a potentially fruitful exchange of theory and empirical evidence between health psychology and social psychology, with new developments in each being potentially useful in the other.

Currently a source of much debate among health scientists is that of the implications of mapping the human genome. This project, recently completed, has promised much in terms of understanding of disease, and also of new ways of treating a variety of conditions currently recognized as major health problems in the developed world. For example, it has been argued that it will soon be possible, on the basis of a simple saliva test, to predict an individual's susceptibility to a full range of health problems from CHD to depression and Alzheimer's disease. In addition, some have argued that genetic predispositions to a variety of behaviours (for example divorce, crime) will be identifiable in the foreseeable future. For some health scientists these are exciting possibilities opening up avenues to a better, healthier society in every sense of the word. Others are more sceptical and view possibilities such as prenatal genetic testing as likely to lead to 'designer babies', while genetic testing of adults may lead those who are susceptible to the development of particular health problems to have difficulties in obtaining employment or insurance. Social psychological theories and research methods are likely to be extensively applied as these developments unfold.

In conclusion, many disciplines have important contributions to make in furthering progress in this field. Medicine, for example, remains a primary source of information on the physiological aspects of health and on new treatments and their implications. Sociology has contributions to make in highlighting structural and demographic factors and their role in health and illness and related behaviours, as well as in accessibility of treatments. Anthropology provides evidence that models of health and illness are important to these experiences and cross cultural examples indicate the importance of sociocultural factors in how individuals construct what constitutes a healthy or a sick body, and the causes and appropriate treatments of illness. Social psychological approaches which can accommodate and synthesize relevant evidence from other disciplines may represent the most promising means of developing more complete understanding of the processes involved in health and illness, and also of translating these into improved quality of life and social capital in order to benefit the individual.

SHORT QUESTIONS

1   What biological factors determine your own health?
2   What psychological factors determine your own health?
3   What social factors determine your own health?
4   What are the problems associated with changing health-related behaviour?
5   How has social psychology contributed to our understanding of health and illness?

CLASS ACTIVITIES

1 Using a case study based either on someone you know or someone who is in the public eye at the moment, consider who should be responsible for the health of that individual. Use this discussion to think more generally about responsibility for individual health.

2 Draw up a list of societies or communities with which you are familiar and draw comparisons in terms of their perceived health. Why do you think that some societies or communities have better health than others, and what can be done to improve health at a social level?

3 Gather together some health promotion materials relating to various health-related behaviours (e.g. diet, stopping smoking, exercise). Review the content of these materials in relation to social aspects of health-related behaviour. How could they be improved?

4 One way to reduce stress is by relaxation. A variety of techniques can be used to achieve this, including visual imagery, biofeedback, progressive muscular relaxation etc. This exercise will illustrate how easily stress can be alleviated by relaxation. First, take and record your resting pulse rate. Next, close your eyes and think of something aversive (an examination, an argument, whatever makes you feel stressed). Concentrate on imagining or visualizing the aversive situation for a couple of minutes, then take and record your pulse rate again. Next, visualize a situation in which you are usually relaxed, maybe resting quietly at home or on a beach. Concentrate on this for a few minutes and then take and record your pulse rate again. Most people will find that they observe an elevation in pulse rate after imagining an aversive situation and a decrease after imagining a relaxing situation.

FURTHER READING

Armitage, C.J. and Conner, M. (2000) 'Social Cognitions and Health Behaviour: A Structured Review', *Psychology and Health*, vol. 15(2), pp. 173–89.

Bennett, P. and Murphy, S. (1998) *Psychology and Health Promotion*. Buckingham: Open University Press.

Hawe, P. and Shiell, A. (2000) 'Social Capital and Health Promotion: A Review', *Social Science and Medicine*, vol. 5(6), pp. 871–85.

Stroebe, W. (2000) *Social Psychology and Health* (2nd edn). Buckingham: Open University Press.

Wilkinson, R.G. (1996) *Unhealthy Societies: The Afflictions of Inequality*. London: Routledge.

Peace and Conflict

5

At the seam between the centuries, Western social psychologists enthusiastically stitch away, trying to mend intergroup tears in the fabric of society and to embroider intragroup patterns of identity.

(Fiske, 2000)

ONCE UPON A TIME...

Helen, a trainee hairdresser, Frank a catering student and Gemma, a student teacher, had been among the thousands of Catholic and Protestant schoolchildren from Northern Ireland selected for funded trips to America for six weeks during the summer holidays. Such holidays, which are funded by American communities, involve both Catholic and Protestant children staying with American families and sharing their way of life. During the trip children experience group activities such as picnics or trips with others from Northern Ireland. Inevitably friendships are made between Protestant and Catholic children but on returning home the children return to their religiously segregated neighbourhoods and schools. The project provided a follow-up programme that enabled the young people to continue to meet friends from different backgrounds in shared youth centres and at residential weekends. The students who had been selected for these projects tended to have very positive opinions of their experience. Gemma noted, 'It gave me a more positive outlook on those of a different denomination and showed me at the time, that basically we were the same and although we had come from different cultural backgrounds as kids we enjoyed the same activities, shared the common interests that all kids do.' Helen, was more direct when she

---

ONCE UPON A TIME... (cont'd)

indicated that, 'I now know that Catholics are human and not monsters. I would always speak to someone of the opposite religion and I'm not bitter at all.' Frank provided a wider view of the impact of the project when he noted. 'The programme sets people on the right path for the future. It helps us to be able to communicate and show respect to each other, as we are as equal as each other regarding politics or religion. As the future of our country, it is up to us to have the confidence in ourselves to end the bitterness and conflict.'

Introduction

Wherever it may appear, the story of peace and conflict typically includes two essential ingredients, group membership and intergroup relations. In relation to the latter, two alternative scenarios present themselves in the social psychological literature. First, successive surveys demonstrate a decline in overt racism, with Western populations recorded as becoming progressively less prejudiced over the last century. This trend, which may reflect changing social norms together with growing acceptance of diversity, has been accompanied by legislative changes designed to promote human rights and to outlaw blatant discrimination and prejudice against minority groups. At the same time it is not hard to find contemporary examples of major conflict between groups, whether defined as organizations, religions, regions or nations. Conflicts between different ethnic, racial and religious groups feature in reports of small-scale incidents of intergroup violence as well as headline accounts of events in major arenas of conflict such as the Middle East, Afghanistan, Bosnia, Rwanda, Zimbabwe and Northern Ireland.

To begin, it should be acknowledged that social psychology is not able to fully explain variations in intergroup relations across time and location. At best, psychological theory and research can be considered as one of the tools that may contribute to efforts which promote tolerance, resolve conflict and reduce dissension. Prejudice and conflict arise from many interrelated factors; there is no simple remedy, and any single method of intervention will be limited regardless of the strength of the theoretical basis. However, as this chapter will hope to demonstrate, there is now considerable optimism that the growing understanding of the processes that contribute to the nature of prejudice and the mechanisms underlying prejudice reduction and conflict resolution will effectively promote acceptance of diversity.

Before considering any of these issues in detail, it may be helpful to provide definitions of key terms and especially two, prejudice and intergroup relations. Most texts represent prejudice as an attitude which is distinct from discrimination or the behaviour associated with that attitude. In a more sophisticated interpretation, Brown (1995) offers an alternative definition which is broader and more inclusive. According to Brown, prejudice must be regarded as roughly synonymous with specific 'ism' terms such as racism, sexism and ageism. From this broad social psychological perspective prejudice is defined as

> the holding of derogatory social attitudes or cognitive beliefs, the expression of negative affect, or the display of hostile or discriminatory behaviour towards members of a group on account of their membership of that group. (Brown, 1995, p. 8)

In a complementary fashion, earlier Sherif (1966) had offered a definition of intergroup relations that is still widely accepted and highlights the importance of the individual's identification with the group in understanding intergroup behaviour:

> Intergroup relations refer to relations between two or more groups and their respective members. Whenever individuals belonging to one group interact, collectively or individually, with another group or its members in terms of their group identifications we have an instance of intergroup behaviour. (Sherif, 1966, p. 12)

Taken together, both definitions help us to understand how intergroup behaviour and prejudice will occur when individuals categorize themselves and others as belonging to different social groups. Stereotypes are the shared beliefs about these groups that help us to cope with the complexity of the social world by providing guidelines for our views and behaviour towards other people. We are not necessarily aware of the powerful influence of negative stereotypes that can be so embedded in the culture that even those who do not see themselves as prejudiced are vulnerable to unconscious biases (Devine, Plant and Buswell, 2000). Efforts to promote fairness and harmony have to address this type of implicit prejudice and discrimination as well as obvious dissensus and conflict between groups.

History and development

A concern with prejudice as a social issue emerged in the 1920s when white Americans' negative attitudes to black Americans began to be seen as problematic. Previously, it was assumed that negative white racial attitudes reflected a 'natural response' to the 'backwardness' of other racial groups. Historical developments following the First World War led psychologists to question accepted wisdom of white racial superiority and to view the racial attitudes of whites as irrational and unjustified. Initially theoretical explanations for such irrational beliefs were found within Sigmund Freud's psychodynamic theory, including the idea of universal intrapsychic processes such as defence mechanisms. Duckitt (1992) shows that these explanations were never explicitly rejected, but instead the rise of fascism and the horrific nature of the holocaust that was revealed after the end of the Second World War came to reflect in a shift of paradigm.

Such atrocities could not easily be encompassed by a view of prejudice as a normal and universal process. They were more readily understood as the outcome of a form of collective madness or pathology that was associated with disturbed or pathological personality structures. Against this backcloth, the new paradigm led social psychologists to try to identify and define the personality structures that were associated with prejudice.

In the 1950s, there was general acceptance of the view that the authoritarian personality (Adorno, Frenkel-Brunswik, Levinson and Sanford, 1950) accounted for individual differences in prejudice. In common with the earlier paradigm, prejudice was primarily seen from a psychodynamic perspective. In this case, prejudice arose from a displacement of unacceptable feelings towards authority figures, the feelings being displaced towards substitute targets such as minority groups. However, by the end of the decade it was clear that individual pathology could not account for regional differences in racism. At this stage there was another radical shift in the search for explanations of prejudice. The ensuing emphasis on social and cultural factors was accompanied by a decline in psychological interest in the causes of prejudice and a growth in sociological explanations. Those psychologists who maintained an interest in racism and prejudice during this period tended to view the two concepts in terms of the social norms of society and questioned how these societal beliefs were learned by children and influenced by factors such as conformity.

In the 1960s and 1970s psychological explanations continued to focus on individual prejudiced beliefs without taking into account the socio-historical nature of group relations. In contrast, sociological theories ignored psychological processes and stressed the importance of social and structural conditions for understanding racism and other intergroup conflicts. However, Sherif's (1966) realistic conflict theory provided the basis for a more social psychological approach that extended beyond the individual to focus on a group-level analysis of intergroup relations. This approach is exemplified by social identity theory developed by Tajfel and his co-workers in the 1980s (Brown, 2000a,b). These theories promoted the growth of widespread social psychological interest in the nature of intergroup relations and the start of the continuing focus on the importance of normal cognitive and motivational processes in understanding complex social behaviour.

No account, however brief, of the history of our understanding of prejudice would be complete without reference to the seminal contribution of Allport's 1954 book, *The Nature of Prejudice*. This work provides the touchstone for all subsequent theoretical examinations of intergroup relations as well as practical approaches to reducing prejudice. Sampson (1999) concludes that even after nearly 50 years, we should follow Allport's counsel and accept that prejudice cannot be understood by any one theory but instead should be viewed through various lenses that focus our attention on different facets of the phenomenon. This chapter focuses on the prejudiced person and the nature of intergroup relations in order to provide an overview of how psychologists are employing current knowledge to influence individuals and groups to live in harmony together.

Concepts, models and theories

The personality, attitudes and values of prejudiced people were of prime importance for earlier generations of psychologists. Nowadays, concern with individual differences must also embrace cognitive processes including their social roots and their ideological antecedents. This perspective provides the foundation for efforts to change the prejudiced person using information gained on the nature of that individual and the functions played by their prejudiced attitudes and beliefs. A complementary approach necessarily involves considering intergroup relations including the need to examine prejudice as an intergroup rather than an interpersonal process. Change, from this viewpoint, arises from interventions that promote changing intergroup relations through contact and cooperation.

Influencing the individual

Prejudice is widely accepted as an affectively/emotionally-based negative attitude. Many choices in life can be influenced by affectively-based attitudes even when it appears that they are based on a rational and considered analysis of the situation. It may be expected that it would be possible to use persuasion in order to change prejudice, in the same way that persuasion is used to change attitudes to consumer products. In general, however, these affective-based attitudes are not governed by logic and may therefore not be changed by rational arguments. Allport (1954) illustrates this feature of blatant prejudice in a dialogue between Mr X and Mr Y:

> **Mr X**: The trouble with the Jews is that they only take care of their own group.
>
> **Mr Y**: But the records of the Community Chest campaigns show that they gave more generously, in proportion to their numbers, to the general charities of the community than did non-Jews.
>
> **Mr X**: That shows they are always trying to buy favour and intrude into Christian affairs. They think of nothing but money; that is why there are so many Jewish bankers.
>
> **Mr Y**: But a recent study shows that the percentage of Jews in the banking business is negligible, far smaller than the percentage of non-Jews.
>
> **Mr X**: That's just it: they don't go in for respectable business; they are only in the movie business or run night clubs. (Allport, 1954, pp. 13–14)

In this scenario, Allport demonstrated how an emotionally-based attitude such as prejudice provides a framework for gross distortion in the processing of information about Jews. Mr X's emotional reactions defy logical challenges and his hatred of Jews leads him to ignore or distort any facts that could change his attitude. Social psychologists now accept that the processing of all social information is distorted to some extent by an individual's past experiences, attitudes and beliefs. The stronger the attitude the greater the distortion that occurs and the greater the impact of the attitude on behaviour.

Prejudice is not governed by logic and it is not necessarily a product of ignorance. It will therefore not be changed by appropriate knowledge, information or rational arguments. At present there does not seem to be any simple persuasive technique that has been found to successfully combat strongly held prejudiced beliefs. Nevertheless, persuasive techniques can provide one approach to challenging assumptions and promoting new ideas, especially with children and young people who are developing their attitudes and learning about their social world.

Influencing children and young people

The research on interventions to reduce prejudice in children and young people is limited. An early review of the evidence (Katz, 1976) which attempted to link educational experiences with measured attitude-change found that academic instruction generally had little impact on prejudice. Attitude-change was found to occur in two studies but only when direct instruction was linked with activities designed to promote emotional involvement. In one case, anti-Semitism was reduced only when new information was combined with a discussion about anti-Semitism. In the other, academic instruction about prejudice had little impact on the attitudes of 14-year-olds but role-playing did produce significant changes in their attitudes.

More recently, Bigler (1999) reviewed evidence from the field of education as well as psychology on the nature and impact of intervention programmes which have used multicultural curricula and materials to reduce racial stereotyping and prejudice. These American projects involved a wide range of techniques and materials that were used in lessons to expose children to minority groups and highlight the contribution of different racial, ethnic and religious groups to the culture. Bigler notes:

> Unfortunately, very little research has systematically examined the effects of intervention content, scope or duration on racial attitude change among children. Empirical data suggest, however, that extant interventions have been largely ineffective in altering children's racial attitudes, and that this is true across the various forms of multicultural programming that have been evaluated. (Bigler, 1999, p. 690)

One of the most popular techniques involves majority-group students engaging in a planned personal experience of discrimination through which they are exposed first-hand to prejudice and discrimination. Byrnes and Kiger (1990) examined the effectiveness of a well-known role-taking exercise as originally designed by Jane Elliott. Eye colour is used in this intervention as the basis for unequal treatment of groups in the classroom. Byrnes and Kiger were concerned that although anecdotal evidence indicated that the simulation exercise was an effective method for changing attitudes and reducing prejudice, they were unable to locate research that supported this view. In their study, student teachers completed two racial attitude scales before being assigned to two experimental conditions. Students who provided the control group attended class as usual where they viewed the film *A Class Divided* that reported on the impact of Jane Elliott's work as part of these normal activities. Students in the experimental group were required to take part in a three-hour cultural awareness workshop that involved them in a simulation exercise based on the work of Jane Elliott. At the end of the term the original racial attitude scales were re-administered. Virtually all the students thought the exercise was useful. While participation in the simulation exercise did not have an impact on social distance attitudes related to contact with African Americans, it did produce an increased willingness to act in an anti-discriminatory way. Neither viewing the film about the exercise nor attending a lecture was found to have an impact on the non-treatment participants. Unfortunately, there was no attempt to measure the long-term impact of the simulation.

Although students were generally positive about the simulation, the ethics of putting children and young people through an experience involving ridicule and unfair treatment that was very stressful for some participants must be considered. Byrnes and Kiger are themselves not wholly convinced of the merits of the intervention. They note that, 'the students' increased awareness of the injustice and pain that discrimination can cause may come at some cost to the students themselves' (Byrnes and Kiger, 1990, p. 353). It may be that the cost is too high for most teachers.

Influencing implicit beliefs

The end of the twentieth century saw many countries adopting human-rights legislation accompanied by strong legislative support for equal rights and sanctions for overt discrimination. The impact of legislation on individual attitudes and beliefs has been closely monitored in the United States since the 1954 Supreme Court ruling on desegregation. There is now overwhelming evidence that these laws did erode racist norms and promote more positive attitudes and behaviour. However, subtle indicators of prejudice such as physiological and nonverbal responses continue to reveal the impact of stereotypes on the reactions of even low-prejudiced people. Devine *et al.* (2000) argue that although their attitudes have changed, most adults acquired negative cultural stereotypes of minority groups as children. The high-prejudiced person reports personal beliefs that are in accord with these stereotypes but the low-prejudiced person has egalitarian beliefs that lead them to reject the stereotype. Although the low-prejudiced person feels guilty and embarrassed by their own responses, they tend to continue responding according to the stereotype when they do not have the time or the cognitive capacity to inhibit their spontaneous responses and thereby replace them with non-prejudiced personal beliefs.

The research evidence suggests that if individuals are motivated to overcome prejudice they can learn to 'break the habit' and respond to members of the stigmatized groups in a way that is consistent with their beliefs. Clear societal and institutional guidelines for promoting equal opportunities and breaking down barriers, along with non-prejudiced media, will undoubtedly help promote change. It also helps if individuals do not mix exclusively with their own group but have the chance of practising their ability to respond to others without prejudice.

Changing the bigot

Recent research suggests that interventions designed to change prejudiced people can backfire if the organizers do not take account of the complex nature of prejudice. Devine *et al.* (2000) demonstrate that people who are personally motivated to respond in a non-prejudiced way and those who respond without prejudice because of external reasons differ in their responses to efforts to promote equality and reduce prejudice. They report a study that examined the impact of a blatant attempt to change participants' views about a race-based affirmative-action policy. Their message had a very positive impact on those who had a high score on a measure of internal motivation to respond without prejudice, but those who had a low score on the scale strongly resisted the message. After receiving the information they showed increased anger and less-favourable attitudes towards the policy. In accord with Brehm's theory of reactance, these respondents displayed a classic pattern of behaviour that occurs when people feel that they are being pressured to do something that constrains their freedom. Further research suggested that those who combined a low level of internal motivation with a high level of external motivation to respond without prejudice were the most likely to show reactance and to 'lash-out' angrily against being forced to endorse a policy that was not in accord with their views. Devine *et al.* consider that their findings indicate that it is important to be aware of the potential resentment that can be encountered when prejudiced people are faced with efforts to promote change. Is there any hope of reaching these bigots with interventions?

Efforts to change the attitudes and values of prejudiced people have not been abandoned. Recent theories embrace social and ideological issues in order to explore the racist mind. One view of prejudice sees change being brought about from information gained on the nature of the prejudiced individual and the function of prejudiced attitudes and beliefs. Altemeyer (1994), for example, attempted to reduce prejudice in right-wing authoritarians (RWAs) following an extensive programme of research. Altemeyer found that RWAs tended to be the most orthodox members of their denominational group and believed most strongly in the teachings of their religion. He also noted that an, 'I don't want to know attitude' towards ego-threatening material distinguished high from low RWAs. The authoritarians' view that prejudice is normal and widespread is exacerbated by a tendency to mix with only a few close friends and acquaintances who share their beliefs, attitudes and prejudices. Altemeyer concluded that it is doubtful that any educational programme based on rational argument and the presentation of facts would promote insight and change if the person denies that they are prejudiced. However, he did seem to have limited success in moderating the views of high RWAs when he used Rokeach's value self-confrontation model of change (Grube, Mayton and Ball-Rokeach, 1994).

Rokeach based his value self-confrontation model of change on a number of assumptions derived from extensive surveys of the values of the American population. First, Rokeach (1973) noted that people who highly value equality are less prejudiced and more likely to support members of minority groups than those who highly value individual freedom. Second, he assumed that there is a structure to individual value systems, and while some values are central others are peripheral. Finally, he argued that changing central, high-ranking values has a major impact on the individual's life whereas change in peripheral values does not.

Individuals rank-order their values during the first stage of the value self-confrontation technique. In America this inevitably involves them ranking freedom higher than equality. They are then given a brief lecture that informs them of their rankings as compared to others and they are told that this pattern of values means that they are more interested in freedom for themselves than the needs of others. Rokeach considers that awareness of inconsistencies should result in a self-regulatory process to reduce the inconsistency between their beliefs and prejudices and their basic values.

Finally the group's attitudes to minority groups and race relations are measured over time. Following a review of studies that had used this technique, Grube *et al.* (1994) concluded that it is possible to change people's attitudes to minorities and even their behaviour towards minority issues by changing key values. They also noted that these changes are not transitory but can be observed in some cases nearly two years afterwards. Altemeyer (1994) found even those who were assessed as RWAs moderated their views on minority-group relations over a period of several months when exposed to the value self-confrontation technique as part of their introductory psychology course.

Devine *et al.* (2000) suggest that the value self-confrontation technique is one of two approaches that may be potentially successful in changing the deep-seated views of those who maintain prejudiced attitudes despite radically changing social norms. This approach does have the merit of enabling people to consider the implications of their attitudes in relation to their understanding of fairness and justice without producing the resentment felt when exposed to direct efforts to change their belief systems. Devine *et al.* also consider that efforts to create empathy with the minority group would help in creating conditions that lead to change.

In sum, it seems that efforts to reduce prejudice and promote tolerance require more than information and simple persuasive messages. However, many interventions designed to promote prejudice reduction have been developed without adequate concern for either the methodological rigour required for the evaluation of their impact or the theoretical rationale that could account for change. There is a need for continuing effort to identify the nature of change and to understand the processes that lead to change. It is also important to remember that there are individual differences in how people respond to any intervention and every effort should be made to ensure that the project does not reinforce or strengthen prejudice in some respondents.

Intergroup relations

Recent reviews of psychological research on intergroup relations (see for example Brown, 2000a,b; Pettigrew, 1998) highlight the vigour of social identity theory as an explanatory framework. Brown (2000a) suggests that the attraction of social identity theory for social psychologist derives from its focus on the relationship between the individual and the group and the possibility it offers for accounting for the emergence of collective phenomena from individual cognitions.

The distinction between interpersonal and intergroup behaviour is central to the social identity approach. It is assumed that once an individual defines him or herself in terms of a social group or category, it is the collective needs and beliefs of that group rather than individual beliefs and motives that primarily determine behaviour. For example imagine two colleagues who enjoy a close and sustained working friendship but who are also members of rival football teams. In work their behaviour and view of the other will be primarily determined by their personal needs and beliefs. On the football field, or at other occasions when their team membership is salient, their actions and thoughts will be dependent on their team membership. Each will define himself as a team member and his views of the other team will be coloured by the nature and history of the relationship between the two teams. In this context, individual differences among team members and friendships between members of different teams will not be relevant.

When people define themselves in terms of their team membership or social categories such as gender, nationality and religion, they tend to act in order to maintain a positive view of themselves and their ingroup as compared to other groups or outgroups. From this perspective it seems that concern to favour the ingroup rather than any specific desire to disparage the outgroup can drive intergroup discrimination (Brewer and Brown, 1998).

Social identity theory has provided a strong theoretical basis for developing interventions to reduce intergroup conflict, with one of the most powerful approaches from this perspective deriving from efforts to promote contact between members of different groups.

The contact hypothesis

Although increased contact between groups can reinforce hostility and confirm stereotypes, Allport (1954) argued that given appropriate conditions, contact can have a positive outcome. Allport's summary of the optimal conditions for contact has been described as the contact hypothesis. It states:

> Prejudice (unless deeply rooted in the character structure of the individuals) may be reduced by equal status contact between majority and minority groups in the pursuit of common goals. The effect is greatly enhanced if this contact is sanctioned by institutional supports (i.e. by law, custom or local atmosphere), and provided it is of a sort that leads to the perception of common interests and common humanity between members of two groups. (Allport, 1954, p. 281)

The contact hypothesis has been greatly refined by the vast body of research it has inspired. Recently, Pettigrew and Tropp (2000) carried out a meta-analysis based on over 200 studies that combined information from 90 000 participants drawn from 25 different nations. Intergroup contact in these studies involved actual face-to-face interaction between members of clearly distinguishable and defined groups. They found that there was an inverse relationship between contact and prejudice in the vast majority of these studies. The few studies that tested whether contact had an impact on perceptions and evaluations of both the immediate participants and the entire outgroup showed significant generalization effects. Sustained contact in work and organizational settings had a stronger effect than the minimal contact offered through travel or recreation but overall contact had different effects within each of the different types of groups.

Pettigrew and Tropp acknowledge that although in some cases it was possible that their findings reflected on the avoidance of contact by the more prejudiced, the strongest impact of contact was found in studies of situations that eliminated choice. Contact did not have a uniform impact. Members of the majority group showed larger effects than minority group members. This implied that minority and majority group members differ in their interpretation of the intergroup encounters. An intervention might aim to create equal status conditions but the minority group may have a different perspective on their status than the majority group. As Pettigrew and Tropp conclude:

> This strong result indicates that we should regard contact theory's specified optimal conditions not as intrinsic features of the situation itself, but as conditions that can be perceived in contrasting ways by members of the interacting groups. (Pettigrew and Tropp, 2000, p. 109)

For many years, psychologists who employed the contact hypothesis focused almost exclusively on the external conditions of contact and there was little debate about the processes involved in intergroup contact. It was generally assumed that the ideal contact conditions would promote interpersonal relationships between members of different groups and provide the opportunity for individuals to correct negative stereotypes and accept the basic similarities between groups. However, the mechanisms which enabled the individual to generalize from specific experiences to the group were not clear.

Hewstone and Brown (1986) argued that lack of knowledge and inaccurate perceptions provided insufficient explanations of intergroup conflict and therefore expectations about the impacts of increasing knowledge through contact should be modest. They proposed that social identity theory could provide an account of the processes that are involved in successful contact. In the event, social identity theory has served as the basis for three related models of contact that indicate different pathways to achieving an improvement in intergroup relations. Each of these approaches accepts that individuals possess multiple social identities derived from their membership of various groups or categories. They also acknowledge that in order for contact to be successful it is important to modify the importance or salience of the conflicting social categories. At the same time the models differ in the methods they see as being most successful in breaking down barriers.

The first approach argues that contact should aim to weaken the boundaries between groups by encouraging a decrease in category use (decategorization). This usually involves participants viewing one another as individuals rather than members of social categories. In these circumstances participants pay less attention to group-based or stereotypical information about members of the other group. Eventually such encounters should ensure that the distinction between ingroup and outgroup members becomes less important. Most interventions designed to break down barriers in Northern Ireland (for example by involving Protestant and Catholic children in shared holidays and community activities) are based on the belief that the decategorization of group members leads to friendship and breaking down group barriers as people see members of the other group sharing their interests and concerns (Trew, 1986). Such an approach has been found to successfully promote friendships between children from different backgrounds, but it has only limited impact on the participants' views of the outgroup. Recently, this model has been extended by developing interventions in which knowledge of close friendships between members of the ingroup and outgroup provides a catalyst for reducing prejudice (Brown, 2000a). In one study, for example, Finnish students exposed to accounts of friendships between other Finnish students and foreigners had more positive attitudes to outsiders than their peers who had not discussed these friendships.

An apparently very different view of intergroup contact is offered by a second model that advocates *recategorization* rather than decategorization as the basis for promoting good intergroup relationships. This model assumes that group barriers will be broken down when a sense of common group membership has united the subgroups involved in the contact. If, for example, students from the two universities in Northern Ireland come together in a joint team to face competition from a Scottish university, it is assumed that the common purpose will transcend existing rivalry between the universities, weaken the team's initial ingroup–outgroup categorization and enable the students to adopt a shared superordinate identity. This approach has been used successfully with experimental groups but would seem to have limited applicability to real life situations. Here divisions between ethnic, racial or religious groups tend to also involve differences in power and status between majority and minority groups. In these circumstances, the powerful majority tend to try and assimilate the members of the lower status group and hence genuine partnerships are rarely feasible.

Although contact is improved by promoting a shared identity, Hewstone and Brown (1986) considered that it is also important to minimize the threat to subgroup identities by preserving a sense of ingroup distinctiveness. Their approach suggests that successful *subcategorization* is possible when intergroup contact is cooperative and pleasant *and* group identity is acknowledged. For example, Dutch students who worked cooperatively with a person who was clearly introduced as Turkish had a more positive attitudes to Turkish people than those for whom the ethnicity of their partner was not made explicit (Brewer and Brown, 1998).

Pettigrew (1998) suggested that decategorization, recategorization and subcategorization could be integrated to promote optimal intergroup contact. His reformulated intergroup contact theory calls for a long-term perspective that allows time for individuals to form cross-group friendships. He argues that personalizing initial contact will help to minimize anxiety associated with the intergroup encounter. It will then be possible to introduce activities that remind people of their group allegiances thereby ensuring that the impact of any change in attitude will generalize beyond the immediate friendship. Finally, efforts should be made to recategorize the subgroups within a shared superordinate category.

Recently a number of theorists (for example Brewer, 2000; Hewstone and Cairns, 2001) have commented on the possible benefits of the dual-identity strategy that results from the crossing of two distinct categories. Research with immigrants suggests that they experience least acculturation stress if they adopt an integration strategy involving high identification with both their own culture and their host community. In contrast, other strategies such as assimilation that involves low identification with their own culture and high identification with the host culture, or marginalization that involves low identification with both own and host cultures are far less successful (Brown, 2000a). There is now growing evidence that favourable outcomes for minority groups in intergroup encounters also result from a dual identity strategy in which both groups maintain both their subgroup identity and a shared superordinate identity. However, this is problematic if there are inequalities in the status and power of the groups or if the groups perceive a threat to their subgroup identity (Stephan and Stephan, 2000). It is noteworthy that Allport's original contact thesis acknowledged problems of status and equality between groups, and current scholarship builds on this theme by suggesting that encounter should also be managed so as to minimize identity threat.

In summary, the contact hypothesis, first proposed almost 50 years ago, has been further validated by recent reviews highlighting the widespread empirical support for the positive impact of intergroup contact under appropriate conditions. Recent theoretical developments from the perspective of social identity theory help to shed light on the processes involved in producing change and provide a basis for clarifying the optimum conditions for contact. However, the impact of any small-scale interventions is limited. As Brown (2000b) has noted, in order to change intergroup relations we must move beyond intergroup processes and consider the wider setting. He concludes:

> Our communities, workplaces and schools must be restructured so that racist, sexist and other pernicious ideologies lose their functional and psychological appeal, and hence become devalued as legitimating devices. How such structural change can be achieved is a task which confronts us all, social psychologists and concerned citizens alike. (Brown, 2000b, p. 769)

Practical issues

Social psychological research and theory on prejudice, contact and intergroup relations contributed to the US Supreme Court's 1954 ruling that mandated the desegregation of public schools in America. The evaluation of the impact of school desegregation on intergroup attitudes has been mixed. Much of the research emphasizes the importance of taking account of the specific conditions within desegregated schools and classrooms. However, evaluations of 'cooperative classrooms' provide some of the most optimistic accounts of successful intervention based on contact. They also serve as very powerful case studies of the benefits derived from integrating social psychological research and theory with practice.

These programmes differ in their organization but share the goal of creating some form of collaborative problem solving (Slavin and Cooper, 1999). The most well-known approach, the jigsaw classroom (Aronson and Bridgeman, 1979) involves groups of six students who differ in terms of a chosen characteristic such as ethnicity, gender, ability, race and so forth. The children meet in these groups for 45 minutes on three days a week for six weeks. Each student in each group is given a part of the information required to answer a set question or complete a project and the group has to cooperate in order to complete the assignments. They cannot complete the project without information from each member of the group.

In the initial evaluation of this technique, it was found that those in the jigsaw classrooms liked one another more and enjoyed school more than those in traditional classrooms. They were also found to have higher self-esteem and they performed better on an objective test on the topic than their peers. Subsequently, the result of many studies have shown that cooperative learning groups are most effective when they involve highly favourable contact conditions and reward interdependence.

The way forward

This chapter has looked at how psychology is working at a number of levels in order to reduce the impact of prejudice on individuals, groups and society. Stephen and Stephen (2000) provide a very optimistic account of the future of intergroup relations when they note:

> Encouragingly, more research is being done on techniques to improve intergroup relations than ever before. More importantly, such techniques are being put into practice at a higher rate than ever before. New techniques are appearing every year. Racial dialogue is being promoted at the highest level of government.

We are far from winning the battle against racism, discrimination, prejudice and stereotypes, but we have developed better weapons with which to fight these enemies. (Stephen and Stephen, 2000, p. 24)

Cairns (2001) assesses the implication of the growing body of research for policies designed to promote world peace. He starts from the premise that in recent years the main threat to peace has tended to be intergroup conflicts based on ethnic, religious or other social and cultural differences. He suggests that there is a range of actions that may help to reduce or even prevent violent conflict arising from such differences. Included in his action plan are many of the approaches outlined in this chapter, including group contacts that are designed to improve intergroup relations at the micro level. In addition, Cairns argues that there is a need to address the psychological causes of existing conflict and to intervene to prevent cycles of revenge. Ameliorative strategies and peaceful alternatives to conflict should be actively endorsed through social policy, education, the law and the media.

In the past, the role of psychologists has tended to be overlooked in the search for peace, but in 1997 the presidents of the US and Canadian psychological associations launched a joint task force in order to create a new profession to enable some psychologists to devote their lives to 'the prediction, prevention, understanding and healing of ethnopolitical conflict' (Seligman, 2001). The first students of the programmes that were set up to develop this new profession have now graduated. It is hoped that they will be able to develop the research and contribute to the scholarship that will help the children of the twenty-first century to grow up in a more peaceful world than that of their parents and grandparents.

SHORT QUESTIONS

1 What is the 'Jigsaw classroom'?
2 According to Altemeyer what are the main characteristics of a right-wing authoritarian?
3 How has Social Identity Theory contributed to our understanding of the impact of social contact between groups?
4 Outline the strengths and weaknesses of persuasion as a technique for combating prejudiced beliefs?
5 Describe and discuss Rokeach's value self-confrontation model of change.

========== **CLASS ACTIVITIES** ==========

1 Primary-school children from rural areas have few opportunities to meet children from other backgrounds. Discuss possible approaches that schools could use to ensure that these children grow up to be tolerant citizens in a multicultural society.

2 Imagine that you are asked to organize a trip to the zoo for two groups of 10-year-olds that come from religiously segregated schools. They have not previously been involved in a programme of shared activities. What are the potential outcomes of this intergroup contact? How would you try and guarantee that the meeting will produce positive outcomes?

3 Discuss how an organization that has an ethnically diverse workforce could promote good working relationships between all members of staff.

========== **FURTHER READING** ==========

Brown, R. (1995) *Prejudice: Its Social Psychology*. Oxford: Blackwell.

Chirot, D. and Seligman M.E.P. (2001) *Ethnopolitical Warfare: Causes, Consequences and Possible Solutions*. Washington, DC: American Psychological Association.

Oskamp, S. (ed.) (2000) *Reducing Prejudice and Discrimination*. New Jersey: Lawrence Erlbaum Associates.

Sampson, E.E. (1999) *Dealing with Differences: An Introduction to the Social Psychology of Prejudice*. Orlando: Harcourt Brace.

Communication
and the Media

6

Children who have been taught, or conditioned, to listen passively most of the day to the warm verbal communications coming from the TV screen, to the deep emotional appeal of the so-called TV personality, are often unable to respond to real persons because they arouse so much less feeling than the skilled actor.

(Bruno Bettelheim)

ONCE UPON A TIME...

A psychology student called Jane decided, as part of a group project, to quantify the amount of violence that was broadcast on television on an average weekday. Jane had a younger brother and sister and had often wondered whether the programmes which they watched had any effect on their behaviour. She set about the task by recording every programme broadcast on each of the major network channels and she then counted up every time a violent act, which she defined as one person or character physically striking another, occurred. The task took rather longer than she had anticipated, but finally she had the answer: children's cartoons are easily the most violent programmes broadcast on an average weekday whereas primetime news broadcasts are among the least violent. Thus, she concluded that the levels of violence on television could be dramatically reduced by curtailing the number of cartoons and increasing the number of news broadcasts. That night she arranged to take her brother and sister to see *The Lord of the Rings* at her local cinema, but at the last minute her brother decided to stay at home to watch the wrestling on television.

Introduction

Technologies for communicating have had a profound impact on the course of human history. Palaeolithic cave drawings constitute the earliest attempts to communicate in a medium based on the technologies of the period. The invention of the written phonetic alphabet in the Tigris–Euphrates valley about 4000 BC marked another revolution in which sounds, rather than pictures, were represented as an alphabet of arbitrary symbols. The invention of the moveable-type printing press in the fifteenth century facilitated an enormous expansion in the recording, production and communication of facts, ideas, beliefs, doctrines and values, and that led to the upheaval of political and religious institutions. Twentieth-century innovations in electronics prompted exponential growth in the nascent communications industry. Within the past twenty years there has been a further revolution through the inter-linking of computing and telecommunication technologies that form the core of the global communications network, including the internet and digital satellite technology.

Debates on the impact of communication technologies, particularly televi-sion and the internet, on audiences and users are steeped in controversy. Increases in crime have been attributed to the adverse consequences of exces-sive exposure to television, while high levels of internet use have been used to explain why so many adolescents appear to be drawn into a world of their own. In approaching these debates, applied social psychologists bring a perspective that questions some of the concepts and language that are central to many arguments. For example, the use of the term 'exposure' – *exposure to too much television* – is itself quite revealing because it suggests that audiences are regarded as passive and uncritical, 'soaking up' whatever it is they are exposed to in ways that induce a pernicious change in values, attitudes and behaviour. Thus, discussions on 'heavy television viewing' and 'heavy internet use' are often couched in a context of social concern about the potentially detrimental consequences. This contrasts with the more positive effects that are attributed to 'heavy reading' of newspapers, novels and reference works. The application of concepts and methods from social psychology has largely focused on mass broadcast media, for example in querying the degree to which audiences are passive and malleable. However, recent technological advances have lead to the introduction of radical changes in communication and interaction within the workplace. For instance, the introduction of e-mail systems allows employees to engage in 'broadcast' communication to groups within their workplace. Even more important, perhaps, is the capacity for e-mail recipients to respond to the 'broadcaster', thereby facilitating the development of new ways of communicating at work. The extent to which these innovations change the nature in which people communicate and alter the formation and maintenance of social networks raises questions that have drawn the involvement of social psychologists.

History and development

Communication is one of those concepts that everyone understands yet stubbornly eludes definition. It includes talking and listening to one another, watching television, listening to the radio, e-mailing and web-surfing. Laswell (1948) provided one of the earliest and most frequently cited models of mass broadcast media when he argued that in order to understand the processes and effects of mass communication it is important to address five interlinked questions: *Who*, says *what*, in which *channel*, to *whom*, with what *effect?* Laswell's model provides a broad psychological agenda for research on communication media. It stipulates that attributes of the communicator, the content of the message, the channel in which it is communicated (for example radio, television, print, internet), the characteristics of the audience (such as their level of knowledge and expertise) and the effect of the message on recipients (for example whether they believe or reject it) are fundamental to understanding the functioning of a communication medium. His model also implies that interactions between stages are important. For example, the effect of a message may be shaped by the manner in which a communication channel influences what is said. The model regards communication as a broadly linear transmission of messages from a sender (*Who*) to a receiver (*Whom*). However, the possibility that audiences may directly or indirectly communicate with message senders is not explicitly recognized; there is no feedback from '*Whom*' to '*Who*'. For example, a listener can use non-verbal cues to feedback to and influence a speaker's speech rate: slow head nods will tend to slow a speaker down whereas rapid head nods will tend to provoke an increase in speech rate. A further drawback of Laswell's model is its focus on the *effect* of what is said rather than the *meaning* of the message and how the meaning was received and understood. Notwithstanding these limitations, much of the research into the psychological processes involved in a wide range of communications media is structured around the main questions posed in that model.

Shannon and Weaver's (1949) mathematical theory of communication has also had a profound impact on the way psychologists have approached the analysis of communication. Their model (see Figure 6.1) is based on the statistical concept of signal transmission. In this model the information

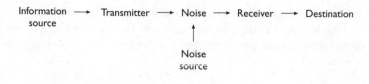

Figure 6.1 Shannon and Weaver's model of communication

source selects a message to be communicated from a range of possible messages. The message may consist of spoken or written words, music, pictures, and so on. The transmitter converts the message to a signal suited to the preferred channel – the channel is the medium that transmits the signal from the transmitter to the receiver. Applied to the analysis of human speech communication, the information source is the brain and the transmitter is the voice mechanism that produces the signal that is sent through the air (the channel). The receiver or listener performs the inverse operation of the transmitter by reconstructing the message from the sensory information collected by the ear.

Other important contributions are Shannon and Weaver's concepts of a message as composed of *entropy* (a measure of the degree to which it is disordered) and *redundancy* (a measure of its predictability) and of achieving the necessary balance between them for efficient communication while offsetting the effects of noise. Noise is anything added to a signal between its transmission and reception that was not intended by the sender. The more noise the greater the need for redundancy in order to reduce the relative entropy of the message. In order to ensure that you correctly understand some of the core concepts in the Shannon–Weaver theory I have used examples (including this very sentence) to add redundancy to my message. By using redundancy to counteract the effects of noise (such as the possibility that you might misinterpret the way Shannon and Weaver define 'noise') I have increased the entropy in my message to you. However, by increasing the redundancy in what I have written I have less space to write about other things in this chapter. The first two sentences (68 words) in this paragraph contains everything I wanted to tell you. Increasing redundancy makes it easier to understand my message, but the cost has been an increase in the number of words (68 + 153) I have written and you have read.

Shannon and Weaver used their model to identify three levels of problem in the study of communication. Level A (technical problems): How accurately can the symbols of communication be transmitted? Level B (semantic problems): How do the transmitted symbols convey the intended meaning?

Level C (effectiveness problems): How effectively does the received meaning affect behaviour in the desired way?

Information theory is essentially a theory of signal transmission which, on first inspection, may seem disappointing because it seems to have nothing to do with the psychology of human communication, and because it equates 'information' with 'uncertainty'. However these were two of the theory's greatest assets because they provided a new way of viewing the communication process. Shannon and Weaver's model implies that all communications are composed of chains of systems and, as with any chain, they are only as strong as their weakest link. A system is any part of an information chain that is capable of existing in one or more states or in which one or more events can occur. A communication system can be an optical cable, the optic nerve or the air used to convey vocal utterances. According to the model, systems must be coupled with one another for information transfer to occur and the state of any system depends on the state of the system adjoining it. If a coupling is broken the information will not be transferred, resulting in communication failure. Interpersonal communication is extremely complex because it consists of several coupled systems, so the potential for communication failure is high. Adding new communication technologies, such as telephones and e-mail, increases its complexity by introducing new systems. This in turn increases the likelihood of communication failure.

The mass media are usually characterized by a relatively high output compared with a low input: relatively few people produce the news items that are seen, heard or read by millions. The mass media themselves are made up of groups of people and, as with any group, communication networks must be established and maintained if a group is to function. Shannon and Weaver refer to this coupling between systems in a larger network as a gatekeeper point. A gatekeeper determines what information is passed along the chain and how faithfully it is reproduced. This concept has been used particularly well to describe what happens when reporters and editorial teams decide what information to use in the media from the vast array of information available for transmission.

Shannon and Weaver's model is particularly accurate when applied to electronic information transmission systems, but less so when applied to human communication. The main reason for this is that the human central nervous system is a functional system – its present state depends on its past operation. Thus, unlike electronic systems the human system can learn. Information received in the past can be learned, recalled from memory and used to inform the interpretation of any future message. In turn message senders may take account of previous communications in the timing and content of planned communications.

Contemporary priorities

The effects of television on children

It is often argued that the weight of evidence favours the conclusion that audiences, and especially children, who view a good deal of television violence – or 'receive' a lot of violent messages – may learn to behave more aggressively (Newson, 1994). The more frequently cited findings come from correlational studies and naturalistic or field experiments. Correlational studies are designed to examine the association between television viewing and the behaviour of audiences. However, they are just that, studies of association and as such they cannot be used to infer causal connections however many times an association may be observed. Naturalistic or field experiments are different in principle because their design can logically accommodate causal inferences. However, field experiments are difficult to control and for each study implicating a causal connection it is usually possible to cite a number of social, economic and lifestyle factors that may have contributed to the emergence of a particular pattern of findings (Cumberbatch and Howitt, 1989).

Intervention studies aim to change beliefs, attitudes and social behaviour. Some television programmes also have as their objective the changing of viewers' behaviours. For example, the North American series 'Mister Rogers' Neighbourhood' was designed to encourage altruistic behaviour in young children and to facilitate understanding and communication of emotions such as anger, fear and aggression. During the 1980s, issues such as abortion, cheating and racism were dealt with in a series 'Up and Coming' intended for teenagers (Johnston and Ettema, 1986). In the UK, there have been several programmes (for example 'Grange Hill', 'Byker Grove') concerned with increasing social awareness about social and moral issues while also providing attractive entertainment.

'Freestyle' was one of the largest and most comprehensively researched interventions (Johnston et al., 1980). It was a 13-part dramatic series for nine- to 12-year-olds designed to change their sex-role stereotypes. There was particular emphasis on portraying girls as competent and capable while occupying traditionally masculine areas, such as science and mechanics. The children were divided into groups and viewed the programmes under one of three conditions:

1 at home with minimal encouragement;
2 at school with no discussion and activities;
3 at school, supplemented by teacher-led discussion and activities.

Seven thousand children in seven US cities participated in the study, which adopted a pre- and post-test design. The children provided self-reports on their beliefs, attitudes and interests in performing non-traditional activities for their gender. The results showed that viewing at school, followed by class discussion, produced large changes on most measures, followed by school viewing on its own and then home viewing. The findings indicated:

- viewing pro-social TV can alter the beliefs, attitudes and interests of children;
- belief and attitude change can generalize beyond programme specific content;
- size of effects interacts with viewer characteristics (girls showed larger changes);
- some topics (e.g. mechanics) show effects more easily than others (e.g. assertiveness or leadership);
- some outcomes are more easily obtained than others (e.g. it was easier to bring about general changes in attitudes and beliefs about the appropriateness of engaging in cross-gender activities than to change personal preferences for participation in these).

A somewhat different intervention (Singer and Singer, 1983) used eight school lessons to teach children, from kindergarten to the fifth grade, about television. The lessons included such topics as: how programmes are created, format and programme type, commercials, TV as a source of information about the world, as well as violence on TV – its unrealistic nature and the value of critical viewing skills. Teachers were shown videotapes, including extracts from current TV programmes, demonstrating the concepts to be taught and supported by discussion ideas and activity sheets for class work and for homework. The teachers were also trained in the use of the various materials.

Younger children, from kindergarten to second grade, showed improvements in understanding the material taught, especially for camera techniques, video editing and realism/fantasy discriminations, and comprehension of the purpose of commercials, again with reality/fantasy distinctions. Small improvements were demonstrated on measures to do with TV violence and critical viewing skills. There were few significant changes on attitude measures, but after the intervention there was a tendency for the children to choose a less violent character as a favourite and to base this choice on attributes other than heroism. After the intervention, third and fourth graders were more likely to choose a realistic rather than a fantasy character as their favourite. Reasons for watching TV shifted from 'exciting' to judgements like 'fun' or 'nothing else to do'. Singer and Singer (1983) suggested this may indicate less reliance on TV for heightened stimulation.

This type of practical intervention requires considerable resources and extensive teacher cooperation, and demonstrates that substantial knowledge gains and some changes in attitudes to TV programmes and characters are possible. The 'Freestyle' project, in contrast, used TV to change beliefs and attitudes about a different social issue (that is, sex-role stereotypes). Both show that well-structured interventions can achieve planned changes in attitudes and ideas, but it is not clear whether these changes in turn lead to behavioural changes. For example, does more critical TV viewing lead to less stereotyped career choices later in life?

Huesmann et al. (1983) took a different approach in their intervention. They considered it may be possible to change children's attitudes and beliefs about TV violence, and thereby attenuate some of the effects attributed to viewing TV violence. Their intervention was on a fairly small scale. Children (six- and eight-year-olds) were given six attitudinal questions to rate on a five-point scale. These included, for example: 'How much of what kids see on TV is fake?'; 'Are TV shows with a lot of hitting and shooting harmless for kids?' These sorts of questions illustrate the need for care when undertaking evaluations in the field: they are not particularly satisfactory because their wording could be taken as suggesting a particular response to a child.

Huesmann et al. aimed to teach children that watching TV violence was undesirable and that it should not be copied. In two training sessions the children wrote reports about negative aspects of TV violence and read them before a video camera. A comparison group encountered the same procedure but their topic was their hobby, rather than TV violence. The results showed that attitudes about TV violence changed in the experimental group but not the comparison group. In the early school years aggression increases with age (Eron et al., 1983), and both the experimental and control group showed increased aggression after the intervention. However, the increase for the experimental group was significantly less than for the control group.

Huesmann et al.'s (1983) intervention did not reduce the children's frequency of violence-viewing or alter perceptions of its realism. The best predictor of aggression in the intervention group was a measure of identification with TV characters. Those children who rated themselves most highly on identification with TV characters were regarded by their peers as being more aggressive. A positive but non-significant correlation was also found in the comparison group, but for this group violence-viewing alone was the best predictor of peer nominations of aggression. Huesmann et al. explain this by suggesting that a change in attitude is not the only cognitive change that reduces aggression. Children who identified least with TV characters also changed their attitudes more and were less aggressive, relative to the control group, after the intervention. Violence-viewing did not change but became uncorrelated with aggression.

Huesmann's intervention emphasizes the importance of identification with television characters. The idea that identification could be an important mediating variable between viewing violent television programmes and aggression comes from social learning theory, the processes by which social factors influence how and what people learn and how they are likely to behave (Bandura, 1977). However, the defining identification poses certain difficulties. In one sense it appears to refer to the extent a viewer may wish to copy or be like a TV character. In a psychodynamic sense identification is a process of internalization (Lefkowitz et al., 1977), involving the acceptance of a character's values, desires goals and standards. Turner and Berkowitz (1972) suggested that identification occurs when an observer imagines him/herself to be the model they see, causing verbalization and other forms of expression of the aggressive model's behaviour. Weiss (1969) suggested that identification is a kind of implicit role-taking which occurs when a person participates vicariously in events, feelings and behaviour with a fantasy TV (or book) character. In their measurement of identification Huesmann et al. (1983) and Eron and Huesmann (1986) chose eight TV characters and asked children how often they did the things the characters did. The children answered 'a lot', 'a little', 'not at all', or 'do not know'. This may seem like a good measure but a closer inspection illustrates the practical difficulties encountered by applied social psychologists. Asking children how often they did the things the characters did is a self-report measure of imitation and does not indicate with which character attributes (for example appearance, personality, behaviour or lifestyle) a child is identifying, nor the reasons for his/her choice. Children's abilities to recognize emotions, infer motives, intentions and reasons and to make attributions develop gradually. This leaves open the possibility that adults may regard particular TV characters as antisocial, aggressive and generally undesirable role models while children may regard them as interesting and attractive for their portrayal of different characteristics to which they are drawn.

Intervention studies can change children's attitudes towards television violence. The level of resource required to bring about a planned outcome is unclear, but studies by Huesmann et al. (Huesmann and Eron, 1986) indicate that modest resources may suffice. The durability of outcomes is uncertain but it is possible that isolated benefits may not endure and can be obliterated by more pervasive, enduring social influences. Even when an intervention achieves planned objectives one must be cautious when using an outcome effect to draw conclusions about causal factors. For example, Huesmann *et al.* have interpreted the success of their intervention as support for their account of the TV violence–viewer aggression relationship. It is tempting to conclude that interventions that change children's attitudes and behaviour towards what they see on television provides evidence of the influence of television on those attitudes and behaviour prior to the intervention. However, this is not necessarily implied by an intervention: the fact that television can be used to change antisocial behaviour does not necessarily mean that it caused the behaviour in the first instance. It is possible that an intervention aimed at teaching children about the unrealistic nature of TV violence and the unsuitability of aggressive solutions to interpersonal problems can alter children's attitudes towards these without implicating TV violence as a causal factor. It could be that formative forces on children's attitudes and behaviours are larger and more pervasive – to do with socioeconomic and lifestyle factors – and an intervention temporarily counters some of these.

One criterion to use when evaluating the success of practical interventions is the durability of their effects. Given the multitude of factors influencing children's daily lives it is doubtful that the effects produced by Huesmann's intervention were sustained. Another criterion for appraising the worth of an intervention relates to the realism of the effects it produces – are the changes socially and psychologically real? Although statistical analyses can identify associations or differences that are unlikely to be due to chance many can be regarded as 'significant' in a statistical sense only. On this criterion the intervention by Huesman *et al.* is somewhat successful – changes in children's understanding of television violence and their perceptions of aggression among peers were brought about. Some of these changes may even endure, and satisfy the first criterion, though the lessons of the intervention are probably subject to memory factors and may be simply forgotten.

One of the questions motivating interest in the potential effects of television on children is whether there is a causal link between the enormous growth in television viewing and increases in crime among children and young adolescents? Psychological interest in this question contrasts with the scant consideration given to it by sociologists, forensic psychologists and criminologists, who place greater importance on family factors, social background, poverty, unemployment, poor housing, alienation and social exclusion (see for example Ainsworth, 2000; Tierney, 1996). Little or no attention is given to the role of the media, and the studies that have examined a potential connection have found it to be unimportant. For example, Hagell and

Newburn (1994) interviewed 78 violent teenage offenders about their uses of, and attitudes towards, the media and compared their experiences with a group of 500 school pupils of the same age. They found that the offenders watched less television and video, had less access to both, had no preference for particularly violent programmes and either enjoyed the same material as the non-offenders or were disinterested.

The rationale for the approach adopted by those interested in understanding the causes of crime is that, in order to explain the problem of violence in society, it is essential to begin with those who engage in crime and examine their biographies. However, studies that have tried to examine connections between crime and the media have almost always adopted a fundamentally different approach: they commence with an analysis of the media and then attempt to describe connections with large social problems. More generally, the interests in media effects have emphasized the importance of individualistic factors and have tended to treat these in a social vacuum. This is reflected in a belief that particular individuals at certain times in specific circumstances may be negatively affected by specific media content, and that the removal of such content would be a positive step.

The media and public perceptions of risk

Many sections of industry and the government appear to hold the view that, just as the media can have a significant impact on child audiences, they also have the potential to exert a powerful negative influence on adult audiences. A particularly striking example of this view is the claim that the mass media distort public perceptions of risk by 'blowing risks out of proportion' (Cohen, 1983). That the public may be concerned about risks that do not particularly worry experts is often attributed to a belief that the media will never let the facts stand in the way of a good story. However, numerous studies of newspapers and television have failed to identify any strong link between media consumption and public perceptions of risk (Wahlberg and Sjoberg, 2000). Nevertheless, ongoing suspicions about the potentially pernicious influence of the media on public perceptions of risk influenced the development of the social amplification of risk framework (SARF), a framework which has come to represent an important attempt to consider how the mass media may shape public perceptions of risk.

The framework starts from the concept of a risk-related 'event', such as media reports of the potential threats to health posed by the release of genetically modified organisms into the environment. Although the concept of 'an event' suggests an accident or incident with specific, immediate effects, the term includes potential events not as yet realized as well as non-physical 'events' such as government policy statements and regulatory actions on a particular issue. The representation of the characteristics of the 'event' is thought to interact with a wide range of psychological, institutional, social and cultural processes. Social amplification describes why some events seem to create ripple effects that spread beyond the initial effects of the hazard or event and impact upon previously unrelated technologies or institutions. These larger impacts include demands for regulatory action, loss of trust in industry and government, and the stigmatization of a company, a local community or product or facility.

SARF adopts the metaphor of amplification derived from the earliest communications theory (Laswell, 1948; Shannon and Weaver, 1949), using this to describe how risk signals are received, interpreted and passed on by a variety of agents in a complex communication chain. These signals are subject to predictable changes as they are filtered through gatekeepers or the various 'amplification' stations. The latter can include individuals or social groups or organizations such as individual scientists, politicians, government agencies and departments, and activist groups. The media are presented as primary amplifiers because of their considerable potential to attend to some issues, and therefore to amplify them, or to downplay or attenuate others.

In a study of 128 hazard stories, Kasperson *et al.* (1992) and Renn *et al.* (1992) measured the volume of media coverage for a range of events from biocidal hazards to natural hazards and compared this to expert and student panel judgements of the risk posed by these events. Once the extent of damage was controlled for, no perception variable – except dread – was found to be correlated with the extent of media coverage. In fact the general pattern that emerged was for full news articles not to overemphasize the gravity of the risks and to offer reassurance. This study focused on hypothetical rather than actual outcomes, and as such it did not address the factors influencing people's responses to real-life hazards. In a qualitative study of six risk events, five of which involved some form of nuclear hazard, sustained and heavy media attention did not of itself ensure risk amplification or significant secondary effects (Kasperson, 1992). Thus SARF's originators have themselves pointed to the ambivalent evidence on the role of the mass media as amplifiers of risk.

Several studies have examined the reporting of risk in relation to environmental issues (for example Anderson, 1997; Campbell, 1998; Allan *et al.*, 1999). These studies have identified consistent criteria in the selection of news selection, all of them touching on psychological processes of one kind or another. These include:

▓ *An orientation to events.* News stories tend to focus on interruptions to the normal flow of activity, such as an accident, a protest or a political speech, rather than on underlying processes or continually unfolding conditions.

▓ *Novelty.* There is a preference for material that introduces new issues or moves an existing story on.

▓ *Scale.* Events are more newsworthy if large numbers of people are affected, such as the risk to health posed by the potential presence of diseased neurological tissue in beef.

▓ *Conflict and drama.* 'The news' places a premium on stories that involve controversy and/or dramatizes the seriousness of actual or potential risks. For example, by drawing attention to disagreements among experts the media may convey the impression that there is confusion on a particular risk and provoke anxiety, leading the public to 'err on the side of safety' (Mazur, 1981).

▓ *Resonance.* News taps into existing public anxieties and frames stories in terms of already familiar events and scenarios. UK media coverage of the presence of genetically modified organisms in food, for example, often makes explicit links with public concern over BSE.

▓ *Personalization.* News seeks to treat issues of public importance with a human face, for example by focusing on specific victims.

▓ *Domestication.* News often looks into the immediate consequences for everyday life in households and families.

▓ *Visualization.* News organizations are continually searching for images that crystallize their interpretation of an event or issue.

There have been several attempts to test SARF empirically, and the findings suggest that some of the underlying causes and factors influencing public reactions can be explained by the framework (Kasperson and Kasperson, 1996). However, the secondary ripple effects which are suggested, such as diminished trust in experts and diluted confidence in government, have proved more difficult to examine. As with intervention studies aimed at children, there are questions over the permanence of any effects, and considerable uncertainty surrounding the precise factors that lead to an issue either remaining controversial or receding (Pidgeon, 1999).

Concepts, models and theories

Over and above the various theories already discussed, it is possible to identify four distinct phases in the way communication media have been studied. Each phase reflects an emphasis on a somewhat different aspect of the person. Phase 1 covers the period 1920–45 and was characterized by the predominance of 'magic bullet' and 'hypodermic needle' theories which assumed that the effects produced by the mass media were strong and relatively enduring. These theories were motivated by an awareness of the enormous impact of political propaganda during the period leading up to the Second World War. Media content was thought to occupy a central role in the effect process: the message was regarded as crucially important and strong messages were thought to produce strong effects. Audiences were considered to react in a relatively uniform way and media effects were thought to occur almost instantly and directly. However, empirical investigations of mass communication campaigns during election periods indicated that audiences can be influenced in a variety of ways. Even when political campaigns are effective in disseminating information they may not alter opinions or voting behaviour.

Phase 2 covers the period 1945–70s and was characterized by the promotion of 'limited-effects' hypotheses that aimed to qualify the claims of the earlier theories. Media content was considered to vary in its persuasiveness and strong messages could have variable effects. In addition, it was considered to have the potential to alter latent psychological processes in audiences. For example, this phase was associated with the study of subliminal effects: the possibility of producing strong, direct effects on audiences by communicating messages below conscious awareness. Studies conducted during this period drew particular attention to the importance of the mediating influences of selective attention (people can vary the amount of attention they give to the media), group processes and group norms (people will talk about and critique what they have heard or seen with family, friends and peers) and opinion leadership (people will take into account what political, business, religious and other leaders have to say on any particular issue). Gerbner's (1956) Cultivation Theory was particularly influential during this period. Gerbner argued that television had become a central cultural arm of American society. His theory contends that television has the potential to impart not only knowledge, and thereby shape people's beliefs, but also cultural values that can shape a person's sense of who they are – their personal identity, and where they belong – their national identity.

Evidence for Gerbner's theory was largely based on questionnaire surveys in which average television viewers (that is, those who watched about four hours per day) were compared with 'heavy' viewers (those who watch even more). These studies found, for example, that heavy viewers tended to overestimate the percentage of the world population living in the United States, thought they were more likely to be the victims of a violent crime and were somewhat less trusting of others. Cultivation theory underwent several significant revisions to take account of the evidence showing that heavy television viewing has different consequences for different social groups. For example, heavy viewers in both low-income and high-income social groups considered fear of crime to be a very serious personal problem. However, light viewers in both these income groups did not share the same opinion. Light viewers in the low-income group were similar to the heavy viewers in both groups. Light viewers in the high-income group tended not to think of fear of crime as a personal problem for them.

One of the implied models of television audiences referred to in the introduction to this chapter is illustrated by the term 'heavy viewer'. 'Heavy' television viewing appeared to imply a diminution of critical thinking abilities:

> Most viewers watch by the clock and either do not know what they will watch, when they turn on the set, or follow established routines rather than choose each program as they would choose a book, a movie or an article. (Gerbner, Gross, Morgan and Signorielli, 1986, p. 19)

Phase 3 covers the period from the 1970s to the early 1990s. It is associated with a partial return to the earlier theories – the 'powerful effects' view of the mass media. Media content was thought to occupy a more central role in the effect process; audiences could be profiled in terms of their reactions; and effects were considered to occur slowly and indirectly. This phase is particularly associated with the development of intervention studies, such as those considered earlier in this chapter. For ethical reasons, certain types of intervention could not be allowed. For example, studies that demonstrate a correlation between television viewing and audience aggression cannot be used to infer that watching television caused the behaviour. The presence of a causal link could be examined through a study in which a sample of children is randomly assigned to one of two conditions. In one the children would be encouraged to routinely view violent films for an extended period of time, and a comparison group would not be supplied with these films. The behaviour of the two groups of children could be compared after some time. Clearly this kind of study is ethically unacceptable although an intervention to reduce the effect of television violence on children would probably be regarded as legitimate. This illustrates a challenge frequently encountered in the application of social psychology: intervention studies seek to bring about a change in one direction only and this imposes a limitation on the kinds of causal inferences that can be drawn. Nevertheless, intervention studies are important because they represent a concerted effort to bring about planned changes for the better.

Phase 4 covers the period from the mid-1990s to the present and includes the impact of changes in information technology and telecommunications systems. Information technology is concerned with the acquisition, processing, storage and communication of information. Information technology (IT) has been made possible by an application of science and engineering to the modelling, processing and retrieval of information. Advances in electronic engineering have provided resources for the storage and manipulation of information on a very large scale, and telecommunications has made possible the technology for the transmission of very large quantities of information in different formats. Affordable applications of advances in science and engineering to the production of information technology have been made possible by the availability of complex, reliable, low-cost microelectronic components. As a consequence of these developments, the communication of information has acquired two functional connotations. First, it has come to be regarded as an economic resource. Communication has come to be associated with trading information in much the same way as labour, material and capital is bought and sold. Information is transacted commercially because its possession and application are considered to increase the effectiveness of physical and human resources. For example possession of climate information helps facilitate the judicious use of natural resources, improves the cost-effectiveness of the agricultural industry and thereby enhances standards of living and quality of life. Second, information is regarded as a commodity. The information service sector is associated with industries concerned with exploration, innovation and design, planning, and financial management. The general effect of these changes has been to provide users with much greater control over the communications media they use – what they choose to access, when and where.

Although information is regarded as a resource and a commodity it has a number of social psychological attributes which distinguish it from other economic entities. First, it is intrinsically diffuse. Second, it reproduces through use; it is not consumed in the way other commodities are consumed. In this sense 'consumers' of information are agents for its reproduction and expansion. Third, information can only be shared, it cannot be transacted. Someone who supplies or communicates information is not automatically dispossessed of it. This greatly complicates commerce in information and introduces a range of psychological and social processes into economic transactions.

Practical issues

One of the most fundamental questions that arises in the study of any kind of communication concerns the definition and measurement of the phenomena in which we are interested. For example, in order to answer the question 'how much violence is there on television?' it is necessary to develop and apply a method of investigation that will yield an accurate picture of the 'quantity of violence'. However, 'violence' is not easily defined. Is the violence one sees in a *Tom and Jerry* cartoon equivalent to the violence seen in a horror film or that broadcast on the evening news? There is no simple, objective way to measure the content of a communication, but one approach often used in applying social psychology is that of content analysis.

Content analysis is based on the systematic identification of specified attributes in a communication. The communication may be written (e.g. newspapers), spoken (e.g. in conversation) or visual (e.g. in pictures). The actual content analysis itself is based on the classification of material in terms of the categories of analysis that the researcher selects. Four types of categories and units of analysis may be used:

- Categories that relate to what you analyse (recording units).
- Categories that relate to where you look (context units).
- Categories that relate to the measurement of what you look at (enumeration units).
- Categories that evaluate or describe what you look at (coding categories).

Figure 6.2 summarizes the relationships between these categories and units of analysis. Once a research hypotheses has been formulated, categories of analysis are constructed. Then recordings units are defined, then context units and then the enumeration system. Each of these will now be considered in a little more detail.

It is essential to formulate the research hypotheses before embarking on a content analysis. The usual way of generating a hypothesis involves

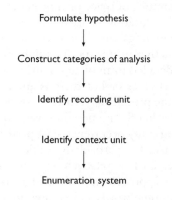

Formulate hypothesis

↓

Construct categories of analysis

↓

Identify recording unit

↓

Identify context unit

↓

Enumeration system

Figure 6.2 Principal parts of a content analysis

familiarization with the research in a particular area in order to conceptualize a testable hypothesis.

Categories of analysis are the elements of the hypothesis that you are testing, and the success of the research investigation will partly depend on translating the hypothesis into discrete categories that can be applied in a content analysis. In the case of a hypothesis, for instance, that television advertisements aimed at children use different devices to those aimed at adults, it is necessary to construct categories that allow advertisements to be coded by the age group of the person to whom the advertisement appears to be directed, as well as the types of devices used to create different kinds of advertisement (for example the use of music, colour, mood).

Recording units are the smallest elements of a communication to be considered in a content analysis. These may be a single word, a part of a sentence, a whole sentence, or even a drawing. It is often not possible to classify a recording unit without detailed reference to the communication in which it appears. In the case of a television advertisement the context unit is normally easy to identify – it is the advertisement. However, there may be age-related differences in children's understanding of what an advertisement is: young children may be less capable of discriminating between something seen and heard on a television programme and similar material presented in an advert. This raises the possibility that researchers may attend to context units to which young children are not sensitive and in so doing inadvertently impose their own view on the child's world.

Five basic systems of enumeration are commonly used in content analysis: the recording unit itself (for example the 'characters'), time/space, appearance/non-appearance, frequency and intensity. Time/space criteria are based on calculations of the amount of space or time allocated to a specified item of content (for example the duration of each advertisement). Appearance/non-appearance involves searching each context unit (each advertisement, for example) and noting whether or not specific things are mentioned. Frequency enumeration is a more detailed form of appearance/non-appearance analysis in which we simply note whether or not there is any reference, for example, to the value for money of the product advertised. However, it could be that some advertisements refer to value for money on several occasions: frequency enumeration involves noting *every* occurrence of a particular item. The measurement of intensity is usually particularly difficult and several alternative techniques are available. Each is relatively technical in nature and need not concern us here, but one approach emphasizes the analysis of language used in a communication where some words and phrases are clearly more intense than others and may allow a message to be coded as particularly intense.

The way forward

The trend towards greater control and activity on the part of the audience – now often referred to as a 'user' – implies that communication theories will need to attend to the interactive nature of new communications media. For example, internet users can quickly become broadcasters either by targeting their own 'audience' through e-mails, advertising their presence in the form of web pages or creating virtual environments (for example chat rooms) in which people with shared interests can create and maintain new social groups. The pace of technological innovation means there has been rapid convergence between the kinds of phenomena that would traditionally have fallen within the remit of mass communication, and those associated with the study of interpersonal dialogue.

Computer-mediated messaging systems impose particular requirements on users and have been shown to have the following characteristics:

1 Participants engage in less overt agreement and more opinion-giving in comparison with face-to-face groups (Hiltz and Turoff, 1987).
2 Computer-mediated group discussion is less likely to produce polarization or shifts to extremes on a risk–caution dimension than is the case in face-to-face interaction (Hiltz and Turoff, 1987).
3 North American findings suggest a greater incidence of swearing, insults, name-calling and hostile comments than occur in comparable face-to-face exchanges (Kiesler, Siegel and McGuire, 1984). However, British findings suggest the contrary (Wilbur, Rubin and Lee, 1986).

The discrepancy between the North American and British findings on the incidence of acrimonious exchanges requires further investigation and illustrates a burgeoning need for more theoretical and empirical work on the kinds of intercultural communication afforded by new technologies.

While computer-mediated dialogues are characterized by high levels of task-related interaction, one cannot conclude that they are entirely task-focused. A significant part of the working day is spent communicating and it is hardly surprising that in one Fortune 500 company 40 per cent of all message traffic was found to be ostensibly frivolous and unrelated to work (Sproull and Kiesler, 1986). That estimate is low relative to the earliest studies of time spent communicating, but reinforces the point that the creation and maintenance of social contacts is crucial to effective coordination and task accomplishment. Knowing who one's co-workers are extends beyond a definition based on competence-on-task. Just as telephone users have invented conventions for overcoming the limitations of that technology, so regular users of e-mail and phone-based text messaging have invented a lexicon of icons to overcome some of the limitations imposed by text-based messaging systems. The following are examples of iconic representations of facial expressions (sometimes called 'emoticons'), and can be more easily understood by rotating the book clockwise:

   :-)   Used to inflect a sarcastic or joking statement.
   ;-)   Used to make a flirtatious or sarcastic remark.
   :-(User did not like the last statement or is upset or depressed.
   :-/   Used to indicate scepticism.
   :-D Used to indicate laughter.

People are prepared to create new ways of communicating in order to overcome functional limitations imposed by the technologies available to them. A relatively neglected aspect of this kind of skill development has to do with the detection and repair of 'trouble'. Co-workers who are hassled, angry, worried or in other ways stressed will send signals – many of them non-verbal – that others can recognize. Most of this recognition can be accomplished as a matter of routine where people share a work environment and can see and be seen. People who become seriously stressed in their work can often convey this to co-workers in the manner in which they conduct themselves in conversation. If we are sufficiently familiar with a colleague we may even be able to detect this in their 'telephone voice'. In this regard point-to-point desktop video-conferencing will pose new challenges for users who will develop subtle skills for presenting and reading a 'video face'. They will do this because face-to-face conversations conventionally involve synchronizing eye-contact, voice characteristics and interpersonal distance. For example, confidential conversations are managed through a subtle combination of close physical proximity, appropriately managed eye-contact and quiet speaking (Argyle, 1989; Argyle and Dean, 1965). Point-to-point desktop video-conferencing supports face-to-face communication while eliminating physical co-presence and introducing subtle transmission time delays. Users will undoubtedly develop new conventions for having different kinds of conversations under these circumstances. It also seems clear that the way people interact with a communications medium *per se* can reveal something about their psychological well-being. A small number of studies have explored how people can become 'addicted' to computer-based communication systems and the following indicators have been identified (Bezilla and Keliner, 1980; Shotton, 1982):

- Logging on unnecessarily many times during a day.
- Excessive irritation when the system is inaccessible.
- Preference for composing thoughts on-line.
- Preference towards developing concepts on-line.
- Preference towards conducting relationships on-line.
- Logging on 'just one more time' before stopping work.

These indicators or 'symptoms' are not unique to computer-based systems; exactly the same kinds of behaviour can be detected in face-to-face dialogue where one of the co-workers is stressed: Unnecessary conversations with the same person several times a day; excessive irritation when a colleague is temporarily unavailable; preference for composing thoughts 'as they come' in conversation, and so on.

The development of good management practice, effective organizations and the fostering of healthy social networks are founded on the acquisition and application of skills for detecting and avoiding impending trouble. Many 'troubles' can be detected and repaired through conversation. Computer-mediated interactions remove many visual and acoustic cues for detecting impending difficulties, but the technology has its own operating characteristics which are likely to capture aspects of a user's broader intentions and needs. In other words, users may learn to convey both propositional content (*what* they say) *and* illocutionary force (*how* they say it) in their interactions with other users (Searle, 1969). We do not yet know what these operating characteristics are for different telematic devices, nor are we yet in a position to describe features which can be used reliably to allow users to identify and resolve impending difficulties, but the history of human engagement with a range of communications technologies suggests that people will develop a range of complex skills to realize the potential in each.

New information and communication technologies (ICTs) are widely regarded as a key element in broad changes in social structures and practices. Growing interest in virtual communities, e-commerce, digital government ('e-democracy') and online media, for example, suggests these will entail changes in practices such as how people socialize, work, shop, obtain the news and receive commercial and public services. However, technology forecasts, because of their focus on scientific, engineering and technical innovation, tend to yield very unreliable estimates of social, economic and cultural impacts. The history of applied social psychology has shown that technological change cannot be separated from social, economic, cultural and political change. For example, research on ICTs has tended to presume that the 'information society' or 'digital age' are inevitable forces for social progress. In reality, economic forces have significantly shaped participation in the information society and have done little to reduce social exclusion. In order to participate in the 'information society', for instance, citizens must have access to the finances required to purchase essential hardware and software and to meet their contractual obligations to internet service providers. Moreover, sustained participation in the information society is constrained by one's ability to upgrade hardware and software over relatively short periods. An emerging conceptual framework that attempts to take account of the interaction between technology and larger social and political forces might consider the potential for restructuring institutions and practices under four headings: the production, use, consumption and governance of information and communication technologies (ICTs) (Dutton, 1999). This approach emphasizes the importance of indeterminate social and psychological processes rather than deterministic forecasts of the social impact of ICTs of a kind that have so often been wrong.

SHORT QUESTIONS

1   Regular viewing of violent movies is thought to increase the likelihood that some audience members will engage in aggressive acts. Should we therefore conclude that psychologists who have spent a lifetime investigating this association are, because of their very high levels of exposure, at particular risk of violent outbursts?

2   To what extent has your use of ICTs impacted on the way in which you make and maintain friendships in your social network?

3   The concept of 'community' as used by social anthropologists, sociologists and psychologists is invariably defined with reference to concepts of 'boundary' and the social production of artefacts for designating boundaries. Are boundaries important in e-communities?

4   The social amplification of risk framework (SARF) implies that risk issues are often treated in a manner that is 'out of proportion'. What would you need to take into account in order to judge whether or not something was given a balanced or proportionate treatment?

5   To what extent does Shannon and Weaver's (1949) information processing theory provide an accurate description of interpersonal communication?

CLASS ACTIVITIES

1   Many web sites are now structured in ways that make it difficult to distinguish between an advertisement and an information display. Collect some examples of web pages you have visited. Using the content analysis techniques described in this chapter, examine the extent of convergence of advertising and more neutral types of information display on www pages. Looking at each page, to what extent can you discriminate advertising and marketing claims from more factual information?

2   Design a study to test the hypothesis that people who make heavy use of e-mail (i.e. those who use the internet for e-mailing for more than an hour a day) have larger social networks that those who never e-mail?

FURTHER READING

Johnson, S. (1999) *Interface Culture: How New Technology Transforms the Way we Create and Communicate*. London: Basic Books.

Livingstone, S.M. (1998) *Making Sense of Television: The Psychology of Audience Interpretations*. London: Routledge.

Livingstone, S.M. and Bovill, M. (2002) *Young People and New Media*. London: Sage.

Price, S. (1997) *The Complete A–Z Media and Communication Studies Handbook*. London: Hodder & Stoughton.

Wallace, P. (2001) *The Psychology of the Internet*. Cambridge: Cambridge University Press.

Education

I have never let my schooling interfere with my education.

(Mark Twain)

ONCE UPON A TIME...

Like many other children before them, Tim and Tina started school at the age of five. Tim and Tina were twins, sharing 50 per cent of their genetic endowment. Tim was viewed by his family as more active and outgoing than Tina, who in turn was generally viewed as the smarter of the two. Their parents intimated this belief to their teachers at school. Tim had some difficulties settling into school, the formality and passivity of the classroom sitting uneasily with his normal boisterous behaviour. His parents and teachers attributed this behaviour to an inability to concentrate and a related difficulty with lessons. Tina settled into school well, she made some friends, kept up with the class when working and was interested in books. As time went on Tim's problems with his school work persisted, whereas Tina flourished academically and became less shy and increasingly confident. Tim's academic performance was often compared to Tina's. On occasions when Tim tried at school, after being punished for poor performances, his efforts appeared to mount to nothing. Each time Tim felt more deflated and he became convinced that he was not capable. By the end of his school years Tim was lagging behind his classmates and his sister quite seriously. However, Tim was no longer bothered by his underachievement, he had long since decided that being good at school was not a guy thing, and being 'a real man' his interests lay beyond the academic domain. Tina left school achieving marks in the top quartile of her cohort and went on to university, Tim didn't.

Introduction

Tim and Tina's story is not unusual, nor indeed is Mark Twain's experience of education. Sadly, formal schooling frequently fails to educate children. For many years, the failure of children at school, was seen as the fault of either the child or their family; either the child was not educatable, being incapable of learning, or the parents placed no value on education debarring child from participating in the learning process. In keeping with this position, educationalists then looked to cognitive psychology to inform their understanding of teaching and learning. In recent years, however, educationalists have been forced to attend to a wider array of social and psychological factors in attempting to explain the successes and failures of school systems. Given the cost of the formal education system to most Western societies, it is not surprising when policy-makers become concerned when it fails. Children afforded access to formal education continue to be able to complete their 'education' without apparently mastering basic literacy and numeracy skills. The need to identify those factors that maximize the utility of formal teaching and those that allow children to learn, thus supporting optimum social and academic development, is the key task in the new millennium. Social psychology is well-placed to inform these issues. This chapter therefore discusses how psychological processes contribute to academic success and failure, as well as considering how wider social factors can influence both motivation to learn and the learning environment.

History and development

Cognitive psychology has been highly influential and continues to shape many aspects of educational practice. By way of example, the assessment of children's learning abilities and the development of IQ (intelligent quotient) testing, a now common practice, has had a widespread effect on educational practices (Ceci, 1999). Likewise, Piaget's theory of cognitive development, which documents children's emerging cognitive capabilities, has aided understanding of students' ways of thinking, thus allowing instructional strategies to be matched to students' developing thought processes. Without question, Piaget's work has had a profound influence on curriculum development in formal education and particularly at primary school level (Woods, 1992). Subsequently, Bruner's theory of discovery learning has emphasized the importance of the structure of a subject together with a need for active learning as a basis for true understanding (Bruner, Goodnow and Austin, 1956). The influence of this theory is exemplified by the rise in the use of inductive reasoning as a learning tool in classrooms (Woolfolk Hoy, 1999).

Paradoxically, perhaps because of the significant early influences of cognitive psychology on the field of education, less attention has been paid as to how other sub-disciplines of psychology can inform educational practice. However, in recent years there has been acknowledgement within the field of cognitive psychology generally that by focusing exclusively on cognitive factors we may fail to offer adequate explanations for individual and group variability in cognitive development and academic performance. For this reason the field of cognitive psychology has undergone something of a revolution and there is now renewed interest in the role that cultural, social and personal affective factors may play in influencing human cognition. Consequently the ability of social psychological theory and research to inform educational policy and practice is now becoming more widely acknowledged than ever in the past.

Given a recognition that social factors are central to the understanding of child development and of children's educational experiences, current thoughts as to what is meant by childhood and what is expected of children must also be considered. The influence of social norms on current concepts is most easily highlighted by referring to child-rearing practices in times past. It is easy to forget that the very concept of childhood has changed radically over the last two centuries. Views of childhood are integrally related to both theories of development and prevailing educational practices. For instance, prior to the eighteenth century the prevailing view in Western societies was that children were inherently depraved. Concern for a child was often expressed in terms of forceful measures that ensured children conformed to religious and social norms. Babies, particularly those who cried frequently, were often believed to be demonic and were sometimes even put to death as a consequence. Education and socialization practices of the day emphasized the importance of strict and stern child-rearing practices, schools emphasized discipline and many children were caned or whipped into obedience, and some even immersed in ice water, confined in dark cupboards and threatened with abandonment or abduction (deMause, 1976) in the belief that this promoted pro-social development.

From the end of the eighteenth century onwards, attitudes to children and childhood, and therefore education, changed considerably. Children came to be treated in a more humane and positive manner. They were no longer thought to be born perverse; rather they were valued for their innocence. Two figures who were central to this change in social attitudes were the social philosophers, Locke and Rousseau (Sroufe, Cooper, DeHart and Marshall, 1996). Locke believed that children were born as blank slates ('tabula rasa') and as such the experiences they encountered in their early lives shaped the person they would become. Rousseau, on the other hand, contended that children had a natural tendency towards healthy growth (the noble savage) and that, all things being equal, children should spontaneously evolve into normal, healthy adults. The power of these ideas was important for two reasons. First, they created a situation whereby harsh treatment of children was no longer justifiable or sanctioned, and second they created the foundation for the long-running nature-nurture debate concerning human development.

Contemporary priorities

The relative impact of nature (genetic factors) and nurture (experiential factors) on all aspects of human development is a debate that is likely to continue to rage for a large part of the twenty-first century (Ceci and Williams, 1999). The current media and research focus on gene therapy, cloning, isolating genetic influences on social behaviours and the human genome project is likely to fuel further controversy. This debate has been fierce at times, especially in relation to intelligence and educatability. For the most part it is fair to say that the majority of theorists now believe that intelligence, like many characteristics such as personality and mental health, is influenced by a combination of hereditary and environmental factors. Belsky (1984) provides a good illustration of this type of integrative model. He highlights the combined influence of genetically determined child characteristics such as early infant temperament, and experiential and social factors such as parental psychological well-being and social support. Children with an easy temperament and with psychologically healthy parents who have adequate social support tend to have the most positive developmental outcomes. In contrast, poorer developmental outcomes are observed in children with a difficult temperament, less psychologically healthy parents and inadequate social support. On average, the poorest developmental outcomes are observed where all three influences are negative, while children with one or two of the three risk factors do better but not as well as those with all three cards stacked in their favour.

It would be fair to say that the ongoing nature vs nurture debate which is still active in the fields of educational and developmental psychology can be attributed as much to social and political issues as to ambiguities in the research findings. For example, characteristics such as intelligence or learning abilities are frequently measured in relation to biopsychosocial categories such as race or gender. While genes may influence both our gender and our race, finding differences in these attributes at a group level does not necessarily imply genetic causation. Mistakenly, evidence of group differences in these attributes is often taken as evidence of the genetic or biological determination of these characteristics. This attribution of causality is wrong for a number of reasons. First, cause and effect relationships have not and cannot be tested in this way. Second, any such differences could have a range of genetic, social or psychological causes as both race and gender have psychosocial components as well as genetic components. Finally, these studies ignore individual differences in these characteristics, differences which are generally far greater than any between group variation.

Concepts, models and theories

In much the same way as the nature vs nurture debate predominates over almost any other debate in developmental psychology, so behavioural models of learning continue to predominate educational theory and practice as they have for many years. The behavioural approach to learning originated from a growing concern in psychology with the lack of testability associated with psychoanalytic theories and theories of the unconscious. The behavioural approach is based on the premise that most human behaviour is voluntary or operant rather than unconscious, and that these voluntary behaviours often occur because of their consequences rather than their inherent value. Essentially, behaviourists argue that repetition of behaviour is most likely to occur when operant acts produce reinforcing consequences. Hence if you wish to encourage a particular behaviour it is best to reinforce that behaviour positively. Therefore if you wish to teach a child to read, reinforcing a child for displaying an interest in books will promote this interest. On the other hand, if you wish to discourage a behaviour such as aggression, the behaviour should be ignored. Attending to the behaviour even by reprimanding the child is still reinforcement, albeit negative reinforcement which is a less powerful reinforcer than generalized positive reinforcers such as money or praise. Behaviourists argue that by reinforcing behaviour, children can be taught many skills, a process known as operant conditioning.

This theory, which has been and continues to be highly influential, is very mechanistic and treats the student as object rather than agent in the learning process. Although behavioural learning theory has been successfully applied in a range of educational and developmental settings, factors other than reinforcement and reward do appear to influence learning. Indeed, many of the failures of behavioural theory can be attributed to the fact that social factors and processes have been ignored. More recently, the social learning approach has attempted to redress this balance. This approach emphasizes the importance of observational learning, imitation and modelling of behaviours. Essentially this approach highlights the learner's role in the learning process where they are seen as active participants. For example, initiation of a behaviour may occur as a result of observation of a model that a child is motivated to imitate. In much the same way as nature and nurture are viewed as having interactive effects, this model emphasizes a role for both teacher and learner in viewing both as active participants in the educational and developmental process.

Practical issues

Social comparison and the self-fulfilling prophecy

Many classic social psychological phenomena are of practical importance in educational contexts. Two such phenomena are the processes of social comparison and the self-fulfilling prophecy effect. The effects of these phenomena are such that they have a pervasive influence on children in educational settings. Reviewing the theory and research relating to them points to the practical utility of social psychology theory and research in the field of education.

Social comparison is a process through which information about the self is acquired, using others as the benchmark against which abilities, traits or feelings are measured. Social comparison theory (Festinger, 1954) suggests that people learn about their own attitudes and abilities by comparing themselves to other people. Two issues are critical to these comparisons. First, a consideration of the contexts within which individuals are motivated to compare themselves to others, and second the individuals or group chosen for the purposes of comparison. Generally, it can be said, social comparison occurs in situations where an individual is unsure of him/herself and no objective standard which is suitable for comparisons exists.

In the real world this means that children and adults often use social comparison to assess their own performance and abilities, and nowhere is this process more obvious than in the context of education. For example, receiving a mark or grade in an examination may give an indication of the extent to which the student has come to grips with the curriculum. However, without knowing the average grade and the range of marks of others then the student cannot accurately assess his or her performance. In the absence of specific feedback derived from continuous assessment throughout much of the academic year, then students will measure their progress in more subjective ways; often comparing their understanding of material with others or monitoring teachers' attitudes or behaviour towards them in comparison to others. Therefore although parents and teachers may try to convince children that 'doing their best' is what is important, in reality this message is likely to have little resonance for two reasons. First, social comparison is a normal and spontaneous psychological process; it is impossible to prevent children from comparing themselves with others and especially if there are any ambiguities about their understanding of their performance. Second, although parents and teachers may insist that performance is assessed individually, and that relative performance is irrelevant, the reality is that the formal education system frequently relies on relative performance measures for decision-making purposes. For example, university entrance criteria rank students' examination performance when offering places, and many second-level schools stream or track children from a certain age, normally by exam performance. This effectively rates academic ability relative to a given cohort. Further to this, primary and secondary schools routinely engage in social comparison exercises by awarding recognition in the form of prizes for a variety of reasons such as sport, academic ability and attendance.

Given the pervasiveness of the social comparison process it is not surprising that the literature on self-perception highlights how our view of ourselves is moulded by social comparison. Self-perceptions can be defined as comprising two elements, self-esteem and self-competence. Self-esteem is typically viewed as the evaluative component of the self which reflects a generalized sense of social worth or an indication of a child's perception of his/her value. Self-competence is a theoretically related construct which reflects a person's sense of efficacy in a particular life domain. Self-perceptions can be viewed as the product of the social comparison process, with the nature of self-perceptions intrinsically related to the groups or individuals against which we compare ourselves. Very often we make comparisons quickly, using any accessible individuals for this purpose. Normally, having compared oneself to our nearest neighbour, we go on to consider the appropriateness of the comparison, as not all comparisons are equally informative. In terms of self-knowledge it is generally most useful to compare ourselves to someone who is similar to us (Wheeler et al., 1982). However, self-knowledge is not always the motivation for comparison; often social-comparison is used as a self-protective or self-enhancing strategy. In such cases we are motivated to compare ourselves to those who are less competent in an area that we rate as important; if you compare yourself to people who are less smart, talented or athletic then you will feel better about yourself. This ego-enhancing process is known as downward social comparison (Aspinwall and Taylor, 1993).

The importance of the group against which a person compares him/herself, and the protective effect of downward social comparison, has been highlighted through a debate now raging in the educational literature. Over recent years there has been a growing tendency for students with learning difficulties to be educated in mainstream schools. Previously many of these students were taught in special schools alongside other differently-abled pupils. The move towards mainstreaming or integrating special-needs students into standard schools has been hailed as progress, not least because it means that those students are no longer socially marginalized. However, recent evidence does suggest that there is a downside for learning-disabled children who are educated in mainstream schools, with research indicating that the effect of this integration on these children's self-perceptions is not always positive. Children who previously may have positive self-perceptions as a result of their favourable comparisons with other students in a special school find that in the mainstream classroom their performance does not always compare well. For this reason, negative self-perceptions can pose a potential threat to the learning-disabled child's academic and social functioning in mainstream educational settings.

This threat may be further exacerbated by the self-fulfilling prophecy effect. A self-fulfilling prophecy can be defined as the tendency by which expectations about a person make that person behave in ways that conform to those expectations. This process was first identified by Rosenthal and Jacobsen (1968) in what is now viewed as a classic social psychological experiment. IQ tests were administered to children attending a primary school in San Francisco. Teachers in the school were told that the test was able to predict which children would 'bloom' or show rapid intellectual development in the near future. However, the children that were identified as 'bloomers' were in fact randomly selected by the researchers and there were no IQ differences between those identified as 'bloomers' and the other children in the sample. Teachers very quickly began to rate the two groups differently; non-bloomers were perceived as less curious, interested and happy at school than bloomers. Essentially, teachers developed stereotypic expectations about the two groups. Grades for the children's work began to reflect these expectations. Subsequent IQ testing of the two groups of children at the end of the school year and the following year showed that significantly greater IQ gains were evident in the bloomer group than in the non-bloomer group. In effect, the children were also living up to their stereotyped expectations.

Although, this finding was viewed with scepticism by some, subsequent replications and extensions of the study have highlighted the robustness of this effect. Rosenthal and Rubin (1978) conducted a meta-analytic review of follow-up studies which confirmed the integrity of the effect. Today this effect also informs our understanding of how ability-streaming or tracking may influence performance. Research now suggests that segregation of classes by ability (streaming or tracking) may benefit high-ability students but may have an adverse effect on low-ability students. Low-ability students appear to receive poorer quality instruction overall because teachers of these classes tend to emphasize lower-level objectives and routine tasks with a less academic focus. Additionally, there are often more management problems resulting in increased stress and decreased teacher enthusiasm. These effects on instruction and teacher attitudes appear to mean that low expectations are communicated to the students which in turn has an adverse effect on student's self-competence and esteem. It would now appear that the best way to deal with diverse student abilities is by having within-class ability groupings. In this way students are clustered by ability but remain in the same class. Groups should be based on actual achievements in the subject being taught, rather than IQ, with different groups being formed for different subjects. Students should be mixed for other activities (Woolfolk Hoy, 1999).

The effects of self-fulfilling prophecies beyond the realm of IQ have also been examined and it would appear that the effect generalizes to other aspects of children's and adult's performance and behaviour. However, it is the applied value of this finding that is central. While many studies have explored the effects of stereotypes ascribed for the purposes of a given study, the effects of naturally occurring stereotypes that are based on real and meaningful social categories are likely to be most powerful of all. The power of naturally occurring social categories to influence teachers' and students' behaviour is related to a number of factors. First, social categories such as gender and race are such fundamental and pervasive categories that they can prompt stereotyped behaviours to which we are oblivious. Second, many social categories have stereotypes related to ability and educatability associated with them and therefore these categorizations are likely to be particularly salient in educational contexts. Third, naturally occurring social categories are often tied to personal and social identities. As such, individuals invest psychologically in their own gender or racial identity, becoming motivated to behave in ways that are consistent with these social identities. Thus it is not just teacher's expectations of young people's behaviour that will influence young people.

Wider social expectations, and in particular the expectations of young people from particular social, racial or cultural backgrounds, influence young people's performance and participation at school at many levels.

Social and cultural influences on educational practices

For this reason social psychology also acknowledges the influence of macro-social factors on educational practices. In recent years, concern has grown as a result of the increased prevalence of school failure and academic under-achievement apparent among boys from minority ethnic groups and socially disadvantaged backgrounds. Increasingly this underachievement is being attributed to a range of social factors, including the absence of positive role models in educational contexts. Disadvantaged, minority-group children and adolescents are taught by middle-class, white and most often female teachers. They may know few people with whom they can readily identify that have formal educational qualifications. The lack of positive educational role models may be further compounded by the lack of employment opportunities in many disadvantaged communities. Seeing little potential for gainful employment around them, the intrinsic value of obtaining educational qualifications is not readily apparent to these young people. In effect these social factors may act to reduce young people's motivation to participate and succeed in educational contexts.

For many young people, this variety of social factors can serve to marginalize and isolate them from school life. Paradoxically, this effect can be inadvertently exacerbated by educational policies aimed at raising standards. For instance, in the UK over the last decade there has been a steady and increasing rise in school exclusion, that is permanent expulsion from the school attended (Parsons, 1996). This increase in exclusions has been attributed at least in part to the introduction of school performance tables or 'league tables'. The increase in discipline and behaviour problems that would be required to account for the increase in exclusions would amount to levels of unacceptable behaviour of epidemic proportions (Rutter, 1991) and at present there is no evidence that this is the case (Office for Standards in Education, 1996). The rise in school exclusions can be better explained by educational policy and the knock-on effect that the between-school comparisons that are required for performance tables have had on subsequent organizational and decision-making processes within schools (Garner, 1994).

The trend that has forced schools to move into the marketplace to compete for students on the basis of past pupil achievement can be been linked to the rise in school exclusions (Garner, 1994). League tables or school performance tables provide a range of information about individual schools, including the attainment levels achieved in public examinations. Often it is this information that parents of prospective students of schools are most interested in when deciding which school their child should attend. Unfortunately, disruptive and challenging students do little to enhance a school's performance in league tables and may in fact adversely affect a school's place in a league table. As such, students that underachieve at school and are adversarial and/or difficult to control may come to be viewed as a burden on teaching time and a liability in terms of the school's performance as a whole. In effect teachers, principals and school governors may be motivated to exclude such students from school. Thus a policy that was designed to improve teaching and learning effectively militates against teaching and learning for the most vulnerable groups within an education system.

The effect of between-school comparisons on organizational practices within schools highlights another important issue. Policies and practices within schools may have both intended and unintended effects. Schools do not operate in a social vacuum; rather they are institutions of society and will often reflect general societal values. The reflection of such values within schools is often referred to as the hidden curriculum. For example, in most co-educational schools there would be a stated policy committing the school to treating male and female students equally. However, the need to stipulate such equality of treatment suggests that gender equality may not be the norm. Further to this, the manner in which male and female students are treated within the school may differ in subtle and often unnoticed ways. Classes may be divided by gender for games and sports, teachers may respond to misbehaviour by males and females in different ways, and pupils' and teachers' expectations regarding their ability in certain subjects may also be related to gender.

In a similar way, as part of the efforts to build a more tolerant and harmonious society in Northern Ireland, a society blighted by political violence, a core aspect of the school curriculum is Education for Mutual Understanding (EMU). This component of the curriculum aims to increase contact between the two opposing groups in the conflict as well as increase understanding of the other group's perspective of the conflict. At the same time, the majority of students in Northern Ireland attend segregated schools, that is students and teachers alike are predominantly if not exclusively either Protestant or Roman Catholic. Students are being taught about the importance of acknowledging diversity and respecting those of another religious tradition, yet in reality the tolerance being advocated is not put into practice. Any effect of messages emphasizing egalitarianism or tolerance is seriously comprised when it is at odds with the wider social message apparent in this type of hidden curriculum.

The way forward

Social psychology can do much to inform educational policy and practice. Perhaps more so than other areas of applied social psychology this area has been blighted by methodological problems that hinder the development of research and knowledge within the field. In the first instance, psychologists need to be particularly cautious when conducting educational research in order that they have time to reflect on the many ethical issues which they are likely to encounter. Basic ethical principles, such as informed consent and voluntary participation, can pose problems in situations where children are the focus of the research. Children themselves often do not give their consent to participate in research; rather parents give consent on their behalf. Further to this, children may not understand why they are completing or undertaking certain tasks, yet feel that they must comply with the adult researcher's requests. Researchers must be cautious and ensure that their recruitment and research practices are not viewed as coercive by their child participants.

There are other ethical difficulties associated with conducting research in this area. While it may be theoretically interesting and of practical importance to understand the many effects of labelling a child as 'slow' or 'dull', undertaking a study to establish the link between labelling in childhood and IQ deficits in later years would be unethical. For a true cause-and-effect relationship to be established, children would have to be randomly assigned into one of two groups, the group subsequently labelled slow or dull and the second equivalent intelligence group, the control group. Any difference between the two groups in their subsequent development could then be directly attributed to the labelling process. Given the long-term effects that this labelling process would be likely to have on children's social, emotional, intellectual and psychological development, however, this experiment could not be justified. In such situations, researchers generally use alternative paradigms. Unfortunately these paradigms are generally less robust and powerful than the true experimental design and may limit the nature of the conclusions, particularly in relation to issues of causality.

Practical problems often arise also when undertaking research in this area. In general the issues and challenges facing the educational system today are complex and multivarious, and the best explanations of problem behaviours often rely on a range of biological, social and psychological factors. For example, antisocial or 'acting-out' behaviour in young children, an increasingly common problem in schools, may be related to a host of factors including genetically determined temperament, hyperactivity, poor parenting, social deprivation and an inadequate school environment. The need to account for all of these factors, as well as consider their additive effects, makes research in this area particularly challenging.

Developmental and educational research endeavours pose further problems in terms of research design. Often issues relating to the medium and long-term effects of social psychological processes are of interest to researchers, and for this reason, the value of traditional cross-sectional, 'snap-shot' designs may be limited. The design of choice in this context is longitudinal; that is, children are assessed on at least two occasions so that the effects of particular risk factors or interventions can be monitored over time, or indeed so that normal developmental processes can be described. This type of design allows research-ers to chart change and is particularly important in developmental and educa-tional research, as we expect change to be the rule rather than the exception as children grow and develop. However, this type of research is also more time-consuming, difficult to conduct and results in data that are more difficult to analyse than is the case with cross-sectional research. Additionally, these studies are likely to be subject to cohort or generational effects; without including at least two cohorts of participants the generalizability and applicability of the research findings may be limited to a particular generation or cohort.

Notwithstanding these problems, research in this area continues to thrive. Increasingly there is evidence of multidisciplinary research projects that are attempting to describe the range of factors that may explain variations in educational and psychological development. Despite their cost, the import-ance and centrality of longitudinal research designs is now widely accepted and the prevalence of longitudinal studies in the research literature is increasing. Moreover, educationalists and cognitive psychologists alike are ever more aware of the importance of social psychological processes in determining educational attainment and school adjustment. It would be naive to suggest that social psychology has the solutions for the many challenges and issues faced by educationalists, but, nonetheless, it is clear that social psychological factors and processes are necessary to inform a full understanding of these problems and must be acknowledged if remedial actions are to be successful.

SHORT QUESTIONS

1 What did Mark Twain mean by saying he never let his schooling interfere with his education?

2 Why did Tina and Tom follow such different paths at school?

3   In the context of the nature–nurture debate, exactly what is meant by the terms 'nature' and 'nurture'?

4   What is meant by the term 'hidden curriculum'?

5   What is meant by the term 'self-fulfilling prophecy'?

CLASS ACTIVITIES

1   Identify five key current educational practices. Would these practices seem unusual to those from other cultures? Discuss how these practices might be viewed by those living in the twenty-second century?

2   A researcher wishes to investigate the causes of academic ability in eight-year-old children. Generate a research protocol that would allow a researcher to examine the influence of genes, family circumstances and school environment on these abilities?

3   How can parents and teachers promote positive self-esteem? Can the same strategies be used with all children?

4   Reflecting on your own childhood, can you think of any occasions where a self-fulfilling prophesy effect may have influenced the choices you made. How can parents and teachers guard against such effects?

5   Break into pairs, each person being assigned one of two roles as either the person attempting to shape (through reinforcement) behaviour or as the person whose behaviour is to be shaped. Each pair must then decide on the reinforcer that they are going to use for this exercise. This could be something like one clap of the hands, a phrase or a click of the fingers. Those who are going to have their behaviour shaped need to leave the room now for a moment. While they are away, decide with the help of your tutor if needs be, what behaviour you are going to try and elicit from your partner. Do not use the same behaviour as anyone else. Possibilities are things like opening a window, writing, walking around a chair; basically any routine behaviour will do. (Hint: Don't use one of these suggestions, it will make it too easy for your partner, they'll have read this.) When you have decided on the behaviour you want to elicit ask your partner to return. Take your seat in the room and ask them to stay at the door until you are ready to begin. Those who are having their behaviour shaped should now move around the room. When they do something that is a precursor or similar to the target behaviour, their partner

should reinforce their behaviour. You should continue to reinforce their behaviour in this manner until they actually perform the target behaviour. Be patient this may take a while and remember you are not allowed to give verbal hints.

After you have achieved this go into groups of 2–3 pairs. Consider the following: What difficulties did you experience? What reinforcement characteristics made the task more difficult? What effect did other pairs have? What implications do you think these problems have for educational settings?

FURTHER READING

Ceci, S.J. and Williams, W.M. (eds) (1999) *The Nature–Nurture Debate: The Essential Readings*. Oxford: Blackwell.

Goodenow, C. (1992) 'Strengthening the Links between Educational Psychology and the Study of Social Contexts', *Educational Psychologist*, vol. 27, pp. 177–96.

Kamins, M.L. and Dweck, C.S. (1999) 'Person versus Process Praise and Criticism: Implications for Contingent Self-Worth and Coping', *Developmental Psychology*, vol. 35, pp. 835–47.

Madon, S., Jussim, L. and Eccles, J. (1997) 'In Search of the Powerful Self-Fulfilling Prophecy', *Journal of Personality and Social Psychology*, vol. 72, pp. 791–809.

Economic Life and Consumerism

Happiness is the deferred fulfilment of a prehistoric wish. That is why wealth brings so little happiness; money is not an infantile wish.

(Sigmund Freud)

ONCE UPON A TIME...

There was an undergraduate called Sam who, on opening the mail one mid-December morning, discovered that she had won a small amount of money. It was just enough to cover the heating and telephone bills that had accumulated over the term. However, she had studied hard all semester, Christmas was just around the corner and it seemed a long time since she had given herself a treat. Since she never expected to win the money in the first place she decided to indulge herself and spend it all on new clothes. Now by coincidence her friend discovered that she too was the recipient of an unexpected cheque – she had paid too much in tax and the excess was being returned to her. Since she never expected to receive a refund she decided to 'forget about it' and put it in a savings account for a rainy day. And they both lived happily, if not prosperously, ever after.

Introduction

Economists and psychologists are both interested in understanding and predicting human behaviour and its consequences, and with formulating and delivering interventions that will lead to sustainable improvements in quality of life. For example, both are concerned with understanding why people work, what motivates people to spend their money and what factors influence saving behaviour. Given these shared interests it would seem reasonable to expect a considerable degree of theoretical and methodological overlap between the two disciplines. However, while economics and psychology have common intellectual roots in the ideas of the seventeenth to nineteenth-century philosophers known as the British Empiricists, in reality the two disciplines have developed somewhat differently and the degree of interaction and cross-fertilization of ideas has not been as great as might have been anticipated. This divergence reflects on many issues including the fact that the development of economics has tended to focus on theoretical issues, as reflected in the emergence of distinct schools of economic thought and on mathematical modelling of economic processes, while the history of psychology has reflected a stronger commitment to empirical enquiry. In particular, psychology has focused on experimental investigation and on pragmatic application, with less commitment to working within particular schools of thought.

One of the most striking differences in the approaches taken by economists and psychologists concerns the importance attached to the idea that people behave in rational ways. Economic theories place considerable emphasis on the idea that people act rationally, whereas psychological theories emphasize the inherently non-rational ways in which people behave. For instance, economic theories start by working out what the most profitable course of action would be for a completely rational person. Other things being equal, someone faced with several job offers would be expected to accept the offer with the highest salary. In reality we know that this is often not the case and that psychological processes may lead people to accept an offer with a lower salary if they believe the work might be more enjoyable and fulfilling. In others words people are prepared to sacrifice tangible financial benefits in favour of nebulous, unquantifiable gains associated with 'personal enjoyment' and 'feeling good about my work'.

The potential benefits to achieving a closer integration of economic and psychological approaches are illustrated by the development of novel working practices that have been made possible by information and communication technologies. The development of virtual organizations has been strongly motivated by economic forces intended to reduce the costs associated with keeping a large workforce in a single building and by the pressing need to reduce the environmental damage caused by very large numbers of people commuting to and from centralized work sites. Allowing employees to 'tele-work' from home would seem to have obvious financial attractions for both employers and employees, but the success of this new way of working will also be determined by social psychological processes, such as the extent to which virtual organizations can sustain a sense of teamwork, group identity and 'belongingness' with a geographically dispersed workforce. Virtual organizations are much more likely to succeed if economic and social psychological factors are appropriately managed.

History and development

Modern economic psychology represents an attempt to develop closer interaction between these two disciplines. Although some early twentieth-century psychologists, such as William McDougall, were interested in economics, the emergence of economic psychology is largely associated with one person, George Katona (1975), who worked within the US government to manage the economy towards the end of the Second World War. Wartime economies tend to have very high rates of inflation, and Katona argued that wartime inflation could be understood using both economic and psychological concepts and that economic instruments, as well as psychological interventions such as publicity and propaganda campaigns, should be combined to manage the economy. After 1945 Katona developed the idea of collecting survey data on business and consumer attitudes to a range of economics activities and concerns, and promoted the use of these measures to predict future economic activity. Although some economists were initially sceptical as to the value of these kinds of indicators for economic forecasting, measures of consumer and business confidence are now treated as important pointers to future economic trends.

The closer alignment of psychology with economics has also been traced to three trends (Lea and Webley, 1994). The first of these concerns the development of experimental techniques within economics, which has provided an important methodological bridge to psychology. The sharing of research concepts and designs means that psychologists and economists have developed closer dialogue on the determinants and correlates of economic behaviour. Second, the commitment of economists to the principal of rationality (the idea that people are rational beings and behave rationally) has increasingly been challenged and augmented with psychological concepts that treat people as non-rational. Third, the development of *socioeconomics* has promoted the emergence of a corpus of intellectual thinking that is sharply critical of major schools of economic thought. Socioeconomists are particularly concerned with achieving a closer integration of the disciplines of sociology, psychology and economics in order to establish a less simplistic, more broad-based and realistic base for economic thinking.

Contemporary priorities

Economics is concerned with the production, distribution and consumption of wealth. Major divisions of economics include microeconomics (which is concerned with the behaviour of individual consumers, companies and traders), and macroeconomics (which focuses on aggregates such as the level of wealth in an economy and the volume of total employment). Psychology, when applied to economic life, sets out to examine two main questions that map onto this distinction between micro- and macro-economics. First, which psychological processes guide an individual's economic behaviour, such as buying and saving? Second, in what ways does the wider economy impact on people's lives? In addressing these questions psychologists have focused their efforts in several areas and most notably buying, saving and work.

Buying

Economists and psychologists are concerned to understand why people buy particular products. Much of the work in consumer psychology examines how people interpret product-related information, make purchasing choices and how memory processes affect their decision-making. For example, experimental techniques are often used to systematically manipulate specific variables, such as the sequence in which information is presented to people, in order to examine effects on hypothetical purchasing decisions. Consumer decision-making is a closely related field of enquiry and has its origins in economics and sociology as well as psychology. Consumer decision-making research has been largely concerned with understanding the influence of costs and normative pressures such as fashion trends. Questionnaire surveys are often used to gather consumers' reports of recent, or intended, purchases and statistical and mathematical techniques are applied to the data to determine latent relationships between decision-making and a range of sociological, economic and psychological variables.

One of the most obvious characteristics of purchasing behaviour is its variability – we don't all purchase the same brand and style of product and service on offer. Consequently psychologists have been interested in exploring ways of dividing large groups of consumers into smaller sectors who behave somewhat differently from one another. Market segmentation, as this is called, is concerned with trying to find a group of like-minded consumers who will respond to advertising and marketing information in similar ways, and contrasting that group with another who will respond differently to the same information. Initial interest focused on segmentation using socio-demographic variables such as age, gender, occupation and socioeconomic background. By way of contrast, more recent work has focused on conspicuously psychological variables such as attitudes, values and information processing strategies. For instance, when processing persuasive marketing communications men appear to prefer a conceptually-driven orientation. This is suggested by their greater attention to overall message themes and the way thematic information seems to trigger memories related to the message content. Women appear to be more 'data driven' and attend more to the details of a commercial claim (Meyers-Levy and Sternthal, 1991).

Prior knowledge also affects how consumers process economic information and make judgements. For example, experts (such as vehicle safety inspectors) and novices (for example people who are interested in purchasing a car) process information contained in car advertisements differently. Furthermore, the type of information that prompts them to engage in dissimilar processing strategies, and the nature of the inferences they may make, differ. Attribute information (for example, 'this is one of the safest cars on the road') prompts experts to engage in detailed analysis of the advertising claim and to expend more effort making inferences that produce an elaborated view of the product. However, benefit information (such as, 'this car is the cheapest to insure in its class') prompts novices to make a detailed examination of an assertion, but not to engage in inferential analyses such as, 'what factors determine insurance premiums?' that could produce an elaborated understanding of the claims made about the car (Maheswaran and Sternthal, 1990).

Experts make more inferences about missing information when an advertising claim is factual (for example, 'this car goes from 0 to 60 in under 6 seconds') and fewer when the claim is evaluative (for example, 'you'll love this car'), whereas novices are less likely to make inferences irrespective of the type of claim. Thus, experts appear to engage in more conceptually-driven analyses whereas novices are more data-driven (Gardial and Biehl, 1991). This parallels the gender difference in information processing noted earlier. It is not yet clear why gender differences in information processing should be similar to those observed for variations in expertise level, and gender stereotypes do not appear to provide a satisfactory account.

Saving

Compared to their investment of effort in understanding buying behaviour, psychologists have devoted relatively little attention to understanding saving. This is somewhat surprising, and especially so because Katona was particularly concerned with understanding and promoting saving behaviour. He showed, first, that people do not regard saving as the opposite of buying, and, second, that not all forms of saving are psychologically similar. *Contractual saving* involves committing to a financial plan that requires regular investments, such as a pension scheme; *discretionary saving* involves deciding to set aside a specific sum of 'spare money'; while *involuntary saving* refers to situations where people may, for instance, unknowingly pay too much tax that is subsequently returned to them. Although it is possible that these three types of saving may yield similar economic returns, they are felt to be quite different in psychological terms. The motivation to engage in these three types of saving is different, the decision processes associated with each are different and in turn savers are likely to use what has been saved in different ways.

Traditional economic models of saving do not reflect the range of psychological processes implicated in this behaviour. Economic models work from the simple assumption that people save in order to maximize the returns on their investment (the interest gained), with the life-cycle model providing the standard explanatory framework. This model states that people try to have a 'smooth utility stream' over their life-cycle. 'Utility' is difficult to measure but is usually defined as the price that people will pay for the goods which they purchase or consume. Having a 'smooth utility stream' means that people try to smooth their expenditure over their remaining lifetime. Most of us will not 'blow all our money' without regard for the long-term consequences. Economic models regard saving and borrowing as instruments that people use to achieve a smooth utility stream so that their expenditure is not tightly coupled to their current income. Since economic models treat people as rational beings they assume that we all attempt to maximize our consumption by searching for the saving or borrowing schemes with the most auspicious terms. There have been some qualifications to this model to accommodate evidence that saving varies across social classes. For example, some of the earliest variations to the model defered to stereotypes of lower socioeconomic classes as characterized by inconsistent or imprudent financial planning. However more recent work acknowledges that saving will be linked to a person's economic situation in more complex ways. It takes into account that a person's economic utility can also be linked to a wish to generate safeguards against unforeseen events or to bequeath money to heirs, and that some social security systems may discourage low-income households from saving.

Sonuga-Barke and Webley (1993) examined the ways in which representations of saving have been used to encourage people to invest in various schemes. They examined advertisements for building societies and leaflets aimed at young savers (and their parents) and found that the advertisements placed most emphasis on interest rates offered by deposit accounts. Thus, the appeal contained in the advertisements reflects the assumption that people will behave rationally and strive to maximize their economic gains. The strongest emphasis was placed on the rate of interest on offer, although other features such as instant access to money were included in some. The material aimed at children appeared to treat saving as a rational behaviour that can be encouraged, provided it is reinforced in an appropriate and timely fashion. Whereas traditional economic approaches have tended to treat saving and thrift as morally laudable, the advertisements did not appeal to potential savers on these grounds. Moreover, the prudential view of saving contrasts with current economic trends that indicate saving rates have dropped across the Western world and buying on credit is now the norm. The empirical evidence suggests that there is a relationship between economic beliefs and saving but we cannot yet conclude that changes in beliefs cause changes in saving behaviour. Whereas cultural values and beliefs almost certainly impact on economic behaviour, saving (or not saving and getting into debt) behaviour is influenced by the lifestyles of other consumers. Hence directly modelling the behaviour of others can cause the emergence of economic values and beliefs some time later.

Work

Psychologists have long been interested in understanding why people work, with improving productivity and with enriching the quality of working lives (see Chapter 3). This has included attention being paid to issues of job design and the management of change in the way work is done. In both of these one can see how economic and psychological concepts have interacted. Improvements in job design have long been thought to lead to gains in the quality of working life. Some of the earliest methods were pioneered by F.W. Taylor and involved designing jobs according to rational, economic principles. The 'rationalization' of jobs usually involved reorganizing them into constituent tasks, the technical streamlining of production processes and the careful use of time. Taylorism, or scientific management as this approach came to be known, led to dramatic increases in productivity in some areas but also tended to lead to low morale among workers and high levels of absenteeism and turnover. Concern with the consequences of rationalization prompted a review of the question: *Why do people work?* Simple economic explanations suggest that earning money is a rational, obvious or 'manifest' reason for working, but they cannot explain why people will not work for as much as they can possibly get. More sophisticated economic explanations take into consideration 'non-pecuniary' motivations and recognize that work can have other 'latent' functions.

One of the first alternatives to Taylorism was Herzberg's (1959) study of job satisfaction. Herzberg asked people to consider times they were satisfied and times they were dissatisfied with work, and found that the reported causes of the 'good' and 'bad' times were quite different. Causes of job satisfaction were usually located in the level of interest in the work, autonomy, responsibility, achievement, recognition or professional advancement. Causes of dissatisfaction were usually to do with job insecurity, poor working relationships with colleagues and supervisors and inadequate pay. Herzberg concluded that the causes of job satisfaction lay in intrinsic factors and the causes of dissatisfaction lay in extrinsic factors. He went on to argue that opportunities for workers to exercise discretion should be reintroduced to jobs in order to reverse the excesses of Taylorism. Herzberg coined the term 'job enrichment' to refer to an approach that emphasized the enhancement of job content as a means to increasing commitment and motivation, and thereby productivity. Although there have been many successful attempts to apply Herzberg's job-enrichment principles, there were also some occasions in which it was clear that not everyone responded positively to enriched jobs and that some people were motivated more by extrinsic than intrinsic factors. This suggests people value work for different reasons and that what work means for different people depends on larger lifestyle issues.

A second major challenge to Taylorism came from sociotechnical systems theory. A basic premise of the theory is that work technologies influence the organization of work activities but not in any simple or easily predicted way. The core idea is illustrated by a classic study of the impact of mechanized methods on coal mining in Britain during the 1950s (Trist *et al.*, 1963). For decades coal was mined by small teams of multiskilled men working in close proximity. Between them they would work the coal-face, move and load the coal onto trucks and build and repair shaft supports as required. Team members were paid the same amount. The introduction of better machines disrupted this arrangement and led to a three-shift system in which one team would mine the coal, another would shift it onto trucks and a third would attend to the infrastructure. The teams were on different rates of pay and supervisors were introduced to oversee the smooth working of the new system. This resulted in reduced morale, increased absenteeism, more accidents and occasionally friction between the three shifts. However, this system was not introduced in all mines. Instead multiskilled teams of miners were retained who rotated between the three shifts and payments were made to each shift as a work unit. Morale was higher in these mines, there were reduced rates of absenteeism and accidents, and productivity was higher too.

Sociotechnical systems theory argues that work technologies influence the social organization of work in significant ways and choices can be made about the nature of the impact. This is illustrated in recent rapid developments in the introduction of communication and information technologies that can sustain virtual work teams located in geographically distributed areas. Coping with unstable economic and political environments, at an increasingly global level, has required significant organizational change and innovation in respect of design and employment practices. Commercial survival requires organizations to be responsive to rapidly changing circumstances by maximizing their flexibility, and a thrust for greater flexibility has provided one of the most important drives for 'teleworking', although it has also been regarded as a way of enhancing product and service quality. Flexibility, in human resource terms, principally involves an expansion of workers' skills and knowledge-bases and the adoption of somewhat unconventional work methods, such as telework. Although telework has been around for more than 25 years, it has not been clearly defined; that is, what counts as telework is a matter of interpretation. In general, teleworking is taken to refer to the performance of work activities at a distant location from employing/contracting organizations where the work is enabled by information and telecommunications technologies.

The potential benefits of teleworking for employers include: increased flexibility, the retention and recruiting of personnel with scarce skills or individuals who would be unable to work in a conventional office (for example people with mobility problems), reduction in employee turnover, increased job satisfaction, motivation and productivity amongst teleworking staff, increased ability to cope with peak demands and reduced office overheads. Employees may choose to telework for one or a combination of reasons including, *inter alia*, home/family responsibilities, mobility problems, commuting, flexibility, desire to live in a community with high unemployment such as a rural area, or perhaps a reluctance to move with the organization. Despite the multiplicity of potential benefits for individuals, organizations and society as a whole, telework has yet to fulfil the expectations of its pioneers. Four possible reasons are that (1) the disadvantages outweigh the benefits for both employers and employees; (2) there is an inherent conflict of interest between the employee and the employer: the benefits perceived for the organization are generally those that are most disadvantageous to the worker and vice versa (for example, employers may see telework as a way of reducing costs by withdrawing full employment status from teleworkers to avoid the payment of benefits such as sick pay and contributory pension schemes); (3) basic problems such as the unsuitability of employees' homes for this work arrangement are overlooked; and (4) enthusiasts have tended to ignore the social and organizational impediments to successful teleworking. This last point is particularly important. Communication is more than a medium for work or a byproduct of organizational life. Organizations are created and maintained through social interactions among their members. For example, organizational structures

Table 8.1   Some characteristics of face-to-face and computer-mediated dialogue

Characteristics of communication channel	Face-to-face	Computer-mediated
Message flow	One-to-few	One-to-many
Source knowledge	Source has knowledge of 'audience'	Source less likely to have knowledge of 'audience'
Degree of interactivity	High	Medium/high
Feedback (quantity)	High	Medium/low
Feedback (speed)	Fast, parallel	Slow, sequential
Ability to preserve communications	Low	High
Socio-emotional content	High	Low
Nonverbal communication	High	Low (usually)
Control of communication	Potential for equal control is high	Potential for equal control is more limited

are just one consequence of organizational communication. Some organizations will sustain hierarchical management structures by encouraging their members to adhere to rules about who talks to whom about what. These rules can include protocols about tone and form of address. On the other hand, less hierarchical organizations can be created and maintained by encouraging members to adopt less formal codes for communication.

Sociotechnical systems theory would also point to the significance of the ways in which telecommunications devices remove, in different ways and in varying degrees, important social cues that are present in face-to-face dialogue. For example, some differences between face-to-face and computer-mediated dialogue are summarized in Table 8.1. Fewer social cues are associated with experiences of: increased psychological distance, diminished social spontaneity and engagement, a greater focus on task completion and diminished rates of compromise. Thus, communications technologies can have a profound impact on the structure and function of organizational activities because they can alter the communications processes and social interactions that sustain their existence. This can be illustrated in more detail by considering how the communications technologies that are used to interconnect people at work can promote the development of different organizational climates. Figure 8.1 depicts three simple configurations (borrowed from sociometry) and describes some of the psychological characteristics associated with each.

The circular topology with bidirectional links between adjacent pairs is associated with high levels of morale and a sense of distributed leadership.

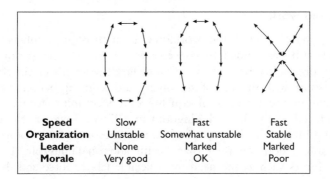

Speed	Slow	Fast	Fast
Organization	Unstable	Somewhat unstable	Stable
Leader	None	Marked	Marked
Morale	Very good	OK	Poor

Figure 8.1   Characteristics of three communication networks

The inverted-U topology is associated with hierarchy, strong leadership and a sense of isolation and lower morale by those at the periphery. The star configuration is associated with perceptions of central control and leadership and a high sense of isolation and low morale among those located at the periphery.

Management teams are increasingly concerned to promote competitiveness through teleworking initiatives that can support high levels of team effectiveness on a low-cost, high-flexibility base (Chapman *et al.*, 1994). In such circumstances managers may be tempted to regard organizational talk as frivolous and to identify opportunities for removing informal networks and 'gossip chains'. The technologies that make teleworking and virtual organizations possible can also support the design of organizational networks and structures of choice. Telematic technologies carry new opportunities – and dangers – in allowing managers to make bespoke organizational structures by editing network connections between individuals. The management of organizational structures has always been concerned with these issues. However, to the extent that an organization's staff share a physical work environment they have opportunities to communicate and work in ways which were not envisaged by managers. There are opportunities in traditional organizations for people to talk to whoever they wish, to share space with colleagues from different departments and to create and use informal communication networks to achieve personal and task objectives. Sustaining this kind of flexibility in virtual organizations will inevitably increase capital and recurrent communications costs and may prove very unattractive for this reason.

Women and work

As women have entered the workforce in increasing numbers since the 1970s, research has tended to concentrate on issues such as power in the workplace, discrimination and the 'glass ceiling', women's career choices and childcare issues, with the aim of identifying and reducing barriers to women's employment in the interests of equality of opportunity (formal legislation was introduced in the United Kingdom in 1975). However, there has also been strong interest in the impact of women entering paid employment outside the home, both on their own health and on family life. In addition, economic forces such as the need for a flexible labour force and the business imperative (or profit motive) are important in understanding patterns of women's employment.

Research in the 1970s indicated that working women benefited in terms of better mental and physical health than those who were not engaged in paid labour. This was largely attributed to the greater number of social roles available for women working outside the home. Later studies suggested that role quality and meaning were as important as role quantity, accounting for the finding that women in paid employment did not enjoy similar levels of health to those found in employed men. This has been related to the types of work done by women; Matthews *et al.* (1998) found that men reported fewer negative work characteristics than women, but also that full-time women workers reported fewer negative characteristics than part-time women workers. The negative aspects reported more by women than men included monotonous work and a lack of learning opportunities.

Bogg and Cooper (1998) also found that women civil servants in the United Kingdom were significantly less satisfied with their work than male colleagues, and had poorer mental and physical health. One factor which has been related to these findings is that of the permeability of the home–work boundary for women but not men. This refers to the degree to which work and home affect each other, often resulting in work–family conflict. Galinsky, Bond and Friedman (1996) found that employees who were parents valued different benefits and workplace policies than non-parents. They also differed in that they had less time for themselves and had poorer quality of life outcomes than non-parents. Analysis of factors which were associated with better outcomes for parent employees indicated that job factors such as autonomy, control and security were important, as well as support in the workplace, which was noted by the authors as being of benefit to all employees. However, family-friendly policies (such as flexible hours and family leave) were not associated with lower work–family conflict.

Women now comprise at least half the workforce in the United Kingdom, but are overrepresented in the atypical workforce. Atypical work is an umbrella term used to describe any form of work which is not permanent, does not fall with the hours of nine to five, and is not carried out at an employer's premises. In fact the term is a misnomer, as atypical forms of work have proliferated over the last two decades and are now more prevalent in modern economies than more traditional permanent jobs – they are now typical. One obvious explanation for the preponderance of women in atypical work is the increased number of mothers in the workforce who wish to combine work and family responsibilities, for example by working part-time during school hours. However, these changing patterns of work are also due to economic influences. Women are concentrated in certain sectors and occupations, with 75 per cent of women workers found in clerical, cleaning, catering, sales or ancillary professions (*Social Trends*, 1995). The growth of '24/7' trading in the retail sector and the increase in demand in the service sector has led to an increase in the number of atypical positions to be filled, and atypical work practices allow employers a great deal of flexibility, thus maximizing profits. Moreover, related to the clustering of women in relatively low-paid occupations, women earn on average around 80 per cent of average male earnings. Breugel and Perrons (1998) note that the form of women's increased participation in employment, particularly their participation in atypical work, has not improved their economic prospects. Clearly any understanding of women in the workplace requires a synthesis of both psychological and economic factors.

Concepts, models and theories

Most economic theories start from the premise that, in order to predict how people will behave under particular economic constraints, one should start by working out what the most profitable course of action would be for a completely rational person. Each of us has a limited income and a restricted number of ways in which to use it. Given these constraints we can ask how a rational person will behave. Within economic theory a rational person is someone who has a thorough understanding of all of the constraints, has all of the information necessary for them to make a decision, and is motivated to gain the maximum amount of money, or money's worth of satisfaction, out of it. The principle of rationality, or of utility maximization as it is also termed, is actually a good deal more complex but its essential features are captured in this description.

Psychologists, by contrast, have been more concerned with understanding human beings as irrational and hence the application of psychology to economics has focused on attacking the assumption of rationality. The contrast between the positions of psychology and economics is captured in a number of biases that pervade the way people collect and interpret information. Collectively these biases are often referred to as heuristics or mental shortcuts, falling under the umbrella term of social cognition in social psychology (Augustinos and Walker, 1995):

- *Confirmation bias*: people tend to seek out and attend mostly to information that supports their preexisting beliefs even in the face of contrary evidence. Thus the confirmation bias states that those with prior experience of an issue, for example the purchase of shoddy merchandise, will attend more to media information that supports their views than that which refutes it, and so their beliefs are reinforced (Gilovich, 1993).
- *Availability heuristic*: information most readily available in memory is more likely to be recalled. Economic information that has high emotional and cognitive content – information that has a perceived direct impact and/or which is controversial – will become *salient* or readily available in memory. For example, media reports about the risk to human health posed by the presence of scrapie in sheep may strongly influence a consumer's judgements about the suitability of purchasing a range of other meat products which pose no health risks.
- *Base-rate fallacy*: when assessing probabilities people tend to make decisions that contradict the *base-rate* or actual likelihood of an event happening. For example, people who routinely spend money on lottery tickets vastly overestimate the likelihood of a win.
- *Anchoring bias*: judgements can be influenced by a previously given figure, called an anchor. For example, if one group of people is asked whether they consider the chance of making a great deal of money on the stock exchange is greater or less than 5 per cent, they may estimate it as 10 per cent. Another group asked whether they consider the chance to be greater than 60 per cent may estimate it as 20 per cent. The higher anchor value (60%) has inflated their estimate.

Irrational thinking is not chaotic nor is it disorganized. Economic psychologist have attempted to identify regularities in irrational thinking in order to qualify and elaborate traditional 'rational' models of economic behaviour. For example, consumers' use of price as an indicator of product quality is consistent with the ideas that consumers are people who process information heuristically. People tend to rely on price as a quality indicator and thus seek higher priced products when quality is important but when quality information is not directly available

(Tellis and Gaeth, 1990). More generally, the concept of the internal reference price (IRP) has been developed to explain systematic biases in the way people interpret price information. The IRP refers to a consumer's expected price and it is used as a standard of comparison for evaluating a product's price. Prices below or above the IRP appear to influence brand evaluations and purchasing choice in the short term. A price falling above the IRP will be interpreted as 'luxurious' or 'expensive', and below as 'cheap' or 'a bargain'. The IRP is not a fixed point. It includes a region of relative price insensitivity such that only price changes outside the region have a significant impact on consumer choice (Kalwani and Yim, 1992). Moreover, people are not equally sensitive to prices falling above and below the IRP, with people tending to react more strongly to price losses (that is, IRP higher than price) than to price gains (Kalwani *et al.*, 1990).

Practical issues

Economic beliefs, values and preferences can be deep-rooted, acquired imperceptibly through socialization and expressed unconsciously through lifestyles and unconscious habitual choices. Such beliefs, values and preferences can be modified through the influence of media and marketing campaigns and without conscious awareness of any change having taken place (see Chapter 6). From a psychological perspective the measurement of economic beliefs and values poses two major problems. First, people may not be aware of their economic beliefs and values and may not appreciate their influence on decision preferences. Consequently, when invited to report their preferences among a set of options, such as spending their money on a holiday or investing it in a savings account, they may find it difficult or impossible to articulate their beliefs and values accurately and reliably. Second, people may not be aware of subtle changes in their beliefs and values and may not be capable of reporting such changes as might have occurred. Consequently, although we may be able to see changes in our economic behaviour over extended time periods, perhaps several years, we may be unable to discern smaller differences that cumulatively lead to these larger changes.

In order to examine these issues consumer psychologists have made extensive use of experimental designs that can detect subtle factors and processes which influence how people interpret economic information and make choices. For example, it is well-established that mood plays an important role in consumers' reactions to advertising and that this can influence purchasing choices. While changes in mood can be induced by advertising and in turn a person's mood may affect their responses to advertising, the direction of the links between advertising and mood are not simple. Some studies suggest that positive moods can decrease the extent to which people actively process the information contained in an advertising message (Batra and Stayman 1990). Thus, positive moods may leave consumers more vulnerable in the sense that they may be less critical or more accepting of what they hear and see in an advertisement. However, other studies suggest the opposite – positive moods may increase attentiveness and critical appreciation (Mathur and Chattopadhyay, 1991). These conflicting results may reflect the fact that a very large number of factors can influence our response to an advertisement, and different studies may have considered some of these factors but not others. For example, consider one factor, the communication medium (radio, television or print). Radio and television broadcasts appear to impose a greater burden on a person's memorial abilities because economic messages are delivered sequentially. When you hear an advertisement for a concert on the radio you have to 're-play' it from memory in order to recover information about the date, location and price. A printed advertisement for the same event can be read and re-read in different orders and a promise of 'a great night out' and other information can thus be examined in greater detail.

Economic information is not interpreted within a psychological vacuum. Knowledge, experience and critical awareness influence how a commercial claim is interpreted and the meaning that is given to it. An important concept in consumer psychology is that the impact of a message is influenced by the elaboration which the message receives in a person's associative memory network. The elaboration of a commercial message influences what consumers will learn about a product or service and the favourableness of judgements they will make. Message elaboration is influenced by whether consumers relate information to themselves and to their own experiences. For example, relating an advertising claim to positive experiences may actually inhibit message learning (Baumgartner *et al.*, 1992) but enhance one's evaluation of the advertisement. This paradoxical effect appears to be because the memory of a positive experience that is triggered by the advertisement is transferred to the goods or services offered, but the relatively limited cognitive effort involved in making this self–advertisement association reduces the likelihood that anything new will be learned. For instance, an advertisement for a new make of car may trigger memories of previous satisfaction with this manufacturer's vehicles and at the same time diminish the likelihood of any new information being learned about the latest model on offer.

Consistent with this notion is the well-established finding that when audience involvement with an advertising campaign is low, then peripheral cues such as the message source can influence judgements. This effect would seem to be due to the fact that secondary or tangential information can be interpreted with relatively little effort. For example, a well-established bank may resort to using media personalities to endorse their mortgage schemes. By contrast, when audience involvement is high, more resource-demanding central cues such as the message content determine judgement. Thus people are likely to invest more effort in attending to and evaluating the details in an advertisement if they are thinking of buying or selling a home. In order to gain the attention of both low and high involvement audiences, advertisers may attempt to forestall audience 'wear out' by using a dual campaign in which one line of an advertisement incorporates a series of cosmetic variations (for example using different media personalities) addressed at low involvement consumers, and another that focuses on substantive variation in the advertising content (Schumann *et al.*, 1990).

The way forward

One issue that is particularly salient to progress towards a full understanding of economic life is that of inclusivity. Both economics and psychology have been charged with largely excluding females from their theorizing and research until the emergence of feminist critiques in the 1970s. Psychology as a discipline tended to be practised by men who took an androcentric (male-centred) approach to the understanding of behaviour. For example, Wilhelm Wundt's (1897) early research into the 'generalized adult mind' was based on data from male students using introspection to understand the structure of the mind. Later psychological research was often conducted using male samples and the results assumed to apply equally to females; if subsequent research revealed that women deviated from the 'male norm', women were assumed to be deficient. Moreover, the research agenda was set by men within the context of a patriarchal society and women's experiences did not feature in this agenda. Where men did study women's experiences, the questions they generated were often viewed by feminists as irrelevant to women's lives. In a discipline which aimed to understand human behaviour, women were largely invisible, whether as researchers or researched. With the emergence of New Wave Feminism in the 1970s, a strong critique of this status quo emerged. As women entered the discipline, research on gender issues was broadened and the concept of 'feminist research' – research conducted by and for women – emerged. Since the 1970s, a wealth of research has examined women's experiences, including their experiences at work.

Similar criticisms have been made in relation to economics, also a male-dominated discipline, but in contrast with psychology one which has focused on what has often been considered as an exclusively male domain. Until the mid-twentieth century, such an approach may have seemed to reflect reality for economists, given that so few women had any paid work outside the home at that time. The concept of the male breadwinner earning a 'family wage' was a powerful one which effectively excluded the majority of women from economic analyses. Nevertheless, feminist critiques served to highlight the importance of women's work inside the home to the economy, arguing that without this 'invisible support' men would be unable to be economically active. It was further pointed out that many women were active consumers, even if their 'housekeeping money' had been earned by a man. As women entered the workforce in larger numbers so the feminist critique was strengthened further. Women's economic participation began to be analysed in earnest, but as with psychology the extent to which gender has been integrated into the mainstream of the discipline remains debatable.

The concept of a 'feminist lens' through which social issues could be examined has been a powerful one which has produced a more inclusive body of research in both psychology and economics. However, recent developments within feminism and within the emerging discipline of masculinity studies have challenged the idea of 'woman' and 'man' as monolithic categories, noting the intersection of gender with race, socioeconomic status, disability, age and a variety of other psychosocial factors to produce a variety of gendered experiences (Burman, 1998). This perspective, embracing diversity, requires social scientists to adopt an inclusive approach in their research and theorizing, and this remains a challenge for the future.

The information economy

As a consequence of developments in communications and computing technologies, information has acquired two functional connotations. First, it has come to be regarded as an economic resource. People buy and sell information in much the same way as labour, material and capital has always been bought and sold. Information is transacted commercially because its possession and application are considered to increase the effectiveness of physical and human resources. For example, possession of climate information will facilitate the judicious use of natural resources, improve the cost-effectiveness of the agricultural industry and thereby enhance standards of living and the quality of life. Second, information is regarded as a commodity. The information services sector is associated with industries concerned with exploration, innovation and design, planning, and financial management. Although information is regarded as a resource and a commodity it has a number of social psychological attributes that distinguish it from other economic entities. First, it is intrinsically diffuse. Second, it reproduces through use – it is not consumed in the way other commodities are consumed. In this sense 'consumers' of information are agents for its reproduction and expansion. Third, information can only be shared, it cannot be transacted. Someone who supplies or communicates information is not automatically dispossessed of it. This greatly complicates commerce in information and introduces a range of psychological and social processes into economic transactions.

A growing interest in globalism, particularly in relation to beliefs about the validity and reliability of information gathered, organized and disseminated from different parts of the world, has stimulated research addressing country-of-origin effects as one of several product features that may influence product evaluation, or by providing an image that informs the development of an impression of a product. Country-of-origin can also indirectly affect product evaluations by influencing the consumer's interpretation of product-attribute information. For example, would you regard financial information services provided from a state in central Africa as being more or less valuable than identical information provided from a country in the UK? This indirect effect appear to be particularly important when consumers are unfamiliar with a country's products (Han, 1989) or have previously formed an evaluative concept of the product based on country of origin because that concept can guide the processing of attribute information received later. For example, Hong and Wyer (1989) suggest that country-of-origin information may stimulate consumer interest, which leads people to think in more general terms about product-attribute information and the evaluative implications of that information. However, much more research is needed to understand how country-of-origin impressions are formed and to explore whether country of origin is indeed a unique product feature with effects that are distinct from those associated with other product features. Yet again, this is a topic which awaits further exploration.

SHORT QUESTIONS

1   Try to construct a definition for 'a bargain'. To what extent is it possible to construct an objective definition?

2   Why do you put so much effort into obtaining a good degree? Is it to maximize the economic return on your effort?

SHORT QUESTION (cont'd)

3 An Armenian proverb states 'When your fortune increases, the columns of your house appear to be crooked.' What is the moral in this proverb?
4 To what extent does the country of origin influence the clothes you buy?
5 How can work benefit psychological well-being?

CLASS ACTIVITIES

1 When assessing probabilities people tend to make decisions that contradict the *base-rate* or actual likelihood of an event happening. It is relatively easy to illustrate the pervasiveness and strength of this fallacy using the following task. Ask a group of people how many people they believe would need to be in a room for there to be a 50:50 probability that two will have the same birth dates? Take a note of their answers and calculate the average. It is very probably that the average will be substantially greater than 23 – which in fact is the correct answer!

To see why you need to consider every possible comparison between each member of a group of 23 and every one of the other 23 members. This produces a surprisingly large number of pair comparisons, and consequently the probability of a shared birthday is higher than most people think. 23 people can actually be paired off in no less than 253 different ways. The chance of finding a shared birthday in a group of 23 people is 50% ($P = 0.5$). This rather high probability illustrates how people tend to underestimate the chances of an event happening when there are a large number of possibilities or combinations to take into account.

With 30 people, as may be found on a typical rugby pitch, the likelihood is 70% that two people will share a birthday.

2 Consider the short scenario at the start of this chapter. Can you identify the 'rational' and 'non-rational' factors that informed your judgment on which of the two students was the wiser?

FURTHER READING

Antonides, G., van Raaij, W.F. and Maital, S. (eds) (1997) *Advances in Economic Psychology*. Chichester: Wiley.

Lewis, A., Webley, P. and Furnham, A. (1995) *The New Economic Mind*. London: Prentice Hall.

Staat, D.A. (1997) *Understanding the Consumer*. London: Palgrave.

Webley, P., Burgoyne, C., Lea, S. and Young, B. (2000) *The Economic Psychology of Everyday Life*. London: Psychology Press.

Weisskopf, W.A. (1999) *The Psychology of Economics*. London: Routledge.

Crime and the Law

ONCE UPON A TIME...

There was a student called Stuart who regarded himself as a law-abiding citizen. He did not have a criminal record and had never been involved with the police. On a wet and dull November afternoon Stuart was driving to an important class that he could not afford to miss. Ordinarily he was a safe and conscientious road user. However, on this occasion he decided to 'run the lights', that is he slipped through a red light unnoticed, no one was hurt and he arrived at his class on time. Stuart continues to regard himself as a law-abiding citizen.

Introduction

The law is concerned with examining the behaviour of people and determining what they had in mind when they were engaged in a particular act. Psychology is defined as the scientific study of behaviour or the science of mental life. Thus, psychological issues are fundamental to the law and it is not surprising that psychologists argue that they can inform legal proceedings by helping to determine how and why people behaved as they did.

The importance of psychological concepts for the law is illustrated most clearly in the legal definition of a crime. A person cannot usually be found guilty of a crime unless two elements are present: an *actus reus*, Latin for guilty act, and *mens rea*, Latin for guilty mind. The legal definition of every crime contains the required *actus reus* and *mens rea* for the offence. For example, in the case of someone accused of shoplifting the accused person is presumed innocent until proven otherwise. The prosecution must establish that the accused committed the guilty act (*actus reus*) – it was they who took the goods, not someone else – and that they intended (*mens rea*) to take them without paying. It may happen that the prosecution can establish that the goods were taken by the accused, thereby showing that the *actus reus* was committed, but they may not be able to prove that the person understood what it is they were doing – that they possessed the *mens rea*. For example, an adult with Alzheimer's disease may suffer memory impairments and therefore may not have the *mens rea* to satisfy the courts they intended to commit an act of theft. However, Alzheimer's is a progressive disease and the courts will require psychological and neurological assessments before deciding whether its effect on the memory of the accused was so great as to make it very likely that they had no memory of taking the goods or of failing to pay for them.

Social psychologists emphasize the importance of situational factors in shaping intentions and behaviour, and the courts also recognize the importance of circumstances and consequences. For example, in criminal law an *actus reus* can consist of more than just a specific act. Criminal actions include all the elements of the offence other than the intentions and actions of the defendant. Depending on the offence, this may include the circumstances in which the act was committed, or the consequences of what was done. For example, the crime of rape requires *unlawful* sexual intercourse by a man with a person without their *consent*. The absence of consent is a circumstance that exists independently of the actions of the accused. Similarly, it is unlawful for an adult to have sexual intercourse with a child; the circumstance of the child's age is a factor that exists independently of a defendant's actions and intentions.

The same behaviour may be part of the *actus reus* of different crimes, depending on the consequences. For instance, shooting someone may lead to their death and so the action would form the *actus reus* of murder. However, the victim may not die, but the wound may form the *actus reus* of grievous bodily harm. The behaviour of the accused is the same in both cases but the consequence for the victim determines whether the *actus reus* of murder or grievous bodily harm has been committed.

History and development

The history of contemporary criminal law can be traced to early Egyptian, Greek and Roman civilizations. For example, in ancient Greece the issue of personal responsibility for criminal actions was first considered under the rule of Draco, when it was decided that a person should not suffer for a crime they did not commit. Thus, the practice of 'vendetta', where sons were punished for the crimes of their fathers, was outlawed. Legal guilt meant that a person had to have personally committed a crime. In AD 230 Modestinus, a Roman lawyer, successfully argued that if an insane person committed murder they may be excused because they were punished enough by their own mental illness: if a person is 'mad' they cannot be rational and therefore are only guilty in action, not in their mind. Thus, the concept of *mens rea* was introduced.

Many fundamental concepts in criminal law antedate the emergence of modern psychology. Thus, it is important to recognize that criminal law makes some fundamental distinctions between different types of *actus reus* and *mens rea*, the validity of which might seem dubious to a psychologist. However, there are at least two reasons why it is important to understand how the law defines guilty actions and guilty minds. First, because these definitions determine how the courts treat the theories and evidence of psychologists, and, second, it is important for psychologists to understand how some of the working concepts of criminal law might be refined and improved.

Actus reus

The law distinguishes between four kinds of crime depending on the nature of the *actus reus*: action crimes, state of affair crimes, result crimes and omissions:

- *Action crimes.* In these crimes the *actus reus* is the action of behaving in a particular way, regardless of the consequence. For example, perjury involves giving false testimony under oath. Whether or not the statement makes a difference to the outcome of the trial is irrelevant.
- *State of affair crimes.* In these crimes the *actus reus* consists of circumstances, and sometimes consequences, but not acts. These are crimes of 'being' rather than 'doing'. For instance, illegal immigrants are charged with *being* a foreigner in a country that they entered without the required permission.
- *Result crimes.* Some kinds of crime are defined by the fact that the behaviour of the accused produced a particular result. Murder, for example, is the result of the actions of one person against another. Result crimes

focus on the analysis of causation: the result must be shown to have been caused by the defendant's act. If the result is caused by an intervening event unconnected with the defendant's act, and which could not have been foreseen, the defendant will not be found guilty of the result. For example, a golfer who is passed a club by his caddy and who, a moment later, is killed by lightning when the club is raised in the air, would not be considered to have been murdered by his caddy.

- *Omissions.* Criminal liability is rarely imposed by a person's failure to behave in a particular way. This is because the law does not place a duty on people to help each other out, or save each other from harm. For instance, an adult pedestrian who notices a child at the kerb-side about to dash into the roadway is not obliged to intervene. A criminal offence is committed by an omission only in those circumstances where the law imposes a duty not to commit that omission. An obvious example of a relationship that imposes a duty to act is that of parents to their children.

The four kinds of *actus reus* require a person to have engaged voluntarily in a particular behaviour. A patient who, while having her patellar reflex tested, kicks and injures her doctor would not be regarded as having done so voluntarily. Neither would the violent movements of someone during an epileptic seizure be considered voluntary, even if they resulted in injury to others. However, juries are often far less convinced that other kinds of neurological disorder can produce complex involuntary behaviour. For example, how could persistent shouting of obscenities, grunting, barking and whistling ever be condoned as 'involuntary'? However, these are some of the symptoms of De Tourette's syndrome, first described in 1885 and which for many years the courts refused to believe could be produced involuntarily.

Mens rea

Mens rea refers to the state of mind of the person committing the crime. The required *mens rea* varies depending on the nature of the offence, but not in ways that might seem familiar to psychologists. English criminal law states that there are four main states of mind that separately or in combination constitute the necessary *mens rea* of a criminal offence. These are intention, Cunningham recklessness, Caldwell recklessness and negligence:

- *Intention.* Intention has different meanings within psychology and within the law; the law distinguishes between direct intention and oblique intention. Direct intention refers to a situation where a person's intention was to produce the desired consequences. For example, a person may take a gun with the intention of shooting and killing another. Oblique intention refers to a situation where a person did not desire a particular outcome, but it is an almost certain consequence of the act, and the accused realizes this and goes ahead anyway. For example, a person might engage in a type of Russian roulette whereby only one of the chambers in a gun is loaded and they 'take a chance' and fire the gun fatally injuring another.

- *Recklessness.* In psychology, the term recklessness follows everyday usage; it refers to the taking of an unjustified risk. However, the courts only recognize two types of recklessness, named after the cases in which they were defined. *Cunningham recklessness* refers to a case in which the defendant, Cunningham, broke a gas meter to steal some money. Gas seeped into the house next door where Cunningham's prospective mother-in-law was sleeping; she became seriously ill. According to this definition recklessness involves foreseeing that the kind of harm that occurred might have happened, and going ahead anyway. *Caldwell recklessness* refers to a case in which Caldwell, an ex-employee of a hotel, held a grudge against the owner. He caused some damage to the hotel by starting a fire and he was charged with arson. Caldwell argued that he had not intended to damage the hotel and that he did not foresee that the small fire would do any damage. In other words, he argued that there was no *mens rea* when he started the fire. However, the courts decided that a person is guilty of behaving recklessly towards property if (a) they perform an act which creates an obvious risk to the property, and (b) where, in committing an act, the person has either not given any thought to the possibility of there being a risk to property, or recognized that there was some risk but proceeded with the action anyway. The intention behind the Caldwell definition was to broaden the legal concept of recklessness, so that people who are considered to be morally at fault cannot escape conviction because it is impossible to prove their actual state of mind at the time they were engaged in a particular act.

- *Negligence.* When a person's behaviour falls below the standards to be expected of a reasonable person they are judged to have behaved in a negligent fashion. The concept of negligence is rarely used in criminal law, partly because the courts have considered that being insensitive to the rights of others is not necessarily morally wrong. Of course punishing negligence may encourage people to think more carefully about the risks to others and to think about others in a more caring way, but callous insensitivity to others is not normally treated as a crime.

Contemporary priorities

What is to be done about law and order? Answers to this question figure in the election manifestos of every political party and as such reflect prevailing concerns with the amount of crime. Research suggests that the issues are rather more complex than indicated by the rhetoric. The criminal statistics that are published annually by most governments are based on police figures of reported crime, and they serve a range of functions including:

- A measure of the total volume of crime that can be used to plan crime-control strategies.
- A map of the statistical distribution of criminal acts by variables such as age, sex, class, etc. The evidence that most crimes are carried out by teenage males living in cities provides the background for focusing research on this group.
- Basic data for theory-building and hypothesis-testing.
- A measure of the enforceability of legal norms.
- A measure of the efficiency of preventive measures and the effectiveness of treatment of different types of offender.
- A measure of changes in crime across time.
- A basis for establishing regional and national variations in crime rates.
- A basis for computing the cost of law enforcement.

While the official figures of crime are useful, most commentators agree that they are far from accurate. This is an endemic problem that arises from the way crime is recorded. Firstly we are dealing with crime not criminals. It is possible for one person to be prosecuted for a list of related offences that were carried out as part of a single attempted burglary, or, alternatively, a single crime might be caused by a group of people. However, new procedures aim to confine measurement to one crime per victim (French, Donnelly and Willis, 2001). Secondly, planned police action can distort crime figures. For example, the police in one area may have chosen to target everyone carrying drugs as part of a drive to remove drugs from their district, whereas in other districts police have other priorities. Thirdly, official statistics exclude some crimes such as those associated with tax and fraud. Finally, it is argued that one of the main problems with official statistics is that there are many more crimes committed than are reported to the police. Crime surveys which look at the public's experience of crime have enabled comparison to be made with official statistics for some but not all crimes. They have not only shown that the gap between victims' and witnesses' reports and the official figure is wide, but also that the pattern of reporting crime varies widely depending on the nature of the crime and the characteristics of the victim. On the basis of the *British Crime Survey*, Kershaw *et al.* (2000) estimate that of all crimes committed against individuals, four out of ten are reported to the police and one in five enter the statistics as a recorded crime.

There are a number of stages in reporting and recording crimes, at each of which it is possible for the crime to disappear from the official statistics. Firstly, a victim has to label an act as a crime and to assess whether it is a minor or serious crime. The victims may then decide that they should call the police. These decisions may in fact have little relationship with the actual seriousness of the crime and much to do with knowledge of the crime or the victim's perception of their own vulnerability and the benefits of calling the police. For example, all but one of the relatives of the people murdered by Dr Harold Shipman were willing to accept that death was the result of natural causes and did not see that a crime had been committed. At a more mundane level, stores and supermarkets are not aware of the nature and number of individual thefts from their premises. They tend to only inform the police if they apprehend a shoplifter. In a very different scenario, a woman who is seriously battered by her husband may not complain to the police because she feels that this will lead to worse violence.

Non-reporting of crime will vary systematically according to the crime. The more serious the crime, the more likely it is to be reported. Almost 97 per cent of vehicle thefts are reported to the police because an insurance claim has to be supported with evidence of a police report. Conversely, if people believe the police will be unhelpful they will not bother to inform them. Almost three-quarters of incidents of vandalism reported in the 1998 *British Crime Survey* were not reported to the police. Young men, who are the most frequent victims of crime, are the least likely to report their victimization, whereas older women are the most likely to report being victimized. If the victim is also engaged in an illegal act or sees him or herself as somewhat to blame for the crime, he or she is not likely to report it. For example, a man who has been drinking heavily and finds that his wallet has been stolen may not feel that it is necessary to report his loss to the police (Ainsworth, 2000).

Even when a crime is reported it may not be recorded by the police, who have some discretion in deciding what is officially notified as a crime. If the police see no basis for a criminal charge, they can deal with the incident with an informal warning or caution rather than sucking the offender into a prolonged legal process. In the past, this was also the case with family violence where conciliation was seen to be more appropriate than prosecution. Changes in government policy has ensured that nowadays incidents of domestic violence are generally reported as a crime.

The use of cautions and conciliation varies widely across time and across regions. In addition, different police forces have different criteria for recording crimes. These are major problems for any cross-cultural analysis of statistics and their interpretation, and must be taken into account in any reading of the trends. However, information about the potential distortions in official figures does provide some safeguards against reaching spurious conclusions about the extent and nature of crime.

The recording of a crime is one step along the pathway between committing an offence and receiving an appropriate legal sanction for this act. Only a quarter of recorded crimes are cleared up by the police, and less than a half of these cleared up crimes result in a person being charged or summoned to appear in court. The remainder result in no further action, a caution, a minor fixed penalty or are 'taken into consideration' when a person is charged with some other crime (Ainsworth, 2000).

Concepts, models and theories

Debates about the insanity defence, whereby the accused pleads that they could not have had a guilty mind because they were insane at the time they committed a particular act, provide an insight into legal and psychological conceptions of the person.

The Enlightenment or Age of Reason heralded the triumph of rationality and scientific medicine. Nevertheless in criminal law the ability to exercise personal will and to understand the difference between right and wrong was determined by the 'wild-beast' test. In order to be considered insane a person had to be so frenzied as to no longer appear to behave like a human. The wild-beast standard was used as late as 1724 in the case of Arnold who shot and wounded one of George II's courtiers. However, the case of Daniel McNaughten is the most important point of reference in the history of the insanity defence. McNaughten attempted to assassinate the Prime Minister Sir Robert Peel, but missed and killed his secretary Edward Drummond. McNaughten believed that Peel had been spreading scurrilous rumours about him and that he, McNaughten, was being persecuted by the Tory Party. McNaughten was labelled 'partially insane' with the ability of reasoning intact. The defence argued that his delusion had caused him to behave as he did and medical testimony was presented that indicated McNaughten was insane. The McNaughten acquittal caused public uproar and Queen Victoria protested at the outcome. The result of the outcry was that the judges were required to explain the law on insanity in what became known as the McNaughten rules. These rules were formulated in 1843 and have been used, with various elaborations and amendments, in England, Wales and Ireland and in some states in America. They are no longer used in Scotland.

One of the causes of controversy on the insanity defence concerns the disparity between the disciplines of law and psychology. The presentation of psychiatric or psychological evidence in court is based on legal concepts of mental disorder. However, the concept of mental illness poses a problem because it does not have a strict legal definition. Neither are there agreed definitions within psychology and psychiatry. Thus, although psychiatric and psychological testimony is supposed to aid the jury in its decision-making process, society is ambivalent to psychological and psychiatric intervention in matters of criminal behaviour. People are often torn between humanitarian feelings and a desire to punish repulsive actions. To what extent does a mental disorder affect the responsibility of an individual and what should this mean in terms of punishment? The concept of an insane person is the juxtaposition of the opposing responses these questions provoke.

Social attitudes are characterized by confusion about the issue of punishment as applied to people judged to be mentally ill. According to American law, for example, prisoners on death row are not allowed to be executed if they are considered to be mentally ill. This raises the obvious question of whether it is possible to regard a murderer as mentally healthy? It is hardly surprising, therefore, that juries are still unwilling to accept that serial sex murderers are not sane, even when psychiatrists apply the label 'paranoid schizophrenic'. In the case of Peter Sutcliffe, known as the 'Yorkshire Ripper', the jury did not accept that he was mentally ill even though psychiatrists testified that he was severely mentally disturbed.

There are many popular misconceptions about the insanity defence. Pasewark (1986) surveyed 1601 members of the public about their opinions on the insanity defence and found that 87 per cent thought that the defence was being used too often by murderers wishing to avoid imprisonment. In reality very few defendants enter an insanity plea, perhaps because they wish to avoid an indefinite period in a mental hospital. Even a so-called 'mentally-ill murderer' may be able to think through the consequences of their plea. For example, Theodore Kaczynski, known as the 'Unabomber', carried out a 17-year bombing campaign that eventually resulted in the death of three people. Although his lawyers and psychiatrists believed him to be a 'classic paranoid schizophrenic', and thus able to enter an insanity plea, Kaczynski refused this defence. Instead he entered a 'mental defect' plea and thereby admitted criminal intent to kill. This meant that his punishment would either be a death sentence or a specified prison sentence but not an uncertain period of incarceration in an institution for the criminally insane.

Cognitive and affective factors

A great deal of evidence presented to the courts is in the form of memories of witnesses to an incident. Thus the accuracy of eyewitness testimony is often crucial to the outcome of many trials. There are discrepancies between psychological and legal views on the reliability of eyewitness memories that further illustrate their different perspectives on human perception, cognition and memory. The courts tend to regard human memory as broadly analogous to a video camera and that people are likely to make particularly good recordings of very important events, such as the criminal actions of others (Ainsworth, 2000). Thus, when a witness is asked to recall what they saw and heard they are thought to do so by locating the pertinent memory and 'playing back' the contents to the court. Psychological theories of memory take a more sophisticated view but the basic question remains: How accurate is eyewitness testimony? One analysis of 1000 experimental conditions in 128 laboratory and field studies of face recognition indicated an accuracy of 68 per cent, suggesting that people make wrong identifications on nearly one-third of occasions (Shapiro and Penrod, 1986).

Psychological investigations of eyewitness testimony sometimes draw a distinction between 'system variables' and 'estimator variables'. System variables are those that can be manipulated by the police, such as the way identification parades are conducted and the type of interrogation techniques used. Estimator variables are those that cannot be controlled, such as the age of an accused, the gender of a witness and so on. Although the distinction between system and estimator variables appears reasonable at first sight, in practice it can be very difficult to discriminate between many important factors in this way. For example, when evaluating the fairness of identification parades it can be very difficult to identify and measure the identification strategies used by individual witnesses, yet is very important to know about those strategies in order to manipulate the system variables effectively. Similarly, when developing guidelines on the optimal time to collect witness statements after a crime it is important to take into consideration the effectiveness of their coping strategies. It may be very difficult to do this in advance of someone actually witnessing a crime, even a staged crime, because people might cope with different kinds of crime in different ways.

An alternative approach is based on a three-stage model of witnesses' experiences: perception of an event, storage of information in memory, and retrieval at a later date. This model corresponds to the natural sequence of events in which someone witnesses a crime, their experiences are stored in memory and retrieved when the police take statements. It has frequently been used to examine how witnesses' memories of an incident can be changed by post-incident experiences. In the first stage, perception, a group of research participants witness a staged crime or accident. In the second stage they are exposed to particular post-incident experiences and in the third stage they are questioned about their original experiences. Typically, research using this model shows that people can experience difficulty distinguishing their memory of the original incident from events that happened afterwards. A classic example is a study by Loftus, Miller and Burns (1978) in which people were shown a sequence of slides depicting a car accident. Later they were asked a series of questions containing potentially misleading information: 'Did another car pass the red Datsun while it was stopped at the stop sign?' There was in fact no 'stop' sign but a 'give way' sign. When they were later (stage three) asked to recall the details of the accident, nearly 60 per cent recalled the false detail that had subsequently been added. They confidently recalled that the Datsun was stopped at the stop sign. This type of research design simulates what can easily happen in real circumstances where police officers may inadvertently, or deliberately, offer information to witnesses that they incorporate into their original memory of what they saw.

The significance of eyewitness accounts for the outcome of many legal proceedings has prompted numerous investigations of factors that may influence their accuracy (Bull and Carson, 1995). Those factors can be grouped into stable and variable characteristics of the witness and of the perpetrator.

Stable characteristics of eye-witnesses

- *Gender.* Up until the mid-1950s it was widely believed that men made more reliable witnesses than women. This gender stereotype is reflected in the relative absence of women as witnesses in criminal trials. Experimental investigations suggest that there are no gender differences in the accuracy of eyewitnesses' testimony.
- *Intelligence.* Common sense suggests that more intelligent people will offer more accurate accounts of an incident. The research evidence indicates otherwise: accuracy is unrelated to variations in intelligence within the normal range, although people with learning disabilities may be less accurate.
- *Personality.* Variations in personality have not been linked with the accuracy of a person's memories.
- *Consistency.* The consistency of a person's testimony is not a reliable indicator of accuracy; people can be consistently wrong as well as consistently right.

EYEWITNESS QUIZ

Before considering the factors that influence the accuracy of eyewitness testimony complete the following quiz. Read each statement and indicate whether you consider it is true or false.

	True	False
Men make more accurate eyewitnesses than woman.		
An eyewitness with an IQ of 110 will be more accurate than another with an IQ of 90.		
Introverts make better eyewitnesses than extraverts.		
People who offer more consistent accounts of what they saw are usually more accurate than those who are less consistent.		
People who are more confident about their testimony are very likely to be more accurate than those who are less confident.		
People who have been trained as eyewitnesses are far more accurate than those who have not.		
Police officers make much more accurate eyewitnesses than members of the general public.		
High levels of stress that people may experience while witnessing a particularly violent crime help create much more accurate memories.		
People who notice superficial features of a perpetrator will find it easier to make a positive identification later on.		
It is easier to remember and to identify the faces of more attractive people than those of less attractive people.		

How did you do? You can find out by skipping to Class Activities at the end of this chapter.

■   *Confidence.* There is a weak association between a person's confidence in their testimony and its accuracy. In general confidence is a poor indicator of accuracy and people who are not confident about their testimony are usually no less accurate than people who are more confident.

Variable characteristics of eye-witnesses

- *Alcohol.* Intoxicated witnesses give less-accurate accounts.
- *Training.* Training witnesses does not substantially increase their accuracy.
- *Depth of processing.* People who notice superficial or transient features in another person's appearance, such as their clothing or jewellery, tend to be less accurate when they later try to identify that person than 'deep processors' – those who attend to details in a person's face.
- *Accuracy of prior descriptions.* The accuracy of witnesses' prior descriptions of a perpetrator are only weakly related to their ability to accurately identify the person some time later.
- *Completeness of prior descriptions.* The completeness of witnesses' prior descriptions of a perpetrator are only very weakly related to their ability to identify them at a later stage.
- *Stress.* Higher levels of stress and anxiety tend to impact negatively on the accuracy and completeness of a person's memories. For example, people who have been in close proximity to a bank raid in which the perpetrators carried lethal weapons are prone to a phenomenon called 'weapon focus'. The presence of the deadly threat may cause witnesses to focus most of their attention on where it is located and where it is pointing. Thus, they can produce very detailed descriptions of the weapons but less complete recollections of the people holding them.

Stable characteristics of the perpetrator

- *Gender.* The gender of the perpetrator does not affect identification accuracy; it is just as easy for people to identify women as to identify men.
- *Attractiveness.* The attractiveness of the perpetrator does not affect identification accuracy.
- *Distinctiveness.* Perpetrators with distinctive features, such as a scar on an ear-lobe, are more accurately identified at a later stage.
- *Race.* Witnesses tend to have greater difficulty identifying the faces of people from a different race.

Variable characteristics of the perpetrator

- *Disguises.* the use of disguises significantly impairs identification accuracy.

The general public tends to believe that police are very accurate in their identification of people based on their memory for them. This belief is usually based on the presumption that people are selected for policing partly because they have good perceptual abilities and good memories, and that these abilities are honed so that 'professional vision' is developed with experience. However, well-publicized cases of police misidentification, such as that of George Davis who was wrongly identified by five policemen despite not being identified by 38 other witnesses (Clifford, 1976) suggest that the police may not be as reliable as commonly believed. It is well-established that memory of an event may be enhanced or distorted by witnesses discussing the events afterwards and modifying what they saw in the light of what others have told them afterwards (Loftus, 1996). The interactive work which is a routine part of police team investigations is such that cases must be repeatedly discussed and reexamined, and this may distort an officer's original memory. In fact, numerous variables such as the types of questioning used by police officers may further decrease the quality of their initial memories.

In addition to the historical evidence of police misidentification, there is a significant amount of experimental work which also suggests that police officers do not have a higher level of accuracy in their identification of suspects than ordinary citizens. For example, Tickner and Poulton (1975) had 24 policemen and 156 civilians view films of a street scene lasting for one, two or four hours, into which various staged events had been inserted. The police identified more alleged thefts than the civilians, but there was no significant difference between the two groups in terms of the true detection of criminal individuals and actions. In other words the police made more misidentifications. In fact the overall detection rate was low, just 31 per cent. This is particularly interesting given that photographs of the relevant 'criminal suspects' were displayed continuously under the screen on which the films were viewed. Moreover, the viewing of a 'softening-up' film of the relevant people, showing the 'criminal suspects' prior to the actual experimental film, raised correct detections to 41 per cent for both police and civilians. In a similar film study, Simmons, Poulton, and Tickner (1975) showed that identification at night is even worse for both police officers and citizens. Experimental investigations of this sort can be criticized for being unrealistic and that a true assessment of the competence of police to offer identifications should involve real-life cases where the consequences of a false identification will be serious for all concerned. However, it is difficult to construct a real-life setting within acceptable ethical parameters. Moreover, it could be argued that the assessment environment of laboratory controlled conditions should provide excellent opportunities to demonstrate the superior 'professional vision' of the police.

Practical issues

Look back to the list of 10 statements in the Eyewitness Quiz. Most people would say some of those statements must be true because common sense suggests they must. Juries consist of 12 members of the general public who are thought to represent the common-sense interests and reasonable views of 'most people'. As such, juries are composed of people who are likely to have a number of false beliefs about the accuracy of eyewitness testimony. Under these circumstances, and given that psychologists have accrued a considerable body of empirically-based ideas about how similarly sized groups function, one might expect the courts to be willing to allow psychologists sit in on and observe the deliberations of real juries. In fact the courts are highly protective of jury deliberations and they are not available to the scrutiny of psychologists or anyone else. Consequently psychologists have, where the law permits, resorted to retrospective investigations of how juries arrived at their decisions, and to examining the dynamics of mock trials that are designed to simulate the real thing.

Retrospective enquiries (see for example Nagel, Lamm and Neef, 1981) have shown that the course of juror decision-making normally follows one of three routes: (1) arrival at a standard of guilt according to the instructions of the judge, personal assessment of a defendant's guilt, and then a decision to convict or acquit; (2) arrival at a tentative decision to convict or acquit, adoption of the standard of guilt, and then progressive adjustment of one's assessment of the defendant's guilt to bring it in to line with the tentative decision and the standard of guilt; (3) arrival at a tentative decision to acquit or convict, personal assessment of the defendant's guilt, and then adjustment of one's perception of the standard of guilt. These different courses illustrate how jury deliberations rely on processes of information-sharing and verdict-negotiation among jurors. Analyses of jurors' requests for clarification also provide an insight into those areas in which they encounter problems (Severance and Loftus, 1984). Jurors often have doubts about the legal elements of criminal offences, particularly the relationships between *actus reus* and *mens rea*. They also experience difficulties understanding the decision criteria they are required to adopt. In criminal proceedings their decision must be 'beyond reasonable doubt', and in civil proceedings 'on the balance of probabilities'. They tend to have particular difficulty with the 'beyond reasonable doubt' criterion. Finally, where multiple charges are involved, they often seek guidance on the procedures they should adopt when reaching a decision.

Mock juries are often used to simulate, using role-play techniques, what may be going on in real jury deliberations. However, simulations cannot capture the degree of responsibility and significance attached to full jury deliberations because the decisions arrived at in role-play situations do not have important implications for 'the accused'. Nevertheless, they may be a useful guide to the conduct of real juries because there is no evidence to suggest that people can easily suspend the normal interpersonal dynamics that occur in all small group activities (Stephenson, 1992).

Studies of mock juries suggest that participants can be divided according to three types of involvement: persuaders, participants and non-participants. On any panel of 12 individuals there tends to be three or four 'persuaders' in the group. These individuals make over 50 per cent of the affirmative statements during the deliberations. They tend to be the ones who build coalitions among themselves and are responsible for most of the introduction of new issues for the jury's consideration. Thus, although there might be one 'fore-person', the focal discussions are divided amongst the three or four persuaders. When a foreperson is ineffective in handling the organization of the deliber-ations, a secondary foreperson tends to emerge informally from among the 'persuaders' and take on the role of the foreperson, without ever actually being identified as such.

Six to eight individuals tend to be active and participate in most of the discussions, but they usually contribute opinions in response to statements made by the 'persuaders'. Therefore the majority tend to be 'joiners' who will follow and support others but who generally will not tend to build coalitions themselves.

Finally, there are usually three or four individuals known as 'non-participants'. These people are usually somewhat uninterested or reluctant to be on the jury, and/or are uncomfortable speaking up. Often their primary concerns are with getting to a verdict as quickly as possible. Consequently they are likely to ask, 'How long is this going to take?' and to say 'If you need another vote to get a majority, you can count me in.' These less-active jurors are more likely to accept arguments contrary to their initial position, but it would be wrong to regard them as completely passive or unquestioningly acquiescent. Juries can only come to an agreed verdict if people are willing to change their position, and less-vocal individuals who are more willing to shift from their original assessment provide role models for others to do likewise. There is a great deal of comprom-ising in the jury deliberation room. For example, in a civil action involving libel there may be a few individuals who strongly believe that the defendant is probably not guilty, but they are persuaded by their colleagues to vote other-wise. If the jury has a role in determining damages against the person, as they do in some jurisdictions, those who pressed jury members to vote for liability will often make some accommodation to those who voted against it during the damages discussion. The negative impact of the votes on liability are accounted for in reduced damages.

One of the most important practical questions raised by the operation of the criminal justice system is whether the remedies handed down are effective in reducing re-offending. There are four primary considerations when offenders are sentenced by the courts: protection of members of the public from the threat posed by the offender, rehabilitation, punishment and deterrence. Applying psychology to each of these considerations typically involves the classification of offenders into different risk groups, the development of treatment or intervention programmes designed to reduce the risk of repeat offending, and researching and evaluating what does and does not work.

Classification

Systems for classifying offenders have a number of important functions. First, they challenge the popular stereotype of prisons as filled with like-minded people. Second, they help prison managers to place offenders in the most appropriate part of the prison. Third, they help in making predictions about recidivism and can inform the decisions of parole boards. Many classification schemes have been proposed but their implementation has been limited and somewhat haphazard. The Adult Internal Management Systems (AIMS) illustrates what classification systems attempt to achieve (Quay, 1984). This system divides inmates into five groups:

Group 1 Prisoners with a history of aggressive and sometimes violent behaviour or who are currently exhibiting such behaviours. These people are most likely to pose the greatest threat to other prisoners and to staffs.

Group 2 These prisoners tend to be as aggressive as Group 1 and in addition are particularly effective manipulators of other prisoners and of staff.

Group 3 These offenders do not have an extended criminal history and are generally those the staff can rely on. They can include people who have murdered a spouse or partner and do not pose a threat to anyone else.

Group 4 This comprises prisoners who are withdrawn, unhappy, unreliable, complaining and 'whiny'. They are easily victimized by other prisoners and may be at increased risk of self-harm and suicide.

Group 5 This group consists of offenders who are depressed, anxious, easily upset, and socially or personally maladjusted. As such they are easily bullied by others and are at increased risk of self-harm and suicide.

Currently available classification systems have the potential to become very powerful tools for decision-making, but their rapid proliferation has made it difficult to conduct empirically sound comparative evaluations of their validity and reliability. Many of the systems are not theoretically sophisticated; they may recognize that the effect of a prison environment may cause many offenders to move from one group to another, but they do not indicate what kinds of movement are desirable.

Treatment and intervention programmes

A quarter of a century ago Carlson concluded that rehabilitation using psychological interventions 'is out of fashion. It is not dead yet, but the literature is littered with death warrants' (Carlson, 1976). One of the reasons for this pessimistic conclusion was the fact that early efforts by psychologists were not sufficiently attentive to the concept of treatment differential. To be maximally effective, any treatment-rehabilitation intervention should be formulated in relation to the needs and capabilities of each person. Therefore, when assessing the effectiveness of any intervention one should not ask 'What works? but 'What works for whom?' Later evaluations of intervention programmes have been more up-beat (Andrews *et al.*, 1990) and have found that effective interventions were usually multidisciplinary in nature: they included a substantial psychological component in addition to elements from social workers, psychiatrists, probation officers and others as appropriate to the needs of the offender. Andrews *et al.* found the most effective interventions to

- be well-structured and focused on changing particular behaviours, such as improved management of anger;
- have enthusiastic staff who work with offenders in a firm but fair manner;
- match the content of the intervention to the needs and characteristics of the offender;
- focus on prisoners with a medium- to high-risk of re-offending;
- aim to generalize beyond the prison setting, for example by targeting enduring attitudes and values that tend to encourage offending behaviour; and
- use problem-solving techniques based on well-established cognitive and social learning principles.

Interventions are likely to be ineffective if they gradually shift away from their original aims; when staff inadvertently use inappropriate behaviours such as becoming hostile when attempting to help offenders improve their anger management skills, or when practitioners start to change the intervention by adding new techniques, modifying targets, and so on.

Effectiveness of interventions

Society has long presumed that punishment and deterrence are very closely linked. Punishment is thought to work in two ways. First, the threat or fear of punishment is thought to act as a potent deterrent. Punishment does act in this way for some individuals and for some crimes but the effect is complex. Debates about the effectiveness of the death penalty as a deterrent to murder often include the observation that someone who is intent on murdering another person will rarely allow the nature of the punishment to deflect them from their objective. Second, punishment applied to the offender will discourage them from repeating the offence in the future. Once again the effect of punishment is complex, partly because prisons and other kinds of detention centres are populated with people who have committed similar offences and the negative influences associated with living with large numbers of other offenders may outweigh the effects of the intended punishment.

The way forward

Much of what has been written by psychologists on the relationship between psychology and law has implicitly adopted an attitude in which psychological theories, principles and techniques are regarded as being in the service of, and contributing to, a fairer and more effective legal system. Psychologists, there-fore, have been criticized for tacitly promulgating the idea that the causes of crime reside in the disturbed minds of a minority of society and for suggesting that psychological concepts and labels can explain the causes of crime. Such an approach could be caricatured as the 'bad apple' theory of crime: if only the bad apples (offenders) could be distinguished from the 'good apples', by identifying the telltale psychological signs that lead to criminal behaviour, they could be given appropriate therapy at an early stage. This focus on individual behaviour tends not to recognize the significant role which social factors can play in shaping individual lifestyles. The latter approach argues we should be less concerned with identifying bad apples and focus greater atten-tion on effects of rotten barrels – the social factors.

Psychologists have also been criticized for adopting a rather naïve view of trial proceedings as fact-finding exercises. Much of what goes on in criminal proceedings bears a superficial resemblance to the way psychologists design studies to explore and test principles of human behaviour. However, the legal trial is not a fact-finding exercise but rather a forum for resolving disagreements on those facts that are disputed. In this respect the legal system is an institution designed to regulate social behaviour and as such it reflects the prevailing values of the culture and society of which it is a product. For example, until recently there was an irrefutable presumption in English law that boys under the age of 14 could not have sexual intercourse and therefore could not commit rape. It was many years before that rule was regarded as absurd and it was only abolished by the Sexual Offences Act 1993. Other equally absurd rules persist: in law a woman cannot commit rape. So, for example, Rosemary West, the wife of the alleged serial killer Frederick West, could not be charged with rape, only with aiding and abetting Frederick West's rape of young girls.

Psychology and law share common interests in the way people behave and the factors that influence their behaviour. However, the legal profession has often doubted the potential value of psychological ideas and evidence. The origins of these concerns lie in differences in the fundamental premises on which psychology and the law operate. The serious pursuit of psychology involves a commitment to scientific method, which involves accepting:

- Nature, including human behaviour, is orderly and regular.
- We can understand nature, and human behaviour as part of nature.
- Nothing in nature, or in human behaviour, should be taken as self-evident.
- Knowledge is acquired from experience.

Psychology places considerable value on a generic approach to investigating and explaining human behaviour based on formulating hypotheses, developing appropriate research designs, using valid and reliable measures, collecting and analysing data in ways that can be easily replicated and in developing empirically-based general statements about human behaviour. The legal system, by contrast, assumes that certain basic truths can be taken as self-evident. Anglo-American law on evidence has its roots in English post-Enlightenment thought. This is based on a correspondence theory of truth – events and states of affairs are regarded as having an existence independently of human observation, and true statements are statements that correspond to the true facts. Thus, according to the 'opinion rule' witnesses are required to state facts, not offer opinions. The 'hearsay rule' prevents witnesses from reporting statements that do not correspond to their direct experience of the facts.

One of the larger implications of this view of truth and reality is that, as noted earlier, the courts tend to regard memory as broadly analogous to the operation of a video camera, so that being an accurate witness is taken to involve an ability to retrieve a relevant memory and 'play back' its contents to the court. Consequently, inaccuracies in testimony are often attributed to witness bias rather than normal imperfections in the way human perception, memory and recall functions. Witnesses whose testimony is tested under cross-examination are often surprised that relatively little attention is given to an assessment of the details of their memories in favour of an investigation of their attitudes, values and beliefs. This is illustrated in the following exchange:

> Barrister: 'At what time did you notice the defendant was Chinese?'
> Witness: 'As soon as he walked in the restaurant'.
> Barrister: 'So you felt that the defendant's race was so significant that you noticed it "as soon as he walked in the restaurant"'?

The Barrister might continue with a line of questioning designed to cast doubt on the impartiality of the witness, who may harbour racist attitudes, rather than the liability of human perception and memory to error.

The concern of psychologists with developing and testing general statements or laws of human behaviour contrasts with the interest of the courts in establishing specific explanations for particular actions performed by named individuals at an exact point in time. The courts would find it enormously helpful if it could be shown that psychologists' pronouncements on human behaviour are so robust that they can be confidently applied to every individual. Indeed, psychologists can sometimes proffer evidence on the limits of human performance with this degree of precision. For example, Haward (1979) showed that a police officer who was said to have recorded the registration numbers of four speeding motorcycles could not have done so under the light and weather conditions prevailing at the time. It is more common for psychologists to find that they can fulfil an actuarial role by offering probabilistic assessments of the links between psychological variables. For instance, where an elderly person claims the allegations of theft against them are false because they have Alzheimer's disease, psychologists may work with neurologists to offer the courts information on the degree of neurological damage and its likely impact on cognitive functioning.

Although the courts are hesitant about introducing psychological testimony, they do not single out the discipline of psychology for special treatment. The courts are not closed to the contributions of any discipline but they do need to be assured that the evidence which is introduced is well-established and not founded on novel research findings that may subsequently be shown to be wrong. It is these concerns that have led some legal experts to conclude that psychiatry and psychology are not yet 'true sciences', and that the 'institution of justice is too important and too fragile to be rented out to evolving technology or quasi-science that captures the popular imagination' (Robinson, 1980).

SHORT QUESTIONS

1 Are official statistics reliable indicators of the true level of crime?
2 Does punishment reduce crime rates?
3 To what extent do the McNaughten rules reflect contemporary ideas and evidence on the nature of psychological well-being?
4 From your knowledge of the psychological processes involved in eyewitness testimony, how would you plan a robbery in such a way as to minimize the likelihood of being accurately identified at a later time?
5 Are systems for classifying offenders of any value?

CLASS ACTIVITIES

1 The Eyewitness Quiz: How did you get on? Psychological research suggests that every one of the statements is actually false! Compare your responses with others in the class and discuss the consequences for the legal system.
2 The following is a modified version of the scenario described at the beginning of this chapter:

> On a wet and dull November afternoon you are driving to an important class that you cannot afford to miss. Ordinarily you are a safe and conscientious road user. However, on this occasion you decide to 'run the lights'. You slip through a red light unnoticed, no one is hurt and you arrive to your class on time. Would you regard your behaviour as criminal, selfish and reckless?
>
> In all likelihood you will have judged your own behaviour – your response to the scenario at the start of this chapter – slightly more leniently. The difference between the two scenarios reflects an attributional bias that people are prone to make. When we see antisocial behaviour in others we tend to judge it more negatively than when we perform the same behaviour ourselves. You can explore this further by reproducing the two scenarios and giving them to different samples of individuals and comparing the judgements they offer.

3   It is possible to create a simulated jury relatively easy. Assemble a group of 10 to 12 fellow students. Your task is to hold a discussion on the probable state of mind of the people who steered the two jets into the World Trade Centre on 11 September 2001. You should try to come to an agreement as to whether or not those people were 'guilty but insane'.

========= **FURTHER READING** =========

Ainsworth, P.B. (2000) *Psychology and Crime: Myth and Reality*. Harlow: Longman.

Harrower, J. (1998) *Applying Psychology to Crime*. London: Hodder & Stoughton.

Hawkins, J.D. (1996) *Delinquency and Crime: Current Theories*. Cambridge: Cambridge University Press.

Loftus, E.F. (1996) *Eyewitness Testimony*. Cambridge, MA: Harvard University Press.

Walklate, S. (1995) *Gender and Crime: An Introduction*. London: Prentice Hall.

Sport and Exercise

10

There's a breathless hush in the Close tonight –
Ten to make and the match to win –
A bumping pitch and a blinding light,
An hour to play and the last man in.
And it's not for the sake of a ribboned coat,
Or the selfish hope of a season's fame,
But his captain's hand on his shoulder smote –
'Play up! play up! and play the game.'

(Sir Henry Newbolt, 1897)

ONCE UPON A TIME...

Before coming to university Rachel had been a keen sportsperson, and had represented both her school and her county at hockey. In particular, Rachel had always enjoyed the social aspects of team sport, with many of her close friends also her teammates. As she became more involved in competitive sport her parents and especially her father began to show more and more interest, often travelling long distances to see her play and to run Rachel to her practices. Although she could not understand why, Rachel never seemed to play as well when her parents were watching and especially when playing in important competitions. When she went to college Rachel joined the hockey club and attended the team trials although she found it difficult to get on with other players whom she felt were unduly competitive. Rachel decided not to play hockey any more but instead spent her spare time with her friends who

---

ONCE UPON A TIME... (cont'd)

were not involved with organized sport. In her second year she heard of
a local sponsored half-marathon run and decided to train for the event with
a close friend. She now runs and swims regularly but is not involved with any
organized sport, much to the disappointment of her father.

Introduction

Sir Henry Newbolt may never have dreamt of a day when sport psychologists would advise cricketers on the significance of intrinsic motivation,
and Rachel may never have realized how her over-zealous parents could
heighten her fear of failure and affect her enjoyment of hockey, but without
doubt sport presents a fascinating arena where psychological principles are at
work daily, as this chapter hopes to illustrate with particular reference to social
psychology.

For those readers who are unfamiliar with sport and exercise psychology,
don't worry – you are not alone. Applied psychology presents itself as a very
varied landscape. On the one hand there are examples of applied areas, most
notably clinical, educational and occupational psychology, which occupy a
central role within the discipline as a whole. On the other hand there are
applied topics which are regarded as more peripheral, and sport and exercise
psychology certainly falls within this latter category. The history of sport and
exercise psychology, and the background of many people who call themselves
sport psychologists, have marked it as outside mainstream psychology and yet
there is no logical reason why this has to be the case (Kremer and Scully,
1994). In recent years there have been increasing efforts to bridge the gap
between sport and exercise psychology and the rest of the discipline (Kremer
and Lavallee, 2002), but it would still be true that most undergraduate courses
in psychology do not include modules dealing with this field. Sport and
exercise play such a significant role in so many people's lives, whether as
participants or spectators, that this omission seems strange. What is more,
much of this activity is social by nature and so the scope for applying social
psychology is immense.

It is a good starting point that the focus of sport and exercise psychology
has traditionally fallen on applied issues. Typically these include topics geared
towards performance enhancement such as imagery and mental rehearsal,

stress management, attention and concentration, participation motivation, exercise and psychological well-being and team processes. While social psychological themes do appear in this list, it is estimated that around 90 per cent of all research in sport psychology continues to centre on aspects of individual performance. This chapter will not follow this trend but instead focus attention on those areas where social psychological perspectives have, and can, further our understanding of behaviour and experience in sport. Topics including participation motivation, social influence, team dynamics, leadership, crowd behaviour and aggression will be highlighted, before moving on to use this particular domain to consider a number of issues associated with practical interventions. This last section focuses on pratical interventions in the world of sport but several of the concerns would apply equally to most other applied areas where theory is being put into practice through direct contact with clients.

History and development

Social psychologists have shown an interest in sport for many decades, indeed as far back as the last years of the nineteenth century. Over the following 60 years while a number of social issues were explored in sporting contexts (including crowd behaviour and social facilitation), in common with social psychology at the time most attention focused not on social processes *per se* but on the individual and especially on performance enhancement. In line with this orientation, the first text on sport psychology appeared in 1926, dealing with principles for successful coaching (*The Psychology of Coaching*). The author, Dr Coleman Griffith, had originally worked as an educational psychologist at the University of Illinois but he then became increasingly interested in sport psychology and subsequently went on to have a profound influence on the development of the subdiscipline. Coleman Griffith was also instrumental in establishing the first sport psychology laboratory where he investigated a wide range of pure and applied topics throughout the 1920s, but again with a primary focus on the individual in sport.

Unfortunately, Griffith was unable to sustain his laboratory through hard economic times in the 1920s, and with no funding forthcoming he eventually turned his considerable energies back towards educational psychology. It was not for over 30 years, and in particular with the growth of sport science in the 1960s, that sport psychology finally came of age as a subdiscipline. At this time the main topics in sport psychology became established and within this list social psychological themes did appear although not as primary concerns in terms of applied work.

Interestingly, since the 1960s the researchers who have been most active in developing sport and exercise psychology have usually come from backgrounds outside psychology, most especially including physical education and sport science. Yet again their primary focus has often been the individual in the sporting context rather than social processes and sport, a domain dominated by sport sociologists. Although many practising sport psychologists may not regard psychology as their parent discipline, they have not been shy of applying existing psychological models and theories to the world of sport including those emanating from social psychology. Within mainstream psychology their contribution to the common stock of psychological knowledge has not always received the recognition which it has deserved, and sport psychology has continued to grow at some distance apart. This has not always fostered a healthy interchange of ideas but, despite its exclusion from the mainstream, sport psychology continues to thrive as an applied science, driven by market demand and responding to issues which present themselves as athletes and teams constantly strive to gain the wining edge.

Contemporary priorities

Until relatively recently attention fell on a small number of topics with a social psychological dimension where very often these topics were seen as discrete issues or problems. Over the last decade this approach has started to change as researchers have cast their nets wider across the social psychological literature, thereby placing greater emphasis on the interactions between topics, on the development of multidimensional constructs, and on the central role played by social context. By way of example, recently sport and exercise scientists have presented a number of comprehensive, multidimensional and integrative models of participation motivation (Busby, 1997), self-efficacy (Feltz, 1992), anxiety (Hardy, 1996), leadership (Riemer and Chelladurai, 1995) and exercise behaviour change (Kimiecik and Lawson, 1996). These models would sit easily alongside many other contemporary approaches in social psychology which likewise highlight the multivariate determinants of our social behaviour. Alongside the development of these models, applied sport and exercise psychology has become increasingly sophisticated in its *modus operandi* (see for example Butler, 1997; Hardy, Jones and Gould, 1998). Taken together, both these developments reflect well on the growing maturity of the subdiscipline and an awareness that simple answers will not suffice to explain complex social phenomenon which happen to be associated with sport and exercise.

In conjunction with these developments, research methodologies have become less hidebound than previously (Duda, 1998), again mirroring changes across social psychology. Earlier sterile debates as to the pros and cons of quantitative vs qualitative techniques have been replaced by an acceptance (albeit reluctant in some quarters) that qualitative methods must enjoy parity of esteem with quantitative procedures (Strean, 1998). At the same time it is hardly surprising that traditional quantitative methods still hold centre-stage. As one index of the attention still afforded to quantification, it is estimated that over 350 psychometric instruments have been specifically designed or adapted to measure behaviour and cognition in sport and exercise settings (Duda, 1998).

Concepts, models and theories

Concept of the person and models of behaviour

Over its long history it would be fair to say that sport and exercise psychology has tended to adopt a pragmatic approach to issues, using practical tools to deal with real-life concerns and not always showing concern with underlying or implicit concepts of the person. Reductionist approaches (that is, taking small aspects of behaviour and looking at each aspect in isolation) have tended to dominate in this research environment. As a consequence, overarching models of the person in sport have been rather thin on the ground. In terms of individual differences in sport, without doubt the trait approach, as associated with writers such as Hans Eysenck and Raymond Cattell, has dominated the literature. This approach is based on the belief that our personality can be defined by a finite number of stable psychological traits. Working from this perspective sport psychologists have spent a great deal of time trying to identify characteristics of those who win and lose, play sport, play different sports or play in different positions. A number of reviews of this work all indicate that we are still no closer to defining the characteristics of either a sportsperson or a 'champion', and that winners are probably more similar to losers psychologically than they are different. With this in mind, if you reflect on the champions in your favourite sport you will probably find it difficult to identify any one personality 'type'. Instead sport is for all, it embraces a wide range of personality types and what is more it is often associated with personality change or development. More generally this perspective illustrates how sport psychology would still be comfortable with a positivist and deterministic view of science, and where the traumas of social psychology's 'crisis', as described in Chapter 1, would not have made a significant impact.

Gender

One aspect of difference has preoccupied sport psychology, gender. Sport continues to be deeply divided by gender and so this interest is very understandable. To begin, by definition sport involves competition and all that goes with competitive behaviour including dominance and aggression. As a consequence sport can be characterized as masculine. In the numerous debates about gender and sport, our biological sex (man; woman) has been found to be less important than our gender or psychological sex (male; female) or, more precisely, our sex-role orientation (masculine; feminine). According to writers such as Sandra Bem (1993) each of us, men and women alike, have two dimensions to our personality, the masculine and the feminine. Contrary to popular belief, these are not inversely related or opposite but are actually independent dimensions. Accordingly men and women can be categorized as either masculine (low feminine; high masculine), feminine (high feminine; low masculine), androgynous (high feminine; high masculine) or undifferentiated (low feminine; low masculine). Within mainstream social psychology, Bem and others have moved away from simply categorizing and instead have developed interactive models of gender beliefs and behaviours within immediate social contexts, arguing that individuals with high scores on either masculinity or femininity are more likely to develop cognitive schemata (that is, ways of interpreting the world) which incorporate a gender component.

Looking at the application of this work to sport, gender schemata may influence the individual's willingness to take up certain sports or to sex-type sports in general. One influential sport psychologist, Diane Gill (1994), has suggested that the gender-schematic processing of adults may be vitally important in influencing the behaviour of young people involved in sport and exercise. In support of her ideas, a number of research studies have indicated that by early adolescence girls have learned that engaging in contact sports can jeopardize their self-image or even popularity as a female, and therefore sport assumes a lower priority in their lives. Other research confirms that despite early interest (typically to the age of 11 years), girls become less and less interested in sport as they move through adolescence while, in contrast, boys' enthusiasm continues to grow (Kremer, Trew and Ogle, 1997).

As with all work dealing with gender relations it is dangerous to rely too heavily on interpretations from the past and including the very recent past. Women in the twenty-first century enjoy greater freedom to experience multiple roles and to make choices about lifestyles. It is argued that the traditional stereotype of the woman as carer, homemaker and provider is being replaced by the 'superwoman ideal' (being all things to all people), especially among young women. As gender stereotypes and sex roles continue to change so rapidly it is argued that both the biological and physical aspects of sport must be considered as part of a social dynamic. The changing gender profiles of the clientele of gyms and leisure centres is one obvious example – even 10 years ago it would have been exceptional to see women in a weights or fitness gym while now women are frequently in the majority. With such trends in mind it is important that the complex interaction of a great many physical, psychological and social variables is incorporated into what Gill describes as *biopsychosocial* models of physical activity and gender. Once more, the picture which emerges here is one of increasing sophistication and complexity and mirrors wider developments across applied social psychology.

Cognitive and affective factors

Sport psychology has long had an interest in social cognition, including how we interpret or perceive our sporting worlds (including winning and losing), how we are motivated to take part in sport and what we derive from our experiences in sport. Some of this work considers personality types in relation to motivation (specifically achievement motivation); other research deals with how we cope with success and failure (causal attribution); and a third branch considers participation motivation, including the factors which influence take-up, continuance and drop-out from sport. Each are interesting illustrations of how social psychological principles have been borrowed or adapted to address important applied concerns, but once more points to the somewhat narrow focus of interest on topics which are of immediate concern to sport and sporting success.

Achievement motivation

From the 1960s, McClelland and Atkinson's work on achievement motivation has been applied in the context of competitive sport, first and foremost because of its perceived practical utility. Their model predicts that in order to be motivated to achieve, in sport as in other life domains, our motive for success or 'need to achieve (Nach) must be higher than our motive to avoid failure or 'fear of failure' (FF). The McClelland–Atkinson model also describes how these motives combine with contextual variables in arousing affective states which in turn dictate approach or avoidance behaviours. Specifically it is predicted that high achievers in sport (those who strive for success and yet do not fear failure – high Nach, low FF) will be drawn towards competition and difficult yet realizable challenges, whereas low achievers (for example high Nach, high FF) will avoid personal challenges, for example by only playing weaker opponents or setting unattainable and hence non-threatening goals. Although considerable work continues to be conducted within the McClelland–Atkinson tradition, the empirical research within sport has generally been inconclusive (Roberts, 1992). Nevertheless the model may still be useful in helping predict long-term patterns of motivation (Cox, 1998) or as a diagnostic tool to be used by applied sport psychologists working with clients. Here the theory has survived almost irrespective of its validation because those in the field continue to recognize its heuristic value, helping explain and understand practical problems.

Participation motivation

Across social psychology as a whole the study of motivation changed significantly with the development of social cognitive paradigms during the 1970s. Effectively, these switched attention from the 'what' or content of motivation to the 'why' or process whereby we are or are not motivated. Within sport and exercise psychology, Weiner's (1986) attribution model quickly rose to prominence at this time, focusing attention on a relatively small issue but one which is hugely important in sport, the explanations which people associate with success and failure. The four main attribution elements in the model are labelled ability, effort, task and luck, and these reflect on the combination of three primary attribution constructs, internal/external, stable/unstable and controllable/uncontrollable. In particular, it has been suggested that the feelings associated with external or internal attributions and the expectancy of future success or failure will be reflected in achievement behaviours (Biddle, 1993). As an example, research has shown that successful performance in sport is more likely to be attributed to stable, internal factors (such as ability), and most especially in sports involving interacting teams and where the attributions relate to team performance. However, there is little support for the prediction that failure will tend to be attributed to external factors (task difficulty or luck).

Within social psychology and sport psychology alike, research interest in attribution theory waned during the 1990s. It was labelled as a nomothetic approach which could operate at the level of generality but had little to say of individual experience or behaviour in particular contexts. In sport, repeated criticisms at that time suggested that what was needed was a comprehensive model of motivation which would consider the bringing together or conceptual convergence between attribution processes and related constructs (Biddle, 1999), and which would then help understand how each individual athlete attributed their performances to different factors. Here is one example of an approach which at a theoretical level could offer some insight but which at a practical level was unable to come to terms with understanding large individual differences and with the influence of changing social contexts.

Over time a steady stream of research has tried to identify the psychological and structural factors which significantly influence initiating, continuing and discontinuing sport and exercise (Cavill, Biddle and Sallis, 2001). A considerable body of evidence now shows that a number of constructs do relate to participation motivation, and these constructs now constitute the bedrock or 'content' on which more recent dynamic 'process' models of participation build. The most important content factors have been identified as perceived competence, self-efficacy, goal orientation, affect, enjoyment, structural barriers, health concerns and significant others. In applied contexts research consistently indicates that attaching importance to intrinsic motives (for example feeling good, enhancing self-esteem) can be predictive of long-term adherence to sport and exercise programmes whereas those who continue to reference extrinsic motives (such as significant others, tangible rewards) are more likely to withdraw from sport (Ryan et al., 1997). Recently, considerable attention has been placed on one particular construct, labelled goal orientation, arguing that motives for participation are primarily a function of this orientation (White and Duda, 1994). Specifically, it is suggested that those identified as task-oriented will participate for reasons linked to skill development, skill mastery, affiliation and fitness (and in turn are likely to continue to be active), while those with an ego orientation tend to mention motives such as social status and recognition (and hence are more prone to dropout). Recent research continues to explore the relationship between goal orientation and participation by modelling the influence of goal orientations on intentions and perceived competence (Wang and Biddle, 2000), but whether these orientations tell the whole story of participation motivation is debatable.

Of the various models which have attempted to bring together or integrate existing research, Weiss and Chaumeton's Motivational Orientation Model (1992) is interesting. Employing a social cognitive approach, the model outlines how personal, social and contextual factors interact to determine an individual's predisposition towards participation. As its name reveals, the model deals primarily with our psychological orientation towards physical activity. While this focus is important it should not detract attention from other structural or social factors (including barriers to participation, social context and social support, individual differences, activity history, self-efficacy, perceived intrinsic and extrinsic rewards, competence, self-esteem and equity). With this in mind, and based more explicitly on expectancy models of work motivation (see Chapter 3), Kremer and Busby (1998) have attempted to demonstrate how all these factors may combine to determine different patterns of behaviour, ranging from complete withdrawal from all physical activities to changes in type of activity and routine continuance. The model reflects a cognitive-behavioural process which leads sequentially from predisposition and decision-making through to participation, evaluation and finally commitment to future action (see Figure 10.1). The model implicitly recognizes that our behaviour is influenced by a whole host of personal, social and structural factors and, what is more, their relative importance will change over time. Although the model is yet to be tested in its entirety, early indications suggest it may help understand the diverse motivational responses to sport and exercise by providing a model which can accommodate large individual differences and priorities.

Social facilitation

The literature dealing with social influence in sport stretches back to 1898 when an American psychologist and amateur cyclist called Norman Triplett carried out a piece of archival research using official cycling records he obtained from the Racing Board of the League of American Wheelmen to compare the times of cyclists training either alone, with others or in competition. The records revealed that those in company consistently rode faster, and those in competition had the fastest times of all. Dynamogism (as he described it), or social facilitation (as it came to be known), is the process whereby the presence of others leads to enhanced performance on certain tasks (that is, well-learnt, dominant responses) but impairs performance on novel tasks (that is, non-dominant responses) and is a topic which appears prominently in almost all social psychology texts, whether pure or applied. The phenomenon has generated scores of experiments over the decades, both laboratory and field-based, and emerges from this examination with a clean bill of health as a robust social phenomenon. As one example, in 1982 Michaels and his co-workers set up an ingenious field experiment in a pool hall in the US. Players were secretly rated as being above or below average ability on the basis of the percentage of successful shots. Subsequently, groups of four people stood by the tables to see how their presence influenced performance. In the presence of spectators, players of above average ability increased their shot accuracy from 71 per cent to 80 per cent, while the below-average players slipped from 36 per cent to 25 per cent (Michaels *et al.*, 1982). The good became better, the bad became worse, social facilitation in action.

Traditionally, one theory was used to explain such findings – Zajonc's (1965) drive theory. The theory posits that the mere presence of others increases

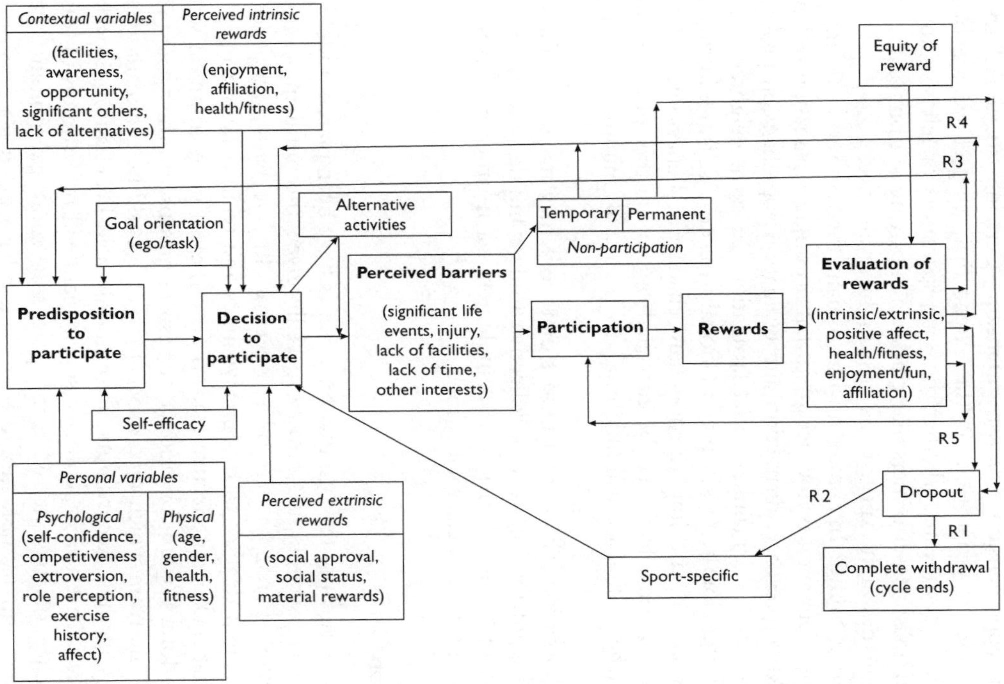

Notes: The influence of each variable may change as the cycle continues and exercise may take on a momentum of its own as certain intrinsic rewards take on greater significance.

Figure 10.1 A cognitive-behavioural process model of participation motivation in sport and exercise

arousal which in turn causes either social facilitation with well-learned, dominant responses or social inhibition with novel, non-dominant responses. Later writers have disagreed as to why this effect occurs, some arguing that conflict of attention (between the task and those present) is paramount, while others say that evaluation apprehension is most significant. Certainly social facilitation effects do increase in proportion to the extent that we feel we are being evaluated by those around us, whether these are spectators or fellow competitors. Even accomplished performers may crack when playing in front of a crowd which they know has high expectations or is highly evaluative.

Which theory is 'right'? In common with so many theories which attempt to explain social phenomena it is now accepted that no single explanation will ever be sufficient. Mere presence, distraction and evaluation apprehension probably each play some part in explaining social facilitation. In turn, heightened self-awareness, self-consciousness, self-presentational concern, self-monitoring or self-attention may well be implicated in any change of behaviour. What is more, social facilitation effects may be cancelled out by another phenomenon, social loafing, where often we will hide in a group so as to minimize the effort we expend.

This is one occasion where each model or theory may make a useful and complementary contribution to our collective understanding, and is a good example of where 'mini-theories' can complement each other in explaining a 'macro' phenomenon, social facilitation.

Team cohesion

It will come as no surprise to learn that team issues have been placed under the spotlight by sport psychologists, most especially given the number of sports where individuals operate as part of a collective. In line with occupational psychology, research dealing with team dynamics and team cohesion in sport reveals that what makes an effective team is far removed from common sense or accepted wisdom. We are conditioned to respect groups and their decisions, to assume that the team which mixes socially together will be the team which plays and wins together. Accordingly, a commonly held belief among coaches and players alike is that a tight, cohesive sports team will be a successful team. As a consequence of these ideas, many practising sport psychologists still believe that their primary task should be to engender a good team spirit. In reality the answer is not so simple and there is now a good deal of research which has begun to help us unravel the complexities of the relationship between team cohesion and performance (Kremer and Scully, 2001). Here practice is beginning to inform theory.

The Canadian sport psychologist Albert Carron has made an important distinction between task cohesion (or group integration) which refers to how well the group or team operates as a working unit, and social cohesion (or individual attraction) which refers to how well members like each other and the extent of team identity. Research generally shows that successful performance does depend on task cohesion, but that social cohesion is far less important, and in addition the relationship between cohesion and performance hinges on context, including the type of sport being played.

The literature continues to struggle with the relationship between cohesion and performance, and especially causality. Does cohesion engender success or does success engender cohesion? A meta-analysis of this literature by Mullen and Cooper (1994) concluded that a cohesion–effectiveness relationship probably does exist, but the effect derives most significantly from task commitment or cohesion and not from social or interpersonal cohesion. The more that the sport requires that team members must rely on each other and are interdependent (*interactive sports*), then the more that cohesion is likely to be significant. In sports where athletes may represent the same team but individual performance does not depend on team work (*coacting sports*), then team cohesion may be less important in determining outcome. These results are important not only for sport but for other applied areas where groups feature and where cohesion may influence performance. This could be one example where sport psychology may be leading the pack in terms of genuinely understanding an applied social phenomenon.

Team maturity

Group or team development is a further issue where sport provides an ideal venue for analysis. Working from Tuckman's stage model of group development (where groups are described as moving through several stages – forming; storming; norming; performing – before operating effectively as a unit, Tuckman and Jensen, 1977), archival research using data derived from sports including soccer, baseball, basketball and gymnastics has demonstrated that team maturity is important in determining success and that player turnover rates and performance are negatively related to success. At the same time there are large differences between sports in terms of the time taken to reach maturity and then the 'shelf-life' of the team – the period for which a successful team is able to sustain a high level of performance and motivation. The effective 'shelf-life' of successful teams is likely to depend on many factors including the age and maturity of players, the type of sport and various facets of group dynamics including cohesiveness and role differentiation. Taken together these factors highlight not the commonalities but the idiosyncracies of groups and including their development, signalling yet again the need for applied social psychology to accommodate diversity.

Leadership

Leadership research in sport draws heavily on applied research derived from occupational psychology, focusing almost all attention on two practical sporting concerns – what defines a good captain and a good coach/manager. As in industry, applied sport research has long since recognized that the search for a unique leadership formula is futile; instead the task should be to determine the contingencies which come together to determine the 'who and when' of leadership effectiveness. The various contingency models described in Chapter 3 have each been applied in sports contexts, and in addition several sport-specific behavioural measures have been developed to evaluate coaches' effectiveness. From the late 1970s onwards sport-specific theories and models of leadership have been developed, including Chelladurai's Multidimensional Model of Leadership. In this model, the effectiveness of the leader is determined by two principal outcomes, how well athletes perform (the task dimension) and how satisfied they are with the process (the socio-emotional dimension). The three aspects of the leader's behaviour which interact to produce these outcomes are, first, the behaviour which is perceived by others to be required of a leader in these circumstances, second, the actual behaviour displayed by the leader, and third, the behaviour which is preferred by the athletes themselves. In turn, each of these is influenced by other factors. The behaviour required of the coach in any situation will depend on the sport itself, the goals of the organization and indeed the whole environment within which the sport exists. His or her actual behaviour as leader will depend on ability, knowledge and interpersonal skills, while his or her preferred behaviour reflects both characteristics of the members and the situation. To date, research, while limited, has been generally supportive of the model (Chelladurai, 2000), although the extent to which the model complements other approaches which identify particular functions of leadership has never been clarified.

Aggression

In social psychology generally, aggression is a topic which has generated considerable experimental research but debate continues to rage as to the practical application of this work, such as the effects of television violence on children's aggression (see Chapter 6). The literature on violence and aggression in sport has focused on two practical concerns, participant's aggression and spectator violence. In terms of the former, sport psychologists have tended to concentrate their attention on behaviour which deliberately and illegally causes physical injury to another competitor, thus highlighting not instrumental or rule-governed aggression but reactive or angry/hostile aggression. In terms of the latter, writers from a great many disciplines have each tried to explain why it should be that sport and fan violence so often go hand in hand.

To some writers, sport represents a cultivation or refinement of the aggressive instinct and, what is more, without sport our aggressive tendencies would probably be vented in other potentially more dangerous and life-threatening pursuits such as violent crime. The evidence to support this Freudian or psychoanalytic idea of catharsis is difficult to find, either with reference to spectators or participants. Instead sport psychology has considered either individual differences in reactive and instrumental aggression or how we are socialized to be aggressive in sport, along with the specific factors which influence displays of predominantly reactive aggression, reflecting an orientation towards quantification. A great many variables have been shown to be associated with an increase in reactive aggression among competitors. These include whether a team or competitor is losing, playing away from home, the distance from home, the type of sport, current values and norms in that particular sport, and the importance of the game to the individual. It is interesting that most research focuses on contact sports which already have some association with violence. High on this list are ice hockey and soccer, and the most common dependent variable which is measured (either through observation or archival research) is the number of fouls or rule infringements. Simple causal relationships are not easy to identify, although the rituals and culture traditionally associated with each sport certainly play a significant role in predetermining the prevalence of violence, alongside the nature of the activity itself and, most especially, physical contact.

As regards fan violence and aggression, sport sociologists and applied social psychologists have for long had an interest in this field, perhaps echoing the long history of hooliganism and fan violence in Europe and particularly England. To understand fan violence it is now accepted that there are no easy answers and no single discipline (or theory) will ever provide all the solutions. This represents a research area which is tailor-made for multidisciplinary research, and indeed there have been attempts to develop psychosocial models which draw on both sociological and psychological traditions and methodologies. Simons and Taylor (1992) have developed such a causal model, incorporating potentiating or general predisposing factors (including socioeconomic conditions, politics and geography, media influences and community norms), critical factors (social and personal identification, group solidarity, de-individuation, dehumanization of the opposition, leadership), on-field contributing factors (type of sport, modelling, score configuration and competitive events) and off-field contributing factors (alcohol, crowd density, frustration and role-modelling). This model incorporates a number of levels of analysis, ranging from the intrapersonal to the societal, and provides a valuable framework for understanding fan violence, demonstrating yet again the value of using a multidimensional approach in order to understand a complex social phenomenon.

Practical issues

As should be evident by now, almost all sport and exercise psychology focuses on practical issues. As should also be clear, psychologists often have been able to help provide sensible and practical solutions for those involved with sport. As one example, in the wake of two catastrophic disasters at soccer games in England (the Hillsborough Stadium stampede in Sheffield on April 15th, 1989, and the fire at Bradford City FC on May 11th, 1985) a major review of safety in sports stadia was undertaken across the UK (known as the Popplewell Inquiry). In the course of this enquiry, applied social psychologists such as David Canter played a significant role in presenting solutions to issues such as the design of exits and seating arrangement (Canter *et al.*, 1989).

This is one example where psychological theory and practice were able to sit easily side by side. Unfortunately the history of sport psychology reveals that the relationship between pure and applied sport psychology has not always been so harmonious, and especially in terms of direct interventions with athletes and teams. On the one hand there are sport psychologists who work in academic settings and who endeavour to develop theories and models which can be applied to the world of sport. On the other hand there are those who regard themselves principally as practitioners whose work is geared towards maximizing the potential of the sportspeople that they advise. The links between these two groups have not always been strong, with practice not always well-informed by theory. As a consequence a number of issues continue to bedevil the delivery or application of sport psychology, as the following sections should reveal. While these issues are often sport-related, the underlying concerns can be read across to many other fields where psychologists apply their work to practical interventions.

Ethics

The idiosyncratic history of sport psychology (Williams and Straub, 1998) has reflected in something of an identity or loyalty crisis among applied sport psychologists. On the one hand there are those who regard themselves primarily as sport scientists but with a specialty in psychology. On the other hand are those who either define themselves as psychologists but who focus their attentions on the world of sport or, far more specifically, clinical/educational psychologists whose clients are athletes. As a consequence of these divided loyalties the professional allegiances of applied sport psychologists do not always coincide and this has led to a degree of confusion as to which professional standards should govern the work.

In the USA, the American Psychological Association's (1992) revised Ethical Standards have been adopted by the two organizations which oversee the work of sport psychologists, the North American Society for the Psychology of Sport and Physical Activity (NASPSPA) and the Association for the Advancement of Applied Sport Psychology (AAASP). This is despite the fact that many of their members may not belong to the APA nor would describe themselves as psychologists. The APA ethical guidelines make reference to 10 principles which are all likely to be relevant to the work of an applied sport psychologist – namely responsibility, competence, moral and legal standards, public statements, confidentiality, welfare of the consumer, professional relationships, assessment techniques and research with human participants (with care and use of animals only relevant in certain cases!). The legal status of these guidelines is not absolutely clear although, as Sachs points out (2000, p. 922), the APA state that the principles should apply to 'psychologists, students of psychology, and to others who do work of a psychological nature under the supervision of a psychologist', and are 'intended for the guidance of non-members of the association who are engaged in psychological research or practice'.

Within the UK, the picture is even less clear. On the one hand, in 1988 the British Association of Sport and Exercise Sciences (BASES; formerly BASS) was instrumental in developing a Code of Conduct for sport psychologists (Biddle, Bull and Seheult, 1992). The Code was introduced in conjunction with the development of a register of accredited sport psychologists and contains 29 statements under five headings: competence, consent and confidentiality, psychological testing, research ethics and personal conduct. On the other hand, under the terms of its Royal Charter the British Psychological

Society (BPS) maintains a code of conduct for *all* its members and for the practice of psychology in the UK. The latest version of the BPS Code of Conduct, Ethical Procedures and Guidelines (BPS, 2000) includes a code of conduct for UK psychologists under the headings: general competence, obtaining consent, confidentiality and personal conduct. Since the late 1980s, BASES and the BPS have continued to engage in a dialogue about the governance of sport psychology and although these discussions continue it is still not clear which code, if any, enjoys primacy among practising sport psychologists. However, for practising psychologists in general the BPS code should always be borne in mind. These ongoing discussions continue to highlight a very significant issue for applied psychology, the regulation of practice – is it sensible to allow market forces to operate, or should professional bodies exercise tight control over those who describe themselves as applied psychologists? The debate continues.

Confidentiality and allegiance

While general ethical principles are routinely cited in the sport psychology literature, there is also an awareness that there are special concerns unique to the role of a practising sport psychologist, whether in the role of counsellor or supervisor (Sachs, 2000). In the words of Sachs (2000):

> The duty of psychologists is towards their client first and foremost. However, in some sports settings the 'client' is not necessarily an individual. It is one thing to be in private practice and have Jane Athlete present with a problem about performance anxiety or an eating disorder, for example. It is another thing to be employed by the New York Knickerbockers and have Joe Athlete come in and discuss some basketball related or other concerns. In the latter case, under what conditions does the practitioner have an obligation to share some/all of the information with the coach/management of the team? (p. 923)

Competency

A further cluster of issues concerns competency, whether in terms of sport science, psychology or knowledge of the sport. In relation to psychological competence there is a serious danger that a sport psychologist may find him/ herself unwittingly crossing the boundaries of professional competency, in the process leaving the athlete and him/herself both extremely vulnerable (but for very different reasons). Heyman and Andersen (1998) suggest that three issues should typically trigger a referral process through to professionals with more specialist skills:

- The length of time a problem has existed, its severity and its relationship with other life events.
- Unusual emotional reactions (for example depression and anger).
- Lack of efficacy of traditional performance enhancement interventions.

The list of client issues which have the potential to become problematic is considerable, although the following are of special note for those without specialist training in counselling, psychotherapy or clinical psychology:

- Eating disorders.
- Drug and alcohol abuse.
- Psychopathology/personality disorders.
- Anger and aggression control.
- Identity issues and sense of self.
- Sexuality and sexual orientation.
- Relationship issues.

An applied psychologist, working in whatever field, must always recognize where the boundaries of professional competence lie. To overstep that mark may not only be harmful to the client, it may also make the practitioner vulnerable to a challenge of professional negligence.

Psychometric tests

The use of psychometric tests in applied sport psychology has attracted considerable attention over the years but with no consensus emerging, or ever likely to emerge, given the diversity of interventions which continue to characterize the field (Andersen, 2000). Perhaps unfortunately lay people often place uncritical faith in results obtained from these tests and hence the need for applied psychologists, in sport as elsewhere, to use tests sensibly and ethically is important. As with all applied areas, where psychological tests are employed then it is imperative that the measures are appropriate, that their psychometric properties (especially in relation to validity and reliability) are known, that they are used for the purpose and population for which they were designed and, in the case of sport psychology, that they are not used to inform selection procedures. Interpretation of the results and subsequent feedback must be appropriate and written consent should be obtained for the release of data.

Drugs, cheating and illegality

Finally, when a sport psychologist becomes aware that a client is using drugs or any illegal means to enhance performance, does this create an ethical dilemma? The answer is no, because it should simply mark an end to the intervention, not only because it may implicate the sport psychologist in an unlawful conspiracy, but also because such actions fly directly in the face of what the sport psychologist is trying to achieve – the fostering of self-control and self-determination and an attempt to maximize the athlete's 'true' potential (Kremer and Scully, 1998).

With all these caveats in mind, through direct interventions it is possible to observe theory in action, to identify which ingredients work and which are less successful. For any academic this type of work can be challenging, while for the discipline it is a challenge which is not only useful but crucial as the ultimate reality check. Too often in the past this has been a challenge which has been sidestepped.

The way forward

There has been a sea change in the relationship between sport and social psychology over the last few years. Sport psychology no longer unceremoniously borrows packaged ideas from social psychology in order to provide simple answers to complex social phenomena. Now the mood is shifting and, in common with social psychology as a whole, sport psychology is beginning to become more critical and self-reflective in recognition of the complexity of the social world with which it deals. Sport psychologists are now willing to recognize the need to develop research methodologies and theoretical frameworks which can cope with a higher level of sophistication. Whether this recognition will act as a spur to future generations of sport psychologists, or as a discouragement, only time will tell but at present the signs are encouraging.

Inevitably, it has only been possible to scratch the surface here, but we hope that it is now obvious not only how much relevant research already exists in key areas, but also the scope for development in others. Many sport psychologists pepper their work with pleas for more theory, and undoubtedly in certain areas the lack of adequate frameworks for understanding have certainly hindered progress. The varied work on social influence is a case in point. At the same time, this plea should not be a naive cry for some ready-made theoretical panacea awaiting to cure all ills. This approach fails to recognize the role of theory in social psychology, and the fundamental nature of social psychological enquiry. In the past, many cures have been offered but far too often they have proved merely to be snakeoils which flatter to deceive. To search for sovereign, grandiose theories with which to tie all loose ends together is to follow a false trail to enlightenment. This search goes against the grain of modern social psychology where multiple perspectives and the judicious employment of mini-theories and the development of multifaceted process models appears to be the order of the day. It is vital that sport psychologists make sure that they take on board not only the successes but also the failures which have led social psychology to this point. The failures, blind alleys and false dawns can be just as revealing of where to go in the future as where not to go, or as sport psychologists are fond of saying, you always learn more from your defeats than your victories. There is no doubt that the gap between social psychology and sport psychology is narrower at present than for some considerable time, and the future certainly looks rosy if challenging. To use that hackneyed Chinese expression, we live in interesting times. To some this will be a source of inspiration, to others this new dawn may be difficult to accept. We side with the former.

SHORT QUESTIONS

1 What special problems do applied sport psychologists face when working directly with atheletes?
2 What techniques can sport psychologists employ to encourage more people to take up sport and to stay in sport?
3 Outline the ways in which applied social psychology can make a contribution to understanding violence in sport.
4 To what extent do men run towards their gender stereotype and to what extent do women run away from theirs?
5 Does the team that drinks together necessarily play together?

CLASS ACTIVITIES

1 Make a list of who you consider to be the ten most successful sportspeople of all time. Consider the personality of each individual. What do they have in common, do they share common personality traits?

2 Imagine that you are working with a team in a sport of your choice. The team contains many talented players but it is underperforming. What advice would you offer the team's coach in terms of team spirit and cohesion?

3 Within your class, compare and contrast your sporting histories, looking at the reasons why you took up, continued and discontinued certain activities. How does the model presented earlier in the chapter help you to undertsand these histories?

4 Devise a field experiment to demonstrate how social facilitation may influence performance in sport. What effects would you expect to find and why?

FURTHER READINGS

Andersen, M.B. (ed.) (2000) *Doing Sport Psychology*. Champaign, IL: Human Kinetics.

Butler, R.J. (1996) *Sports Psychology in Action*. Oxford: Butterworth-Heinemann.

Cockerill, I. (ed.) (2001) *Solutions in Sport Psychology*. London: Thompson Learning.

Kremer, J. and Scully, D. (1994) *Psychology in Sport*. London: Taylor & Francis.

Singer, R.N., Murphey, M. and Tennant, L.K. (eds) (2000) *Handbook of Research on Sport Psychology*. London: Palgrave Macmillan.

Swotting

11

The rest is silence.

(Shakespeare, 1601)

To bring this book to a natural conclusion has not been easy. As should now be apparent, the business of applying social psychology remains unfinished and so at this time any endpoint is bound to appear fairly arbitrary. One possibility for drawing to a close may lie in returning once more to earlier issues, thereby endeavouring to throw even fresher light on old problems. Having already covered so many applied fields and having outlined the key issues facing applied social psychology in the introductory chapter we felt the scope for this endeavour was limited. As a more radical alternative we decided it may be interesting to end by bringing theory to practice, employing a technique familiar to many practising psychologists while at the same time hopefully remaining true to many of the theoretical aspirations of contemporary applied social psychology.

The applied technique in question is widely used by consultants in social evaluation research and is known as SWOT analysis. In practical settings this type of analysis often involves workshop participants or focus-group members, either individually or more often collectively, discussing and listing what they consider to be the Strengths, Weaknesses, Opportunities and Threats (hence SWOT) of the topic under discussion. This topic could be, for example, a policy proposal, a social issue, a new product line, a marketing strategy, a political campaign, a team, an organization, indeed almost anything that happens to be the focus of attention at the time. The technique is widely used because it works – it provides a coherent and easily understandable framework for evaluation which can be revealing of both internal and external factors, and which is not time-bound. Quite naturally, the past, present and future all emerge for comment as you work through the four stages of a SWOT analysis. (Strengths and Weaknesses offer an internal focus while Opportunities and Threats provide an external focus.)

Below, the five contributors to this book, as practising applied social psychologists, have each provided an unedited version of a SWOT analysis of 'Applying Social Psychology'. Quite deliberately no attempt has been made to aim for a consensus or to focus on our own particular areas of interest. Instead, each SWOT analysis stands alone, and we hope the orientation of each analysis will spontaneously reflect our personal perceptions and priorities. It is also hoped that the five will act as independent commentaries or evaluations of what it means to apply social psychology to the real world and in combination we hope the five contributions may exemplify what we believe are core values of applied social psychology in the twenty-first century: At the risk of covering ground already well-trodden these include:

Social construction – we each have the capacity to construe the world in a unique and idiosyncratic way. Each construction is valid in its own right, and tells us as much about the person who construes as the object/topic under investigation

Multiple perspectives – a wide range of complementary approaches should operate in tandem and not in competition to help us understand social behaviour and experience. There should be no no winners or losers in this endeavour; no single perspective can ever provide all the answers, and most especially as each is likely to operate at a different level of analysis.

Diversity – while we may feel comfortable with sameness it is our difference that makes the difference and should be enjoyed as such. This diversity should reflect in the interests and orientations of those carrying out the research as well as the topics under investigation.

In keeping with this philosophy we would encourage you, either before or after reading our five contributions, to attempt your own SWOT analysis of Applying Social Psychology. Having provided your own perspective then consider points of difference and similarity between your analysis and ours. In the process, reflect on how each analysis may reflect on you, on us and on applying social psychology, past present and future. Your aim should not be to seek concurrence but aspire to a higher goal, to enjoy difference!

SWOT I

SWOT I: strengths

Social psychology has a well-established theoretical tradition stretching back over at least a century. During this time the subdiscipline has grown exponentially while the number of social psychological theories has also mushroomed. Earlier, hugely influential writers such as Sigmund Freud, George Herbert Mead and Erving Goffman offered grand social theories to explain the relationship between the individual and society. More latterly attention has turned to finer-grained analyses of particular social processes and phenomena. Together all these contributions, whether micro or macro in orientation, offer a considerable theoretical resource which any practising social psychologist has the opportunity to draw upon. Equally, the number of people across the globe who would now define themselves as social psychologists is enormous and many would regard application as an integral and necessary part of their work. In the past, too often the applied field would have been treated at arm's length, somehow as rather 'cheap' in comparison with 'pure' or academic social psychology. Market forces, and including the stated priorities of research funding bodies, have led to a sea-change in the research agenda over the last 30 years, with an applied focus increasingly taking centre-stage as the main breadwinner of the psychology family. Running alongside this trend in research, social psychology would now be far less hidebound in terms of methodology than was previously the case. Today the subdiscipline embraces a much broader range of research methods than in the past. For example, most social psychologists would have few problems in affording equal status to both qualitative and quantitative methods, using whichever technique is appropriate for the task at hand. This eclectic approach to methodology has facilitated greater flexibility in response to understanding social issues, very often drawing on a wide range of qualitative procedures to develop deeper understanding of behaviour and experience, sometimes (but not always) in applied social contexts. A glance through the social psychology literature will also reveal an increasing orientation towards applied concerns in the subject matter of many key journals. The potential subject matter of social psychology is almost limitless; at long last social psychology may be starting to explore the true extent of its domain by locating application at the heart of its business.

SWOT I: weaknesses

Against these positive trends, a significant number of mainstream and influential social psychologists would still argue that their primary business relates not to the appliance of science but to the advancement of science for its own sake.

This is underpinned by an assumption that somehow, somewhere, their words will be translated into the common tongue and as if by magic their work will have an impact on real people and how they live their lives. Unfortunately in the past the reality has been that very often social psychological research has failed to make any significant impact on the outside world; in the true sense of the phrase it has been an academic exercise, run by academics for academic audiences. Perhaps one reason for this may be a reluctance to subject the material to outside scrutiny, where very often the emporer's new clothes can be revealed for what they truly are – fine words but little of genuine substance to interest practitioners. Some social psychologists would still struggle with the idea of 'selling' the subject to outsiders, but horizons must be broadened if any impact is to be made. On the other side of this coin are to be found the ubiquitous 'pop psychologists' who seem to have thrived in the current multi-channel, multimedia world. In contrast with their recalcitrant academic colleagues, pop psychologists are willing to talk on any subject at any time, and will often portray social psychology in its worst light – as the blindingly obvious and the instantly forgettable. While the media must carry some blame for this situation, those who feed the frenzy must also bear some responsibility. Applied social psychology must aim to steer a safe course between these twin imposters, on the one hand ensuring that the material is well-grounded in sound science, on the other ensuring that the material is accessible to those who may wish to be informed. Not all social psychological research will be sensational, it may merely confirm commonsense or what we all suspected was the case all along. Where the blatantly obvious comes to light there is always a temptation to 'gild the lily' or embellish. Instead, all that is needed is honesty, to acknowledge when we have something useful to say and, when we haven't, to say nothing.

SWOT 1: opportunities

That said, social psychology has the potential to say at least something about almost any aspect of our social lives, the opportunities for comment are almost immeasurable. For example, when a community faces the ravages of foot and mouth disease, a social psychologist could be on hand to help explain and understand what have been the individual and collective responses and why. When two planes fly into the World Trade Centre, the short, medium and long-term effects nationally and internationally could be informed by commentators from within the subdiscipline. When a celebrity dies, patterns of behaviour or emotion may be predictable. More typically, social psychologists will later interpret what happened and why, but the prediction of social behaviour before it has happened is far less common. There is a need to shorten the response time, to bridge the gap between the thinkers and the doers, and for social psychologists to market themselves as useful people in relation to a range of situations involving social behaviour. For example, how many organizations would think of consulting with a social psychologist before constructing a new office or embarking on a new venture or operating a new strategy or policy? How many advertising or marketing companies would routinely employ or consult with social psychologists when developing a campaign? How many authors, politicians, journalists or speech writers would look to social psychology when constructing their messages? In all these situations and a great many more there is scope for positive interventions at the planning or development stage, yet too often the interventions, if they take place at all, only occur after the event by way of evaluation. To market social psychology successfully there is a need to present the common stock of knowledge in a user-friendly way and to acknowledge where our competence begins and ends. In this way a sensible role can be defined within a mutlidisciplinary team, working alongside those with other skills and areas of expertise.

SWOT I: threats

In one sense, applied social psychology is still shackled by its own history. Generally content to define itself primarily as an academic endeavour, it has not carved out a recognizable niche in the applied arena; instead it has been left to individuals time and again to demonstrate their worth to a sceptical public, almost despite not because of their background in the subdiscipline. Other fields have been far more proactive in marketing their skills – management consultants being an obvious example. Unless social psychology engages in more active self-promotion then there is a real danger that others may corner the applied market and we will be left as the perpetual bridesmaid. Equally there is a danger that we promise more than we can deliver and to hide our inadequacies we put up a smokescreen of jargon. It goes without saying that people are not stupid and they know when a spade is being called an earth transfer implement, and if anything is bound to ruin a good working relationship it will be pretention for its own sake. The social world is not static, it is constantly changing and in turn applied social psychology must be responsive to the *zeitgeist*, to social forces and notable events. In this way the threat of change can be turned into an opportunity for advancement, and applied social psychology can begin to mark its claim as a prime player in understanding and interpreting social behaviour and experience.

SWOT 2

SWOT 2: strengths

Applied social psychology is problem-focused and applications-oriented. Rooted in the study of real-world problems it is strongly committed to naturalistic modes of investigation. It is cautious of the value attached to laboratory-based experimental investigations of social processes and of the mistaken belief that the processes observed therein are necessarily a pure form of the processes that operate outside the lab. Applied social psychology is not averse to laboratory-based enquiry. Applications-oriented research can bring issues to the laboratory for closer scrutiny and thereby support the development of theory through systematic investigations of constructs of interest. However, the psychology laboratory is itself a socially-constructed device, and quite an unusual one at that, so generalizing from the lab back to the application domain is rarely straightforward.

SWOT 2: weaknesses

One of the criticisms levelled against applied social psychology is that it is problem-focused rather than solution-focused. This criticism is largely a reflection of the fact that many of the theories from which applied social psychologists draw are descriptive rather than prescriptive. Descriptive theories seek to describe, predict and explain behaviour but they do not offer guidance on what should be done. For example, the application of social psychology to environmental issues can provide insights into how people are likely to behave in response to particular innovations. It can predict, for instance, the extent to which local communities will tend to respond according to the 'Not in my back yard' (NIMBY) principle. However, it does not give any direction as to the appropriateness of challenging a NIMBY attitude, nor how and when a challenge should be made. Prescriptive or normative theories seek to prescribe or direct behaviour in order that people may optimize their own interests. These kinds of theories are more common in economics. In Chapter 8 we noted that economics and psychology are concerned with understanding why people work, what motivates people to spend their money and what factors influence saving behaviour. But whereas psychological theories tend to focus on explaining and predicting consumer behaviour, economic theories work from the principle that people are rational and as such act to optimize their interests. Certain prescriptions follow from this position and these are routinely used to inform government policies as well as the plans of both large and small-scale commercial concerns. Psychologists may eschew the rather simplistic, rationalist view espoused by applied economists, but the fact of the matter is that with the notable exception of therapeutic applications, psychology has generally failed to come up with prescriptive theories of the type offered by economists and taken up by those trying to formulate practical solutions.

SWOT 2: opportunities

Applied social psychology is keenly aware of the fact that practical problems do not recognize disciplinary or conceptual boundaries. The effective application of social psychology entails a commitment to sharing its methods and concepts with other disciplines and an openness to the value of working within a framework where the approach offered by other disciplines is equally valued. This means that it is particularly well-suited to taking a proactive approach to the investigation of novel problems as they arise. Rather than asking 'What's the social psychological question here?' applied psychologists explore various ways of framing a particular problem and in their consideration of the relative merits of each seek to identify conceptual lacunae which could be filled by expanding a multidisciplinary team. Thus, in the vast majority of cases, applied social psychologists work within a multidisciplinary framework that offers a flexible and robust approach that can be used to tacke a range of complex, novel problems.

SWOT 2: threats

There is nothing so practical as a good theory; applied social psychologists make a great deal of use of some very good psychological theories. However, in taking from those theories there is an obligation to feed something back in return. Applied social psychologists need to attend to the balance between taking from theory and giving something back in return. Many of the practical lessons learned in dealing with a practical problem can also shed light on the underlying theories that were used to inform a particular intervention. If psychologists fail to complete this feedback loop then research messages cannot be used to further develop, refine or challenge theory which, in the long term, may lead to a reliance on obsolete ideas and approaches.

SWOT 3

SWOT 3: strengths

A major strength of applied social psychology is undoubtedly the range and scale of issues to which the discipline addresses itself. Applied social psychology informs some of the most pressing social and global problems of our times, such as terrorism and intergroup conflict, global warming and environmental issues and social inequality. Applied social psychology also informs other disciplines, aiding for instance the understanding of social processes in science, education and medicine. While this breadth of application represents one of the major strengths of the discipline, it pales in comparison to the potential that arises as a result of the fuller understanding of current social problems. It is only when we understand the origins and course of these social issues that we can hope to address them. The chances of alleviating child poverty or terrorism is low if we do not understand the human processes that contribute to their bases. A second major strength of applied social psychology is reflected in the vitality and vigour of the current discipline. Many recent conferences in this area have been marked by the enthusiastic and dynamic debates in areas such as racism, social identity and social inequality. Further to this many of these debates are strongly associated with theoretical issues, highlighting the fact that theory informs this area and is continually informed by research findings. These theories, in many ways, are unusual in modern psychology. More often than not they are theories that have readily apparent real-world application. The centrality of theory to the discipline has been underlined throughout this text and the vibrancy of current theoretical debates and developments represents a significant strength. The final strength lies in the range of research methods which it embraces. Social psychology more than any other subdiscipline in psychology is willing to take an eclectic approach to addressing research questions. This approach has a number of advantages. First it means that the social psychologist has more tools in the methodological kit bag. Second, evidence of convergence from a multitude of methods strengthens our confidence in particular findings. Finally, this approach maximizes the likelihood that real-world problems are explored and means that social psychologists can often add value to extant explanations.

SWOT 3: weaknesses

One of the major weaknesses of the discipline as it currently stands is its success in informing policy and politics. Many of the issues that applied social psychologists address are contentious political and social issues. While work on these subjects continues to be published in peer-reviewed journals, often these results do not permeate into the real world. In general, applied social psychologists have been wary of engaging in wider social and political debates. This nervousness is often borne of a fear that research or researchers will be labelled as biased. All research is affected by biases to a greater or lesser extent, though it is less biased than naked political opinion. Applied social psychologists need to become confident in their discipline's theories, research and methods and become proactive in their attempts to inform social issues. Failing to apply the knowledge available within the discipline undermines its value and defeats its purpose.

SWOT 3: opportunities

The opportunities for applied social psychology in the future are manifold. Biological science is currently dedicating itself to the mapping of the human genome, and as a result of this programme genetic explanations of behaviour are increasingly popular. However, some claims are exaggerated and a sense of perspective on reductionist viewpoints associated with this trend is essential. Social psychologists are particularly well-suited to this role. The exploration of the role of both genetic or hereditary factors alongside social or environmental factors on human development and behaviour is key. Few human behaviours are likely to be determined by genetics alone, however the need to examine the interacting effects of genetics and environment is critical. This can only be achieved if biologists and social scientists work alongside each other exploring these issues. This type of research represents a real opportunity for social psychologists and biologists who want to develop a holistic understanding of human behaviour. The fallacy of the reductionist approach is further undermined by the changing nature of science as an endeavour. It is fair to say that science has now become more evolutionary rather than revolutionary. Major breakthroughs that change the way we view the world are few and far between, but nonetheless the workings of the human brain continue to be poorly understood. Again there is real opportunity for social psychologists working alongside neuro-psychologists to consider how biological, social and psychological factors interact in the control of behaviour. Such collaborative endeavour represents real and exciting opportunities for applied social psychologists.

SWOT 3: threats

Paradoxically, the application of social psychology to a range of areas has resulted in the development of one of the subdiscipline's major threats. Too often, social psychology is undermined by beliefs of other psychologist and scientists. These beliefs are based in a perception of the discipline as being unscientific and/or commonsensical. The accusation of 'unscientific' is most often levelled due to the use of alternative methodologies to the traditional lab-based experiment. However, it is important to remember that the problems associated with overreliance on this method have been well-documented. The second accusation, that the findings of research undertaken in the area are self-evident or commonsensical is even more disingenuous, in particular when levelled by fellow scientists. Commonsense beliefs are often contradictory (for example those who hesitate are lost vs look before you leap) and if we believe everything is self-evident we wouldn't 'do' science at all. This coupled with the fact that applied science if often seen as the poor relation of pure science results in a situation where the discipline is not taken seriously. There is a need for social psychologist to sell the discipline more effectively, to dispel misconceptions regarding its value and to be more proactive in underlining the strengths and achievements in the field.

SWOT 4

SWOT 4: strengths

This volume provides a snapshot of the some of the topics that benefit from analysis based on social psychological research and methods. One of the major strengths of the subdiscipline is that it provides tools and theories that enable this wide range of issues to be approached from multiple perspectives and at different levels of analysis. Social psychology does not necessarily provide solutions to problems but a set of strategies for answering questions. It does not just focus on the individual or the situation but it emphasizes both the power of the situation and the importance of individual differences. It stresses the socially constructed interpretations of events and the role of culture in shaping social understanding. It incorporates the analytical insights and precision of experimental research with the wider perspective gained from analysis of social behaviour, group and intergroup processes and the influence of cultural norms. The unique contribution of social psychological analysis to policy and societal change is that, unlike other social sciences, it includes the analysis of the situational processes that mediate between the macro-structural or societal and the micro-individual level of analysis. Pettigrew (1998) summarized this particular strength of social psychology when he acknowledged that:

> Other social sciences consider situations, but only social psychology focuses on situational mediation systematically. In doing so, the discipline provides both distinctive variables and distinctive explanations that usually involve subjective interpretations of the social environment. This situational and subjective perspective is the discipline's unique contribution and forms the core of its potential application. (p. 666)

SWOT 4: weaknesses

One of the most widely-cited occasions where social psychology was applied to government policy involved the contribution of social scientists to the 1954 supreme court's ruling on desegregation in the United States, following the *Brown* v. *Board of Education* case. Allport's contact hypothesis, which argued that increasing contact between members of different groups under appropriate conditions could reduce prejudice, is widely associated with this victory. Unfortunately, the subsequent fate of the contact thesis also illustrates potential weaknesses in applying social psychology. Perhaps, it was inevitable that the impact of desegregation would be disappointing. At that time the contact hypothesis was largely untested and the process and conditions for successful implementation of desegregation had not been specified. In practice, black and white young people in desegregated schools failed to develop the close relationships that would lead to racial harmony. Social psychologists still have a tendency to offer prescriptions for society, but while it is natural to assume that scholarship can be applied to resolve society's problems it is essential that the limitations are acknowledged. It is tempting to oversimplify theories, such as the contact hypothesis for political purposes, and ignore the importance of the processes involved in the implementation of change.

Ironically, the development of the contact theory suffered from its apparent success in influencing policy as, following the supreme court ruling, a vast number of small-scale research studies were carried out to test its limitations. Other areas have suffered a similar fate as the press for publications leads researchers to focus on testable minor variations of an apparently succesful paradigm rather than analysing basic processes. This is potentially a major weakness in the development of applicable concepts such as 'stereotype threat' and 'implicit prejudice' which are currently seizing the imagination of academic social psychologists. However, it may not be a serious weakness in the development of ideas. Important theoretical concepts such as the contact thesis tend to be discoverd by new generations of scholars who seek to replace the theoretical sterility of earlier work by efforts to understand the mechanisms that lead to change.

SWOT 4: opportunities

Pettigrew (1998), identifies a number of historical factors that have contributed to social psychology's failure to have the impact on social policy it expected. Some of these factors such as the nature of social psychology as an inductive science and its historical retreat to the laboratory cannot be changed. However, there is no reason why social psychologists cannot become more directly involved in the application of theories and research to solving problems and developing policies. For example, major research funding agencies in the United Kingdom such as the Economic and Social Research Council now require a commitment that research findings will be fully exploited either commercially or in the public interest. Opportunities for applying social psychology have also grown as government and industry has increasingly become committed to evidence-based policies that require clear objectives. It seems that there is increasing recognition by policy-makers that social psychologists have the methodological tools and conceptual understanding that enables them to monitor performance and establish the impact of programmes and procedures.

SWOT 4: threats

Threats to the acceptance of applied social psychology derive from, on the one hand, the failure of the discipline to engage with the real world, and on the other the simplistic application of social psychological concepts to complex social problems such as racial tensions. The tendency for social psychologists to assume that their role is completed once they make their findings available for peer-review is a further threat to efforts to bridge the gap between research and practice. This problem is exacerbated by the failure of the academic community to acknowledge that scholarship is not only demonstrated through publications in prestigious academic journals, but it is also served by efforts to translate research so that it is readily available for users such as students and policy-makers as well as those who translate research into practice.

SWOT 5

SWOT 5: strengths

Major strengths are derived first from the inherently social nature of the discipline, and second from the general theories and models developed within mainstream social psychology. However, an equally important contribution has been the concept of analysis taking place at multiple levels, a mainstay of social psychology and one which has had an important influence in applied research. For example, a particular strength of social psychology when applied to the analysis of relationships between health and behaviour is that contextual factors are afforded their due importance. These factors may be sociocultural, local or interpersonal, but those interested in researching health and illness ignore the social element of the processes involved at their peril. Health-related behaviours on the part of the individual do not take place in a socio-cultural vacuum, and a social psychological approach uniquely offers the opportunity to examine a full range of relevant contextual factors which may impact at any point on the health–illness continuum, and moreover may do so at an individual, family or community level. In terms of applying the theories of mainstream social psychology in a variety of contexts, these generic approaches have often proved a useful starting point for those seeking to address more specific issues. For example several currently influential models of health-related behaviour have their origins in traditional mainstream social psychology. These generic models have been adapted and developed for use in health research and promise a more complete understanding of the processes and pathways involved in health and illness and hence the opportunity to develop effective interventions. Again, such interventions may operate at multiple levels, ranging from individual programmes for behavioural change to community-level interventions aimed at increasing social capital and hence significantly improving health and well-being.

SWOT 5: weaknesses

The strengths also determine, at least to some extent, the weaknesses of applying this approach. Models and theories which were developed to account for broad relationships, such as those between attitudes and behaviour, tend to be overly general when applied in specific contexts and often have little predictive power at the level of the individual. This is a serious problem for those attempting to use social psychological theory to design interventions, such as in the field of health promotion, but one to which social psychology may also provide the solution. Within mainstream social psychology, it has long been acknowledged that measuring specific attitudes in relation to corresponding behaviours increases predictive power. Increasingly within health psychology it is being acknowledged that behaviour-specific models may need to be developed and that some models may be well-suited to examining a few specific health-related behaviours, but less useful in relation to others. An example is that of the distinction emerging between health-related behaviours which are or become habitual (such as smoking, toothbrushing), and those which are purposeful. Another weakness of social psychological approaches to applied research is that they have often failed to illuminate the relationships between individual and social factors. This is illustrated by the ongoing debate over the extent to which sociocultural factors may be related to the development of eating disorders in some individuals in the context of industrialized societies.

SWOT 5: opportunities

Social psychological theory when applied in a variety of contexts provides opportunities to contribute to an improved understanding of the processes and pathways to a variety of outcomes (for example health or illness, educational attainment). More importantly, as understanding of these processes and pathways develops, the way opens for effective interventions to improve outcome not only at the individual level but also on a much larger scale. For example, recent theorizing in relation to social capital promises improved health at a community and eventually a national level. In emphasizing social influences in applied areas, social psychologists have the opportunity to influence policy and hence improve social conditions on a broad scale with concomitant benefits for the individuals whose outcomes improve as a result of the implementation of such policies. Hence, applying social psychology may afford opportunities to advance towards social reform on the basis of sound evidence.

SWOT 5: threats

The rise of evolutionary psychology, the human genome project and advances in genetic medicine and behavioural genetics may all be viewed as either threats or opportunities by those interested in social psychological approaches in a variety of applied areas. Biological determinism in all its guises appears to be on the rise. Hence, the causes of most behaviours and indeed outcomes are thought by some evolutionary psychologists to be largely attributable to nature rather than nurture. Nevertheless, it is possible to reconcile recent advances in genetics with a social psychological approach by acknowledging that most human behaviours are likely to be socially mediated to some extent. For example, while an individual may be genetically predisposed to develop specific diseases, in the majority of cases environmental factors or behavioural factors are also necessary for the manifestation of those diseases. While genetics may have a relatively large effect on intelligence, factors such as motivation, relevant role models and social support mediate these effects, making outcomes amenable to interventions. Similarly, the number of diseases determined solely by genetic factors is small, and for the most part those interested in the application of social psychology will find it still has much to offer in the face of advances in genetic science.

References

Abraham, J. (1973) *The Origins and Growth of Sociology*. Harmondsworth: Penguin.

Abramson, L.Y., Seligman, M.E.P. and Teasdale, J.D. (1978) 'Learned Helplessness in Humans: Critique and Reformulation', *Journal of Abnormal Psychology*, vol. 87, pp. 49–74.

Adams, J.S. (1965) 'Inequity in Social Exchange', in I. Berkowitz (ed.), *Advances in Experimental Social Psychology* (vol. 2, pp. 267–99). New York: Academic Press.

Adler, N.E., Boyce, T., Chesney, M.A., Cohen S., Folkman S., Kahn, R.L. and Syme S.L. (1994) 'Socioeconomic Status and Health: The Challenge of the Gradient', *American Psychologist*, vol. 49, pp. 15–24.

Adorno, T.W., Frenkel-Brunswik, E., Levinson, D.J. and Sanford, R.N. (1950) *The Authoritarian Personality*. New York: Wiley Science Series.

Ainsworth, P.B. (1998) *Psychology, Law and Eyewitness Testimony*. Chichester: Wiley.

Ainsworth, P.B. (2000) *Psychology and Crime: Myth and Reality*. Harlow: Longman.

Ajzen, I. (1991) 'The Theory of Planned Behavior', *Organizational Behavior and Human Decision Processes*, vol. 50, pp. 179–211.

Ajzen, I. and Fishbein, M. (1980) *Understanding Attitudes and Predicting Behaviour*. Englewood Cliffs, New Jersey: Prentice Hall.

Allan, S., Adam, B. and Carter, C. (eds) (1999) *Environmental Risks and the Media*. London: Routledge.

Allport, G.W. (1935) 'Attitudes', in C.M. Murchison (ed.), *Handbook of Social Psychology* (pp. 798–844). Worcester, MA: Clark University Press.

Allport, G.W. (1954) *The Nature of Prejudice*. Reading, MA: Addison-Wesley.

Allport, G.W. (1985) 'The Historical Background of Social Psychology', in G. Lindzey and E. Aronson (eds), *Handbook of Social Psychology* (vol. 1, 3rd ed., pp. 1–46). New York: Random House.

Altemeyer, B. (1994) 'Reducing Prejudice in Right-Wing Authoritarians', in M.P. Zanna and J.M. Olson (eds), *The Psychology of Prejudice: The Ontario Symposium* (vol. 7, pp. 131–48). Hillsdale, New Jersey: Lawrence Erlbaum Associates.

American Psychological Association (1992) 'Ethical Principles of Psychologists and Code of Conduct', *American Psychologist*, vol. 47, pp. 1597–611.

Andersen, M.B. (ed.) (2000) *Doing Sport Psychology*. Champaign, IL: Human Kinetics.

Anderson, A. (1997) *Media, Culture and the Environment*. London: University College of London Press.

Anderson, L.M. (1981) 'Land Use Designations Affect Perception of Scenic Beauty in Forest Landscapes', *Forest Science*, vol. 27, pp. 392–400.

Andrews, D.A., Zinger, I. and Hoge, R.D. (1990) 'Does Correctional Treatment Work? A Clinically Relevant and Psychologically Informed Meta-Analysis', *Criminology*, vol. 28, pp. 369–404.

Argyle, M. (1989) *The Social Psychology of Work*. Harmondsworth: Penguin.

Argyle, M. and Dean, J. (1965) 'Eye Contact, Distance and Affiliation', *Sociometry*, vol. 28, pp. 289–364.

Armistead, N. (1974) *Reconstructing Social Psychology*. London: Penguin.

Armitage, C.J. and Conner, M. (2000) 'Social Cognitions and Health Behaviour: A Structured Review', *Psychology and Health*, vol. 15, pp. 173–89.

Arnetz, B.B., Wasserman, J., Petrini, B., Brenner, S.O., Levi, L., Eneroth, P., Salovaara, H., Hjelm, R., Salovaara, L., Theorell, T. and Petterson, I.L. (1987) 'Immune Function in Unemployed Women', *Psychosomatic Medicine*, vol. 49, pp. 3–12.

Aronson, E. and Bridgeman, D. (1979) 'Jigsaw Groups and the Desegregated Classroom: In Pursuit of Common Goals', *Personality and Social Psychology Bulletin*, vol. 5, pp. 438–46.

Asch, S.E. (1956) 'Studies of Independence and Conformity: A Minority of One against a Unanimous Majority', *Psychological Monographs: General and Applied*, vol. 70, pp. 1–70 (whole no. 416).

Aspinwall, L.G. and Taylor, S.E. (1993) 'Effects of Social Comparison Direction, Threat, and Self-Esteem on Affect Evaluation and Expected Success', *Journal of Personality and Social Psychology*, vol. 64, pp. 708–22.

Augoustinos, M. and Walker, I. (1995) *Social Cognition*. London: Sage Publications.

Azjen, I. and Fishbein, M. (1977) 'Attitude–Behavior Relations: A Theoretical Analysis and Review of Empirical Research', *Psychological Bulletin*, vol. 84, pp. 888–918.

Bandura, A. (1977) 'Self-Efficacy: Towards a Unifying Theory of Behavioral Change', *Psychological Review*, vol. 84, pp. 191–215.

Bandura, A. (1977) *Social Learning Theory*. Englewood Cliffs: Prentice Hall.

Barker, R. (1968) *Ecological Psychology*. Stanford, CA: Stanford University Press.

Bass, B.M. (1990) *Bass and Stogdill's Handbook of Leadership: Theory, Research and Managerial Applications*. (3rd ed.). New York: Free Press.

Bass, B.M. and Avolio, B.J. (eds) (1992) *Improving Organizational Effectiveness through Transformational Leadership*. London: Sage Publications.

Batra, R. and Stayman, D.M. (1990) 'The Role of Mood in Advertising Effectiveness', *Journal of Consumer Research*, vol. 17, pp. 203–14.

Baumgartner, H., Sujan, J. and Bettman, J.R. (1992) 'Autobiographical Memories, Affect, and Consumer Information Processing', *Journal of Consumer Psychology*, vol. 1, pp. 53–82.

Belsky, J. (1984) 'The Determinants of Parenting: A Process Model', *Child Development*, vol. 55, pp. 83–96.

Bem, D.J. (1967) 'Self-Perception: An Alternative Interpretation of Cognitive Dissonance Phenomena', *Psychological Review*, vol. 74, pp. 198–200.

Bem, S.L. (1993). *The Lenses of Gender: Transforming the Debate on Sexual Inequality*. New Haven and London: Yale University Press.

Bennett, P. and Murphy, S. (1997) *Psychology and Health Promotion*. Buckingham: Open University Press.

Berlyne, D.E. (1960) *Conflict, Arousal and Curiosity*. New York: McGraw-Hill.

Bezilla, R. and Keliner, A. (1980) *Electronic Network Addiction*. Paper presented at the National Computer Conference. Arnheim, California.

Biddle, S. (1993) 'Attribution Research and Sport Psychology', in R.N. Singer, M. Murphey and L.K. Tennant (eds), *Handbook of Research on Sport Psychology* (pp. 437–64). New York: Macmillan.

Biddle, S., Bull, S. and Seheult, C. (1992) 'Ethical and Professional Issues in Contemporary British Sport Psychology', *The Sport Psychologist*, vol. 6, pp. 66–76.

Biddle, S.J. (1999) 'Adherence to Sport and Physical Activity in Children and Youth', in S. Bull (ed.), *Adherence Issues in Sport and Exercise* (pp. 111–44). Chichester: John Wiley and Sons Ltd.

Bigler, R.S. (1999) 'The Use of Multicultural Curricula and Materials to Counter Racism in Children', *Journal of Social Issues*, vol. 55, pp. 687–705.

Bogg, J. and Cooper, C.L. (1998) 'An Examination of Gender Differences for Job Satisfaction, Mental Health and Occupational Stress among Senior UK Civil Servants', *International Journal of Stress Management*, vol. 1, pp. 159–72.

Breakwell, G.M. (1990) *Interviewing*. Leicester: British Psychological Society.

Breugel, I., and Perrons, D. (1998) 'Deregulation and Women's Employment: The Diverse Experiences of Women in Britain', *Feminist Economics*, vol. 4, pp. 103–25.

Brewer, M.B. (2000) 'Reducing Prejudice through Cross-Categorization: Effects of Multiple Social Identities', in S. Oskamp (ed.), *Reducing Prejudice and Discrimination* (pp. 165–83). New Jersey: Lawrence Erlbaum Associates.

Brewer, M.B. and Brown, R.J. (1998) 'Intergroup Relations', in D. Gilbert, S. Fiske and G. Lindzey (eds), *The Handbook of Social Psychology* (4th ed., pp. 554–94). New York: McGraw-Hill.

British Psychological Society (2000). *Code of Conduct: Ethical Principles and Guidelines*. Leicester: BPS.

Brotherton, C. (1999) *Social Psychology and Management: Issues for a Changing Society*. Buckingham: Open University Press.

Brown, R.J. (1995). *Prejudice: Its Social Psychology*. Oxford, Blackwell.

Brown, R.J. (2000a). *Group Processes: Dynamics within and between Groups*. Second edition. Oxford: Blackwell.

Brown, R.J. (2000b) 'Social Identity Theory: Past Achievements, Current Problems and Future Challenges', *European Journal of Social Psychology*, vol. 30, pp. 745–78.

Bruner, J.S., Goodnow, J.J. and Austin, G.A. (1956) *A Study of Thinking*. New York: Wiley.

Bryant, F.B., Edwrads, J., Scott Tindale, R., Posavac, E.J., Heath, L., Henderson, E. and Suarez-Balcazar, Y. (1992) *Methodological Issues in Applied Social Psychology*. New York: Plenum Press.

Bull, R. and Carson, D. (eds) (1995) *Handbook of Psychology in Legal Contexts*. Chichester: Wiley.

Bunn, G. (2001) 'Charlie and the Chocolate Factory', *The Psychologist*, vol. 14, pp. 576–79.

Burman, E. (1998) 'Deconstructing Feminist Psychology', in Burman, E. (ed.) (1998), *Deconstructing Feminist Psychology*. London: Sage Publications (pp. 1–29).

Busby, G. (1997) 'Modelling Participation Motivation in Sport', in J. Kremer, K. Trew and S. Ogle (eds), *Young People's Involvement in Sport* (pp. 178–210). London: Routledge.

Byrnes, D.A. and Kiger, G. (1990) 'The Effect of a Prejudice-Reduction Simulation on Attitude Change', *Journal of Applied Social Psychology*, vol. 20, pp. 341–56.

Cairns, E. (2001) 'War and Peace', *The Psychologist*, vol. 14, pp. 292–93.

Campbell, D., Converse, P.E., Miller, W.E. and Stokes, D.E. (1960) *The American Voter*. New York: Wiley.

Campbell, F. (1998) *The Construction of Environmental News: A Study of Scottish Journalism*. Aldershot: Asgate.

Canter, D., Comber, M. and Uzzell, D.L. (1989) *Football in its Place: An Environmental Psychology of Football Grounds*. London: Routledge.

Carlson, R.J. (1976) *The Dilemmas of Corrections*. Lexington, MA: Lexington Books.

Cavill, N., Biddle, S. and Sallis, J.F. (2001) 'Health Enhancing Physical Activity for Young People: Statement of the United Kingdom Expert Consensus Conference', *Pediatric Exercise Science*, vol. 13, pp. 12–25.

Ceci, S.J. (1999) 'Schooling and Intelligence', in S.J. Ceci and W.M. Williams (eds), *The Nature-Nurture Debate: The Essential Readings* (pp. 168–76). Oxford: Blackwell.

Ceci, S.J. and Williams, W.M. (1999) 'Born vs. made: Nature-Nurture in the New Millennium', in S.J. Ceci and W.M. Williams (eds), *The Nature-Nurture Debate: The Essential Readings* (pp. 1–10). Oxford: Blackwell.

Chapman, A.J., Sheehy, N., Heywood, S., Dooley, B. and Collins, S.C. (1994) 'The Organizational Implications of Teleworking', *International Review of Industrial and Organizational Psychology*, vol. 10, pp. 229–48. Chichester: Wiley.

Chelladurai, P. (2000) 'Leadership', in R.N. Singer, M. Murphey and L.K. Tennant (eds), *Handbook of Research on Sport Psychology* (pp. 647–71). New York: Macmillan.

Clifford, B.R. (1976) 'Police as Eyewitnesses', *New Society*, vol. 22, pp. 176–77.

Cochrane, R. and Stopes-Roe, M. (1981) 'Women, Marriage, Employment and Mental Health', *British Journal of Psychiatry*, vol. 139, pp. 373–81. Cohen, S. and Wills, T.A. (1985) 'Stress, Social Support and the Buffering Hypothesis', *Psychological Bulletin*, vol. 98, pp. 310–57.

Cohen, B. (1983) 'Nuclear Journalism: Lies, Dammed Lies and New Reports', *Policy Review*, vol. 26, pp. 70–4.

Conner, M. and Norman, P. (eds) (1996) *Predicting Health Behaviour*. Buckingham: Open University Press.

Cooper, D. and Robertson, I.T. (1995) *The Psychology of Personnel Selection*. London: Routledge.

Cox, R. (1998) *Sport Psychology: Concepts and Applications* (4th edn). Boston, MA: McGraw Hill.

Crosby, F.J. (1987) *Spouse, Parent, Worker*. New Hampshire: Yale University Press.

Dennerstein, L. (1995) 'Mental-Health, Work, and Gender', *International Journal of Health Services*, vol. 25, pp. 503–09.

Cumberbatch, G. and Howitt, D. (1989) *A Measure of Uncertainty: The Effects of the Mass Media*. London: Broadcasting Standards Council.

Daniel, T.C. and Boster, R.S. (1976) 'Measuring Landscape Aesthetics: The Scenic Beauty Evaluation Method', *Research Paper RM-167*. Fort Collins, CO: USDA Forest Service.

Daniel, T.C. and Vining, J. (1983) 'Methodological Issues in the Assessment of Landscape Quality', in I. Altman and J.F. Wohwill (eds), *Behavior and the Natural Environment* (pp. 39–84). New York: Plenum.

deMause, L. (ed.) (1976) *The History of Childhood*. London: Souvenir Press.

Devine, P.G., Plant, A. and Buswell, B.N. (2000) 'Breaking the Prejudice Habit: Progress and Obstacles', in S. Oskamp (ed.), *Reducing Prejudice and Discrimination* (pp. 93–114). New Jersey: Lawrence Erlbaum Associates.

Doise, W. (1986) *Levels of Explanation in Social Psychology*. Cambridge: Cambridge Univ. Press.

Duckitt, J. (1992) 'Psychology and Prejudice: A Historical Analysis an Integrative Framework', *American Psychologist*, vol. 47, pp. 1182–193.

Duda, J.L. (ed.) (1998) *Advances in Sport and Exercise Psychology Measurement*. Morgantown, WV: Fitness Information Technology, Inc.

Dunlap, R. and Van Liere, K. (1978) The 'New Environmental Paradigm', *Journal of Environmental Education*, vol. 9, pp. 10–19.

Dutton W.H. (1999) 'The Web of Technology and People', *Prometheus*, vol. 17, pp. 5–20.

Ernsberger, P. and Koletsky, R.J. (1999) 'Biomedical Rationale for a Wellness Approach to Obesity: An Alternative to a Focus on Weight Loss', *Journal of Social Issues*, vol. 55, pp. 221–60.

Eron, L.D. and Huesmann, L.R. (1986) 'The Cross-National Approach to Research on Aggression: Measures and Procedures', in L.R. Huesmann and L.D. Eron (eds), *Television and the Aggressive Child: A Cross-National Comparison*. Hillsdale, NJ: Erlbaum.

Eron, L.D., Huesmann, L.R., Brice, P., Fischer, P. and Mermelstein, R. (1983) 'Age Trends in the Development of Aggression, Stereotyping and Related Television Habits', *Developmental Psychology*, vol. 19, pp. 71–7.

Espego, R. (1994) 'What is Systemic Thinking?', *System Dynamics Review*, vol. 10, pp. 119–212.

Fazio, R.H. (1990) 'Multiple Processes by which Attitudes Guide Behaviour: The Mode Model as an Integrative Framework', *Advances in Experimental Social Psychology*, vol. 23, pp. 75–109.

Feltz, D.L. (1992) 'The Nature of Sport Psychology', in T.S. Horn (ed.), *Advances in Sport Psychology* (pp. 3–11). Champaign, IL: Human Kinetics.

Festinger, L. (1954) 'A Theory of Social Comparison Processes', *Human Relations*, vol. 7, pp. 117–40.

Festinger, L. (1957) *A Theory of Cognitive Dissonance*. Stanford, CA: Stanford University Press.

Fiske, S.T. (2000) 'Stereotyping, Prejudice and Discrimination at the Seam between the Centuries: Evolution, Culture, Mind and Brain', *European Journal of Social Psychology*, vol. 30, pp. 299–322.

Forsyth, D. (1991) *Group Dynamics* (2nd edn). Pacific Grove, CA: Brooks/Cole.

French, B., Donnelly, D. and Willis, M. (2001) *Experience of Crime in Northern Ireland. NIO Research and Statistical Bulletin 5/2001.* Belfast: Northern Ireland Statistics and Research Agency.

French, D.P., Senior, V., Weinman, J. and Marteau, T.M. (2001) 'Causal Attributions for Heart Disease: A Systematic Review', *Psychology and Health*, vol. 16, pp. 77–98.

Furnham, A. (1986) *Social Behaviour in Context.* Newton, MA: Allyn & Bacon.

Galinsky, E., Bond, J.T., and Friedman, D.E. (1996) 'The Role of Employers in Addressing the Needs of Employed Parents', *Journal of Social Issues*, vol. 52, pp. 111–36.

Gardial, S. and Biehl, G. (1991) 'Evaluative and Factual ad Claims, Knowledge Level and Making Inferences', *Marketing Letters*, vol. 2, pp. 349–58.

Garner, P. (1994) 'Exclusion from School: Towards a New Agenda', *Pastoral Care in Education*, vol. 12, pp. 3–9.

Gerbner, G. (1956) 'Toward a General Model of Communication', *Audio-Visual Communication Review*, vol. 4, pp. 171–99.

Gerbner, G., Gross, L., Morgan, M. and Signorielli, N. (1986) 'Living with Television: The Dynamics of the Cultivation Process', in J. Bryant and D. Zillmann (eds), *Perspectives on Media Effects.* Hillsdale, NJ: Erlbaum.

Gifford, R. (1996) *Environmental Psychology: Principles and Practice.* Boston, MA.: Allyn & Bacon.

Gill, D. (1994) 'Psychological Perspectives on Women in Sport and Exercise', in D.M. Costa and S.R. Guthrie (eds), *Women and Sport* (pp. 253–84). Champaign, IL: Human Kinetics.

Gilovich, T. (1993) *How We Know What isn't So: The Fallibility of Human Reason in Everyday Life.* New York: Free Press.

Gough, B. and McFadden, M. (2001) *Critical Social Psychology.* London: Palgrave Macmillan.

Gove, W.R. (1984) 'Gender Differences in Mental and Physical Illness: The Effects of Fixed Roles and Nurturant Roles', *Social Science and Medicine*, vol. 19, pp. 77–91.

Gray, D. (1985) *Ecological Beliefs and Behaviors.* Westport: Greenwood.

Green, S.G. and Mitchell, T.R. (1979) 'Attributional Processes of Leaders in Leader Member Interaction', *Organizational Behavior and Human Performance*, vol. 23, pp. 429–58.

Grube, J.W., Mayton, D.M. and Ball-Rokeach, S.J. (1994) 'Inducing Change in Values, Attitudes and Behaviours: Belief System Theory and the Method of Value Self-Confrontation', *Journal of Social Issues*, vol. 50, pp. 153–73.

Gyllenhammer, P.G. (1977) *People at Work.* Reading, MA: Addison Wesley.

Haavio-Mannila, E. (1986) 'Inequalities in Health and Gender', *Social Science and Medicine*, vol. 22, pp. 141–49.

Hagell, A. and Newburn, T. (1994) *Young Offenders and the Media: Viewing Habits and Preferences*. London: Policy Studies Institute.

Han, C.M. (1989) 'Country Image: Halo or Summary Construct?', *Journal of Marketing Research*, vol. 26, pp. 222–29.

Hardin, G. (1968) 'The Tragedy of the Commons', *Science*, vol. 162, pp. 1243–8.

Hardy, L. (1996) 'Testing the Predictions of the Cusp Catastrophe Model of Anxiety and Performance', *The Sport Psychologist*, vol. 10, pp. 140–56.

Hardy, L., Jones, G. and Gould, D. (1996) *Understanding Psychological Preparation for Sport*. London: John Wiley & Sons.

Haward, L.R.C. (1979) 'The Psychologist as Expert Witness', in D.P. Farrington, K. Hawkins and S. Lloyd-Bostock (eds), *Psychology, Law and Legal Processes* (pp. 44–53). London: Guilford.

Hawe, P. and Shiell, A. (2000) 'Social Capital and Health Promotion: A Review', *Social Science and Medicine*, vol. 5, pp. 871–85.

Healy, B. (1991) 'The Yentl Syndrome', *The New England Journal of Medicine*, vol. 325, pp. 274–76.

Heider, F. (1958) *The Psychology of Interpersonal Relations*. New York: Wiley.

Helmreich, R. (1975) 'Applied Social Psychology: The Unfulfilled Promise', *Personality and Social Psychology Bulletin*, vol. 1, pp. 548–60.

Herriot, P. (1989) *Assessment and Selection in Organizations*. London: John Wiley & Sons.

Herzberg, F., Mausner, B. and Snyderman, B. (1959) *The Motivation to Work*. New York: Wiley.

Hewstone, M. and Brown, R. (eds) (1986) *Contact and Conflict in Intergroup Encounters*. Oxford: Blackwell.

Hewstone, M. and Cairns, E. (2001) 'Social Psychology and Intergroup Conflict', in D. Chirot and M.E.P. Seligman (eds), *Ethnopolitical Warfare: Causes, Consequences and Possible Solutions* (pp. 319–43). Washington, DC: American Psychological Association.

Heyman, S.R. and Andersen, M.B. (1998) 'When to Offer Athletes for Counseling or Psychotherapy', in J.M. Williams (ed.), *Applied Sport Psychology* (pp. 359–71). Mountain View, CA: Mayfield Publishing.

Hiltz, S.R. and Turoff, M. (1987) *The Network Nation*. Massachusetts: Addison-Wesley.

Himmelweit, H.T., Humphreys, P. and Jaeger, M. (1985) *How Voters Decide*. Milton Keynes: Open University Press.

Hodgson, R. and Thayer, R. (1980) 'Implied Human Influence Reduces Landscape Beauty', *Landscape Planning*, vol. 7, pp. 171–79.

Hong, S.T. and Wyer, R.S. (1989) 'Effects of Country-of-Origin and Product-Attribute Information on Product Evaluation: An Information Processing Perspective', *Journal of Consumer Research*, vol. 16, pp. 175–87.

House, J.S., Landis, K.R. and Umberson, D. (1988) 'Social Relationships and Health', *Science*, vol. 241, pp. 540–5.

Hraba, J., Lorenz, F., Lee, G. and Pechacova, Z. (1996) 'Gender Differences in Health: Evidence from the Czech Republic', *Social Science and Medicine*, vol. 43, pp. 1443–51.

Huesmann, L.R. and Eron, L.D. (eds) (1986) *Television and the Aggressive Child: A Cross-National Comparison*. Hillsdale, NJ: Erlbaum.

Huesmann, L.R., Eron, L.D., Klein, R., Brice, P. and Fischer, P. (1983) 'Mitigating the Imitation of Aggressive Behaviors by Changing Children's Attitudes about Media Violence', *Journal of Personality and Social Psychology*, vol. 44, pp. 899–910.

Hughes, D.L. and Galinsky, E. (1994) 'Gender, Job and Family Conditions, and Psychological Symptoms', *Psychology of Women Quarterly*, vol. 18, pp. 251–70.

Ibanez, T. (1990) 'Henri, Serge and the Next Generation', *British Psychological Society Social Psychology Newsletter*, vol. 24, pp. 5–14.

Israel, J. and Tajfel, H. (1972) *The Context of Social Psychology: A Critical Assessment*. London: Academic Press.

Jackson, J.M. (1988) *Social Psychology: Past and Present: An Integrative Orientation*. Hillsdale, NJ: Lawrence Erlbaum.

Janis, I.L. (1982) *Groupthink*. Boston, MA: Houghton Mifflin.

Jaspars, J. (1986) 'The Future of Social Psychology: Taking the Past to Heart', in A. Furnham (ed.), *Social Behaviour in Context* (pp. 273–310). Newton, MA: Allyn & Bacon.

Jin, R.L. (1995) 'The Impact of Unemployment on Health: A Review of the Evidence', *Canadian Medical Association Journal*, vol. 153, pp. 529–40.

Johnston, J. and Ettema, J. (1986) 'Using Television to Best Advantage: Research for Prosocial Television', in J. Bryant and D. Zillmann (eds), *Perspectives on Media Effects*. Hillsdale, NJ: Erlbaum.

Johnston, J., Ettema, J. and Davidson, T. (1980) *An Evaluation of Freestyle: A Television Series to Reduce Sex-Role Stereotypes*. University of Michigan: Institute for Social Research.

Jones, E.E. (1998) 'Major Developments in Five Decades of Social Psychology', in D.T. Gilbert, S.T. Fiske and G. Lindzey (eds), *The Handbook of Social Psychology, volume One.* (4th edn) (pp. 3–57). New York: Oxford Univesity Press.

Kalwani, M.U. and Yim, C.K. (1992) 'Consumer Price and Promotion Expectations: An Experimental Study', *Journal of Marketing Research*, vol. 29, pp. 90–100.

Kalwani, M.U., Yim, C.K., Rinne, H.J. and Sugita, Y. (1990) 'A Price Expectations Model of Consumer Brand Choice', *Journal of Marketing Research*, vol. 27, pp. 251–62.

Kandola, B. and Fullerton, J. (1994) *Managing the Mosaic: Diversity in Action*. London: Institute of Personnel Development.

Kaplan, R. and Kaplan, S. (1979) *The Experience of Nature: A Psychological Perspective*. New York: Cambridge University Press.

Kasperson, R.E. (1992) 'The Social Amplification of Risk: Progress in Developing an Integrative Framework', in S. Krimsky and D. Golding (eds) *Social Theories of Risk*. Westport, CT: Praeger.

Kasperson, R.E. and Kasperson, J.X. (1996) 'The Social Amplification and Attenuation of Risk', *Annals of the American Academy of Political and Social Science*, vol. 545, pp. 95–106

Kasperson, R.E., Golding, D. and Tuler, P. (1992) 'Social Distrust as a Factor in Citing Hazardous Facilities and Communicating Risks', *Journal of Social Issues*, vol. 48, pp. 161–87.

Katona, G. (1975) *Psychological Economics*. New York: Elsevier.

Katz, P.A. (1976) *Toward the Elimination of Racism*. London: Pergamon Press.

Keashly, L. (1997) 'Conflict and Conflict Management', in S.W. Savada and D.R. McCreary (eds), *Applying Social Psychology* (pp. 248–73). Upper Saddle River, NJ: Prentice Hall.

Kershaw, C., Budd, T., Kinshott, G., Mattinson, J., Mayhew, P. and Myhill, A. (2000) *The 2000 British Crime Survey, England and Wales. Home Office Statistical Bulletin 18/00*. London: Home Office.

Kiesler, S., Siegel, J. and McGuire, T.W. (1984) 'Social Psychological Aspects of Computer-Mediated Communication', *American Psychologist*, vol. 39, pp. 1123–34.

Kimiecik, J.C. and Lawson, H.A. (1996) 'Toward New Approaches for Exercise Behavior Change and Health Promotion', *Quest*, vol. 48, pp. 102–25.

Kremer, J. and Busby, G. (1998) 'Modelling Participation in Sport and Exercise: An Integrative Approach', *Irish Journal of Psychology*, vol. 19, pp. 447–63.

Kremer, J. and Lavallee, D. (eds) (2002) *Special Issue of The Psychologist, Sport and Exercise Psychology*. BPS: Leicester.

Kremer, J. and Montgomery, P. (eds) (1993) *Women's Working Lives*. London: HMSO.

Kremer, J. and Scully, D. (1998) 'What Sport Psychologists Often don't Do: On Empowerment and Independence', in H. Steinberg, I. Cockerill and A. Dewey (eds), *What Sport Psychologists Do* (pp. 75–88). Leicester: BPS.

Kremer, J. and Scully, D. (2001) 'The Team Just won't Gell', in I. Cockerill (ed.), *Solutions in Sport Psychology*. London: Thompson Learning.

Kremer, J., Steele, R., Cassidy, F. and Jones, B. (1999) *The Essential Guide to Combating Harassment at Work*. Belfast: APAS.

Kremer, J., Trew, K. and Ogle, S. (eds) (1997) *Young People's Involvement in Sport*. London: Routledge.

Laswell, H. (1948) 'The Structure and Function of Communication in Society', in L. Bryson (ed.) The *Communication of Ideas*. New York: Institute for Religious and Social Studies.

Lazarus, R.S. and Folkman, S. (1984) *Stress, Appraisal and Coping*. New York: Springer.

Lea, S. and Webley, P. (1994) 'Economic Psychology', in P. Spurgeon, R. Davies and T. Chapman (eds), *Elements of Applied Psychology* (pp. 279–96). Reading: Harwood.

Lefkowitz, M.M., Eron, L.D., Walder, L.O. and Huesmann, L.R. (1977) *Growing Up to be Violent: A Longitudinal Study of the Development of Aggression*. New York: Pergamon.

Lewin, K. (1917) Kriegslandschaft. *Zeitschrift Fur Angewandte Psychologie*, vol. 12, pp. 440–7.

Lewin, K. (1936) *Principles of Topological Psychology*. New York: McGraw-Hill.

Lewin, K. (1951) *Field Theory in Social Science*. New York: Harper.

Light, K.A. and Girdler, S.S. (1993) 'Cardiovascular Health and Disease in Women', in C. Niven and D. Carroll (eds), *The Health Psychology of Women*. Harwood: Academic Press.

Loftus, E.F. (1996) *Eyewitness Testimony*. Cambridge, MA: Harvard University Press.

Loftus, E.F., Miller, D.G. and Burns, H.J. (1978) 'Semantic Integration of Verbal Information into a Visual Memory', *Journal of Experimental Psychology: Human Learning and Memory*, vol. 4, pp. 19–31.

Lord, R.G. and Maher, K.M. (1991) 'Cognitive Theory in Industrial and Organizational Psychology', in M. Dunnette and L. Hough (eds), *Handbook of Industrial Organizational Psychology* (2nd ed., vol. 2, pp. 1–62). Palo Alto, CA: Consulting Psychological Press.

Maheswaran, D. and Sternthal, B. (1990) 'The Effects of Knowledge, Motivation, and Type of Message on ad Processing and Product Judgments', *Journal of Consumer Research*, 1990, vol. 17, pp. 66–73.

Major, B., McFarlin, D.B. and Gagnon, D. (1984) 'Overworked and Underpaid: On the Nature of Gender Differences in Personal Entitlement', *Journal of Personality and Social Psychology*, vol. 47, pp. 1399–412.

Mathur, M. and Chattopadhyay, A. (1991) 'The Impact of Moods Generated by Television Programs on Responses to Advertising', *Psychology of Marketing*, vol. 8, pp. 59–77.

Matsumoto, D. (2000) *Culture and Psychology: People around the World*. Stamford, CT: Wadsworth/Thompson learning.

Matthews, S., Hertzman, C., Ostry, A. and Power, C. (1998) 'Gender, Work Roles and Psychosocial Work Characteristics as Determinants of Health', *Social Science and Medicine*, vol. 46, pp. 1417–4.

Mazur, A. (1981) *The Dynamics of Technical Controversy*. Washington, DC: Communications Press.

McDougall, W. (1908) *An Introduction to Social Psychology*. London: Methuen.

McKechnie, G. (1978) 'The Environmental Response Inventory in Application', in K. Craik and G. McKechnie (eds), *Personality and the Environment*. London: Sage.

Mead, G.H. (1950) *Mind, Self and Society from the Standpoint of a Behaviourist*. Chicago: University of Chicago Press.

Meyers-Levy, J. and Sternthal, B. (1991) 'Gender Differences in the Use of Message Cues and Judgments', *Journal of Marketing Research*, vol. 18, pp. 84–96.

Michaels, J.W., Blommel, J.M., Brocato, R.M., Linkous, R.A. and Rowe, J.S. (1982) 'Social Facilitation and Inhibition in a Natural Setting', *Replications in Social Psychology*, vol. 2, pp. 21–4.

Milgram, S. (1974) *Obedience to Authority*. London: Tavistock.

Morrow, V. (1999) 'Conceptualizing Social Capital in Relation to the Well-Being of Children and Young People: A Critical Review', *Sociological Review*, vol. 47, pp. 744–65.

Mullen, B. and Cooper, C. (1994) 'The Relation Between Group Cohesion and Performance: An Integration', *Psychological Bulletin*, vol. 115, pp. 210–27.

Munsterberg, H. (1909) *Psychology and Crime*. London: Fisher Unwin.

Murray, M. (2000) 'Reconstructing Health Psychology: An Introduction', *Journal of Health Psychology*, vol. 5, pp. 267–71.

Nagel, S., Lamm, D. and Neef, M. (1981) 'Decision Theory and Juror Decision Making', in B.D. Sales (ed.), *The Trial: Perspectives in Law and Psychology* (vol. 2, pp. 27–39). London: Plenum.

Newson, E. (1994) 'Video Violence and the Protection of Children', *The Psychologist*, vol. 7, pp. 272–74.

Oakley, A. (1992) *Social Support and Motherhood*. Oxford: Basil Blackwell.

Office for Standards in Education. (1996) *Exclusions from Secondary Schools 1995/96*. London: HMSO.

Okojie, C.E.E. (1994) 'Gender Inequalities of Health in the Third-World', *Social Science and Medicine*, vol. 39, pp. 1237–47.

Orland, B. Vining, J. and Ebreo, A. (1992) 'The Effect of Street Trees on Perceived Values of Residential Property', *Environment and Behavior*, vol. 24, pp. 298–325.

Ortega, G. (1972) *Meditations on Hunting*. London: Scribners.

Parker, I. (1989) *The Crisis in Modern Social Psychology and how to End it*. London: Routledge.

Parker, I. and Shotter, J. (1990) *Deconstructing Social Psychology*. London: Sage.

Parsons, C. (1996) *Counting the Cost*. London: Commission for Racial Equality.

Pasewark, R.A. (1986) 'A Review of Research on the Insanity Defence', in S.A. Shah (ed.), *Annals of the American Academy of Political and Social Science: The Law and Mental Health; Research and Policy* (vol. 484, pp. 100–14). London: Sage.

Paulus, P.B., Dzindolet, M.T., Poletes, G. and Camacho, L.M. (1993) 'Perception of Performance in Group Brainstorming: The Illusion of Group Productivity', *Personality and Social Psychology Bulletin*, vol. 19, pp. 78–89.

Pepitone, A. (1981) 'Lessons from the History of Social Psychology', *American Psychologist*, vol. 36, pp. 972–85.

Pettigrew, T.F. (1998) 'Intergroup Contact Theory', *Annual Review of Psychology*, vol. 49, pp. 65–85.

Pettigrew, T.F. and Tropp, L.R. (2000) 'Does Intergroup Contact Reduce Prejudice? Recent Meta-Analytic Findings', in S. Oskamp (ed.), *Reducing Prejudice and Discrimination* (pp. 93–114). New Jersey: Lawrence Erlbaum Associates.

Pettigrew, T.P. (1998) 'Applying social psychology to international social issues', *Journal of Social Issues*, vol. 54, pp. 663–75.

Pidgeon, N. (1999) 'Risk Communication and the Social Amplification of Risk: Theory, Evidence and Policy Implications', *Risk, Decision and Policy*, vol. 4, pp. 145–59

Porter, L. and Lawler, E.E. (1968) *Managerial Attitudes and Performance*. Homewood, IL: Irwin.

Potter, J. and Wetherell, M. (1987) *Discourse and Social Psychology*. London: Sage.

Prochaska, J.O. and DiClemente, C.C. (1983) 'Stages and Processes of Self-Change in Smoking: Towards an Integrative Model of Change', *Journal of Consulting and Clinical Psychology*, vol. 5, pp. 390–95.

Proshanky, H.M. (1981) 'Uses and Abuses of Theory in Applied Research', *Applied Social Psychology Annual*, vol. 2, pp. 97–136.

Quay, H.C. (1984) *Managing Adult Inmates*. College Park, Maryland: American Correctional Association.

Renn, O., Burns, W.J., Kasperson, J.X., Kasperson, R.E. and Slovic, P. (1992) 'The Social Amplification of Risk: Theoretical Foundations and Empirical Applications', *Journal of Social Issues*, vol. 48, pp. 137–60.

Riemer, H. and Chelladurai, P. (1995) 'Athletic Leadership and Satisfaction', *Journal of Sport and Exercise Psychology*, vol. 17, pp. 276–93.

Roberts, G.C. (ed.) (1992) *Motivation in Sport and Exercise*. Champaign, IL: Human Kinetics.

Robinson, D.N. (1980) *Psychology and Law*. New York: Oxford University Press.

Rokeach, M. (1973) *The Nature of Human Values*. New York: Free Press.

Rosenthal, R. and Jacobson, L.F. (1968) *Pygmalion in the Classroom*. New York: Holt, Rinehart & Wilson.

Rosenthal, R. and Rubin, D.B. (1978) 'Interpersonal Expectancy Effects: The First 345 Studies', *Behavioural and Brain Sciences*, vol. 3, pp. 377–86.

Ross, E.A. (1908) *Social Psychology*. New York: Macmillan.

Ross, R. and Schneider, R. (1992) *From Equality to Diversity: A Business Case for Equal Opportunities*. London: Pitman Publishing.

Rowbotham, S. (1977) *Hidden from History: 300 Years of Women's Oppression and the Fight Against it*. London: Pluto Press.

Rushing, B. and Schwabe, A. (1995) 'The Health-Effects of Work and Family Role Characteristics: Gender and Race Comparisons', *Sex Roles* vol. 33, pp. 59–75.

Rutter, M. (1991) 'Services for Children with Emotional Disorders: Needs, Accomplishments and Future Developments', *Young Minds*, vol. 9, pp. 1–5.

Ryan, R.M., Frederick, C.M., Lepes, D., Rubio, N. and Sheldon, K.M. (1997) 'Intrinsic Motivation and Exercise Adherence', *International Journal of Sport Psychology*, vol. 28, pp. 335–54.

Sachs, M. (2000) 'Professional Ethics in Sport Psychology', in R. Singer, M., Murphey and L.K. Tennant (eds), *Handbook of Research on Sport Psychology* (pp. 921–32) New York: Macmillan.

Sahakian, W.S. (1982) *History and Systems of Social Psychology*. New York: Hemisphere Pubs.

Sampson, E.E. (1999) *Dealing with Differences: An Introduction to the Social Psychology of Prejudice*. Orlando: Harcourt Brace.

Schumann, D.W., Petty, R.E. and Clemons, D.S. (1990) 'Predicting the Effectiveness of Different Strategies on Advertising Variation: A Test of the Repetition-Variation Hypothesis', *Journal of Consumer Research*, vol. 17, pp. 192–202.

Searle, J.R. (1969) *Speech Acts*. Cambridge: University Press.

Seligman, M.E.P. (1975) *Helplessness*. San Francisco: W.H. Freeman.

Seligman, M.E.P. (2001) 'Preface', in D. Chirot and M.E.P. Seligman (eds), *Ethnopolitical Warfare: Causes, Consequences and Possible Solutions* (pp. xiii–xvi). Washington DC: American Psychological Association.

Seligman, M.P. and Csikszentmihalyi, M. (2001) 'Positive Psychology', An introduction. *American Psychologist*, vol. 55, pp. 5–14.

Severance, L.J., Greene, E. and Loftus, E.F. (1984) 'Toward Criminal Jury Instructions that Jurors can Understand', *Journal of Criminal Law and Criminology*, vol. 75, pp. 198–233.

Shackelton, V. (1995) *Business Leadership*. London: Routledge.

Shannon, C. and Weaver, W. (1949) *The Mathematical Theory of Communication*. Illinois: University Illinois Press.

Shapiro, P. and Penrod, S. (1986) 'A Meta-Analysis of Facial Identification Studies', *Psychological Bulletin*, vol. 100, pp. 139–56.

Sheehy, N., Wylie, J.W., McGuinness, C. and Orchard, G. (2000) 'How Children Solve Environmental Problems', *Environmental Education Research*, vol. 4, pp. 117–37.

Sheeran, P., Conner, M. and Norman, P. (2001) 'Can the Theory of Planned Behavior Explain Patterns of Health Behavior Change?', *Health Psychology*, vol. 20, pp. 12–19.

Sherif, M. (1966) *Group Conflict and Co-Operation: Their Social Psychology*. London: Routledge & Kegan Paul.

Shifren, K., Bauserman, R. and Carter, D.B. (1993) 'Gender-Role Orientation and Physical Health : A Study Among Young-Adults', *Sex Roles*, vol. 29, pp. 421–32.

Shotter, J. (1975) *Images of Man in Psychological Research*. London: Methuen.

Shotton, M.A. (1982) *Computer Addiction?* London: Taylor & Francis.

Simmons, D.C.V., Poulton, E.C. and Tickner, A.H. (1975) 'Identifying People in a Videotape Recording made at Night', *Ergonomics*, vol. 18, p. 6.

Simon, R.W. (1995) 'Gender, Multiple Roles, Role Meaning, and Mental Health', *Journal of Health and Social Behavior*, vol. 36, pp. 182–94. Stampfer, M.J. and Colditz, G.A. (1991) 'Estrogen Replacement Therapy and Coronary Heart Disease: A Quantitative Assessment of the Epidemiologic Evidence', *Preventive Medicine*, vol. 20, pp. 47–63.

Simons, Y. and Taylor, J. (1992) 'A Psychosocial Model of Fan Violence in Sports', *International Journal of Sport Psychology*, vol. 23, pp. 207–26.

Sims, R.R. (1992) 'Linking Groupthink to Unethical Behaviour in Organizations', *Journal of Business Ethics*, vol. 11, pp. 651–62.

Singer, D.G. and Singer J.L. (1983) 'Learning how to be Intelligent Consumers of Television', in M.J.A. Howe (ed.), *Learning from Television: Psychological and Educational Research*. London: Academic Press.

Slavin, R.E. and Cooper, R. (1999) 'Improving Intergroup Relations: Lessons Learned from Co-Operative Learning Programs', *Journal of Social Issues*, vol. 55, pp. 647–64.

Smith, M. and Robertson, I.T. (1993) *The Theory and Practice of Systematic Personnel Selection*. London: Macmillan.

Smith, M.B. (1972) 'Is Experimental Social Psychology Advancing?', *Journal of Experimental Social Psychology*, vol. 8, pp. 89–96.

Social Trends (1995) London: Office for National Statistics.

Sonuga-Barke, E.J.S. and Webley, P. (1993) *Children's Saving*. Hove: Erlbaum.

Sproull, L. and Kiesler, S. (1986) 'Reducing Social Context Cues: Electronic Mail in Organizational Communication', *Management Science*, vol. 11, pp. 1492–512.

Squire, C. (1989) *Significant Differences: Feminism in Psychology*. London: Routledge.

Sroufe, L.A., Cooper, R.G., DeHart, G.B. and Marshall, M.E. (1996) *Child Development: Its Nature and Course*. New York: McGraw-Hill.

Steers, R.M. and Porter, L.W. (1991) *Motivation and Work Behaviour*. New York: McGraw-Hill.

Stephan, W.G. and Stephan, C.W. (2000) 'An Integrated Threat Theory of Prejudice', in S. Oskamp (ed.), *Reducing Prejudice and Discrimination* (pp. 23–45). Hillsdale, NJ: Lawrence Erlbaum Associates.

Stephenson, G.M. (1992) *The Psychology of Criminal Justice*. London: Blackwell.

Sterman, J.D. (1994) 'Learning in and About Complex Systems', *System Dynamics Review*, vol. 10, pp. 291–330.

Stern, P.C. (1992) 'Psychological Determinants of Global Environmental Change', *Annual Review of Psychology*, vol. 43, pp. 269–302.

Strean, W.B. (1998) 'Possibilities for Qualitative Research in Sport Psychology', *The Sport Psychologist*, vol. 12, pp. 333–45.

Strickland, L.H., Aboud, F.E. and Gergen, K.J. (1976) *Social Psychology in Transition*. New York: Plenum Press.

Stroebe, W. (2000) *Social Psychology and Health* (2nd edn) Buckingham: Open University Press. Thoits, P.A. (1995) 'Stress, Coping, and Social Support Processes: Where are We? What Next?', *Journal of Health and Social Behavior*, Special Issue, pp. 53–79.

Tellis, G.J. and Gaeth, G.J (1990) 'Best value, Price Seeking and Price Aversion: The Impact of Information and Learning on Consumer Choices', *Journal of Marketing*, vol. 54, pp. 34–45.

Thomas, K.W. (1992) 'Conflict and Negotiation Processes in Organizations', in M.D. Dunette (ed.), *Handbook of Industrial and Organizational Psychology* (2nd edn, pp. 651–718). Palo Alto, CA: Consulting Psychologists Press.

Thompson, R.A. and Sherman, R.T. (1993) *Helping Athletes with Eating Disorders*. Champaign, IL: Human Kinetics.

Tickner, A.H. and Poulton, E.C. (1975) 'Watching for People and Actions', *Ergonomics*, vol. 18, pp. 35–51.

Tierney, J. (1996) *Criminology: Theory and Context*. London: Prentice Hall.

Trew, K. (1986) 'Catholic-Protestant Contact in Northern Ireland', in Hewstone, M. and Brown, R. (eds), *Contact and Conflict in Intergroup Encounters* (pp. 93–106). Oxford: Blackwell.

Trist, E.L., Higgin, G., Murray, H. and Pollock, A.B. (1963) *Organizational Choice*. London: Tavistock.

Tuckman, B.W. and Jensen, M.A. (1977) 'Stages of Small Group Development Revisited', *Group and Organizational Studies*, vol. 2, pp. 419–27.

Turner, C.W. and Berkowitz, L. (1972) 'Identification with Film Aggressor (Covert Role Taking) and Reactions to Film Violence', *Journal of Personality and Social Psychology*, vol. 21, pp. 256–64.

Turner, M.E. and Pratkanis, A.R. (1994) 'Affirmative Action as Help: A Review of Recipient Reactions to Preferential Selection and Affirmative Action', *Basic and Applied Social Psychology*, vol. 15, pp. 43–69.

Ulrich, R.S. (1977) 'Visual Landscape Preference: A Model and Application', *Man Environment Systems*, vol. 7, pp. 279–93.

Van de Ven, A.H. and Delbecq, A.L. (1974) 'The Effectiveness of Nominal, Delphi and Interacting Group Decision Making Processes', *Academy of Management Journal*, vol. 17, pp. 605–21.

Verbrugge, L.M. (1989) 'The Twain Meet: Empirical Explanations of Sex Differences in Health and Mortality', *Journal of Health and Social Behavior*, vol. 30, pp. 282–304.

Wahlberg, A.A.F and Sjoberg, L. (2000) 'Risk Perception and the Media', *Journal of Risk Research*, vol. 3, pp. 31–50.

Waldron, I. (1987) 'Patterns and Causes of Excess Female Mortality Among Children in Developing Countries', *World Health Statistical Report*, vol. 40, p. 194.

Wang, C. and Biddle, S. (2000) 'The Conceptions of the Nature of Athletic Ability Questionnaire for Children: Evidence on Psychometric Properties and its Use in Predicting Physical Activity Intentions', *Journal of Sports Sciences*, vol. 18, p. 61.

Wech, B.A. (1983) 'Sex-Role Orientation, Stress, and Subsequent Health-Status Demonstrated by Two Scoring Procedures for Bem Scale', *Psychological Reports*, vol. 52, pp. 69–70.

Weiner, B. (1986) *An Attributional Theory of Motivation and Emotion*. New York: Springer-Verlag.

Weinstein, N.D. (1987) 'Unrealistic Optimism About Susceptibility to Health Problems: Conclusions from a Community-Wide Sample', *Journal of Behavioral Medicine*, vol. 10, pp. 481–500. Weinstein, N.D. (1993) 'Testing Four Competing Theories of Health-Protective Behavior', *Health Psychology*, vol. 12, pp. 324–33.

Weiss, M.R. and Chaumeton, N. (1992) 'Motivational Orientations in Sport', in T.S. Horn (ed.), *Advances in Sport Psychology* (pp. 61–99). Champaign, IL: Human Kinetics.

Weiss, W. (1969) 'Effects of the Mass Media of Communication', in G. Lindzey and E. Aronson (eds), *Handbook of Social Psychology* (vol. 5). Reading, MA: Addison Wesley.

Wheeler, L., Koestner, R. and Driver, R. (1982) 'Related Attributes in the Choice of Comparison Others: It's there but it isn't all there is', *Journal of Experimental Social Psychology*, vol. 18, pp. 489–500.

White, S. and Duda, J. (1994) 'The Relationship of Gender, Level of Sport Involvement, and Participation Motivation to Task and Ego Orientation', *International Journal of Sport Psychology*, vol. 25, pp. 4–18.

Wilbur, S., Rubin, T. and Lee, S. (1986) 'A Study of Group Interaction Over a Computer-Based Message System', in M.D. Harrison and A.F. Monk (eds), *People and Computers: Designing for Usability*. Cambridge: University Press.

Wilkinson, R.G. (1996) *Unhealthy Societies: The Afflictions of Inequality*. London: Routledge.

Wilkinson, S. (1986) *Feminist Social Psychology: Developing Theory and Practice*. Milton Keynes: Open University Press.

Williams, J.M. and Straub, W.F. (1998) 'Sport Psychology: Past, Present and Future', in J.M. Williams (ed.), *Applied Sport Psychology* (pp. 1–12). Mountain View, CA: Mayfield Publishing.

Wohwill, J.F. (1974) 'Human Response to Levels of Environmental Stimulation', *Human Ecology*, vol. 2, pp. 127–47.

Woods, D. (1992) *How Children Think and Learn*. Oxford: Blackwell.

Woolfolk Hoy, A. (1999) 'Psychology Applied to Education', in A.M. Stec and D.A. Bernstein (eds), *Psychology: Fields of Application* (pp. 78–92). Boston: Houghton Mifflin.

Wundt, W. (1897) *Outlines of Psychology*. New York: Stechert.

Wylie, J.W., Sheehy, N., McGuinness, C. and Orchard, G. (1998) 'Children's Thinking About Air Pollution: A Systems Theory Analysis', *Environmental Education Research*, vol. 4, pp. 117–37.

Young, B.M. (1990) *Television Advertising and Children*. Oxford: Clarendon.

Yukl, G. (1994) *Leadership in Organizations*. Englewood Cliffs, NJ: Prentice Hall.

Zajonc, R.B. (1965) 'Social Facilitation', *Science*, vol. 1429, pp. 269–74.

Zimbardo, P. and Ebbeson, E.B. (1970) *Influencing Attitudes and Changing Behavior*. Reading, MA: Addison Wesley.

Author Index

Subject Index